PN
81
.T425
1991

Theoretical Issues in Literary History

Edited by
David Perkins

Harvard University Press
Cambridge, Massachusetts
London, England
1991

LIBRARY
FLORIDA KEYS COMMUNITY COLLEGE
5901 West Junior College Road
Key West, Florida 33040

D1531208

LIBRARY OF CONGRESS
5
JUL 18 1991
COPY
CIP

Copyright © 1991 by the President and Fellows of Harvard College
All rights reserved
Printed in the United States of America
10   9   8   7   6   5   4   3   2   1

This book is printed on acid-free paper, and its binding materials
have been chosen for strength and durability.

Library of Congress Cataloging-in-Publication Data

Theoretical issues in literary history / edited by David Perkins.
   p.   cm.—(Harvard English studies ; 16)
   ISBN 0-674-87912-0 (alk. paper).—ISBN 0-674-87913-9 (pbk. :
   alk. paper)
   1. Literature—History and criticism—Theory, etc.   2. Criticism.
   I. Perkins, David, 1928–   .   II. Series.
PN81.T425   1991
809—dc20   90-22331
                                                      CIP

Contents

LIBRARY OF CONGRESS
DUPLICATE

Theoretical Issues in
Literary History

DAVID PERKINS

Introduction: The State of the Discussion

Literary history began in antiquarian works of the eighteenth century. Assimilating ideas of Herder and the Schlegels, the discipline soon became intellectually profound. Its major modes have been Hegelian, positivist, *geistesgeschichtlich,* Marxist, Formalist, sociological, and, paradoxically, post-modern. In variants the theories of Darwin, Spengler, Wölf-flin, Weber, Adorno, Foucault, Bloom, Geertz, and many others have been pressed into service. The genre includes works on the literature of nations, periods, traditions, schools, regions, social classes, political movements, ethnic groups, women, and gays, and these studies may focus on the genesis or production of texts, on their impact on society or on subsequent literature, on their reception, or on all these moments synthetically.

For approximately the first seventy-five years of the nineteenth century, literary history enjoyed popularity and unquestioned prestige. As a synthesis of history and criticism, it seemed more powerful, in some ways, than either discipline separately. Because literary historians viewed texts in relation to their historical contexts, literary history could achieve, its proponents argued, a juster interpretation and a more complete appreciation than was otherwise possible. As a mode of his-

1

toriography, it revealed the "spirit," mentality, or Weltanschauung of a time and place with unrivaled precision and in-
timacy.

This flourishing discipline eventually came under attack.
From its beginning it had been accompanied by strenuous
probing of grounds and debating of methods. But for a long
time this theorizing was only a struggle of different schools of
literary history. Gradually, however, the worth of the whole
discipline was questioned. In the name of a revived classicism
Matthew Arnold marked the difference between the "real" and
the merely "historical" estimate of texts.[1] Arnold had no argument, for his "real" estimate could only be his own estimate, and he did not wish to substitute a personal relativism
for a historical one. But he showed how the wind was blowing.
Under the impact of late nineteenth-century aestheticism,
other critics, such as Edmond Scherer and Emile Faguet, made
the point more profoundly. They pointed out that historical
contextualism can explain everything except what, perhaps,
one most wants to explain—genius; in other words, the qualitative difference between works of art produced in exactly the
same time and place.[2] Historical contextualism can interpret
and account for elements of texts by referring them to relevant
bits of the social and literary matrix. But it cannot grasp texts
as aesthetic designs. This argument has often been forgotten
but never answered. Others made the complaint, also still
valid, that because literary history emphasizes the social, collective determinants of creativity and reception, it wallows in
the minor works, drearily reviewing insignificant authors. And
it was pointed out, for example by Brunetière, that the historical context of any text is infinite, and hence that the historical
or sociological explanation of the literary series must, if rig-

1. Matthew Arnold, "The Study of Poetry," *Essays in Criticism,* 2nd ser.
(London: Macmillan, 1896), p. 7.

2. Edmond Scherer, *Essays on English Literature* (New York: Charles
Scribner's Sons, 1891), p. 76; Emile Faguet, *Politiques et moralistes du dix-
neuvième siècle,* 3rd. ser. (Paris: Lecène, Oudin, n.d.), p. 268. These critics
are merely cited as representative. The argument was made repeatedly and
by many persons.

orously pursued in detail, focus not on literature but on the social totality of which literature is one manifestation.

The theories of the Russian Formalists were a response to the last objection. The Formalists did not question the value or the possibility of writing literary history, but denied that the literary series could be accounted for by events external to literature. Instead, they traced the immanent laws and mechanisms of literary change. At about the same time as the Formalists, Croce mounted his powerful attack on literary history (explored in this volume by John Paul Russo). The essence of Croce's position was that since every work of art is unique, it cannot be reduced to the classification and generalization that are essential in writing a literary history. For Croce the uniqueness of a text is the locus of its value, its "art"; hence literary history, which is useful for certain practical purposes, perforce exhibits less important aspects of the texts it considers. In the United States the New Critics programmatically rejected historical contextualism as a mode of "reading" or interpretation. Reacting to abuses of *Geistesgeschichte* during the Nazi period, scholars in Germany taught and practiced a similarly "immanent" criticism after the Second World War. Deconstructive criticism exposed the logical aporias involved in periods, genres, and other classifications hitherto essential to literary history,[3] and, deploying arguments different from the Aesthetes and Croce, undermined the confidence of the discipline as it confronts literaticity. Objects as self-contradictory, indeterminate, and uninterpretable as are texts in deconstructive readings are not easily subject to generalizations.

The debates within history and the philosophy of history—for example, of Sartre against Lévi-Strauss, of the Annales school and its opponents, and of Hayden White against his critics concerning the rhetorical determinants of historical representations—also had an impact on thinking about literary

3. Paul de Man, "Literary History and Literary Modernity," in *Blindness and Insight,* 2nd ed. rev. (Minneapolis, Minnesota: Minnesota University Press, 1983); Jacques Derrida, "The Law of Genre," in *On Narrative,* ed. W. J. T. Mitchell (Chicago: University of Chicago Press, 1981).

history, though this impact is not yet as large as one might expect. Foucault, however, has been a major influence. He encouraged his readers to reject the traditional Romantic model of literary change as continuous development, to resituate literary texts by relating them to discourses and representations that were not literary, and to explore the ideological aspects of texts from the past in order to intervene in the social struggles of the present, and these remain characteristic practices of present-day historical contextualism—of New Historicism, feminist historiography, and cultural criticism.

With Foucault we come to the 1960s, from which it is conventional to date the reviving theoretical cachet of historical contextualism. The reason usually given for this revival is itself contextual: students of the 1960s are professors of the 1980s, and have not completely lost the political motivations of their youth. They stress the interconnections between social realities and literature because society remains a prime object of their concern. As *Ideologiekritik,* their scholarship engages in the political struggles of the present even when its subject is discourses in the past. To deny the involution of social conflict and power relations in literary and critical texts would leave our profession politically irrelevant. The movements for liberation of women, blacks, and gays have produced literary histories for the same motives, essentially, that inspired the national and regional literary histories of the nineteenth century. These groups turn to the past in search of identity, tradition, and self-understanding. Their histories do not usually stress discontinuity but the opposite. They find their own situation reflected in the past and partly explained by it, not (in their opinion) because they are projecting their situation on the past, but because the same situation of suppression or marginalization continues from the past into the present. To see it this way is part of their protest.

Of course, the changing arguments, tendencies, and practices within literary history are its history and can be explained contextually. We can always show factors that, in a given time and place, brought forward a particular view and caused it to be favorably received. From one point of view there is no reason to do this. Whatever determines a statement to be made has no bearing on its truth or falsity, which is assessed by asking quite other questions. But literary history inevitably reflects on itself by its own methods. Just as the political turmoil of the 1960s was a matrix of the New Historicism, the positions of the Aesthetes, the Russian Formalists, Croce, the New Critics, and the deconstructionists were related to the symbolist-modernist assertion of the autonomy of art and the artist's sense of alienation from society. They were projections within critical discourse of the sociological situation of the modern, avant-garde writer. The doctrine of historical discontinuity in Foucault and his followers is also characteristic of modernist and postmodernist literature from the 1910s to now. Innumerable scholars and critics have explored the sociological determinants of these modern feelings of alienation, dissociation, and discontinuity. For a Marxist literary historian they are ideological expressions of a class situation as a general one.

Contextual explanations can never be conclusive. Mediation, the paths leading from the alleged context to the text, is an insurmountable problem. The paths can never be fully known, and if this were possible, a book could not be long enough to trace them. In fact, the task is infinite, for between each link in the mediating chain mediations must be specified. Moreover, since the context of any text is infinite, and any contextualizing study reports only fragments of it, the literary historian must explain why any particular fragments are privileged. Other studies may place the same text or textual element in equally relevant but altogether different contexts and networks of mediations. If these different studies cannot be synthesized, we must usually admit that we do not know which is correct or whether any one is. The historical, contextual explanation of literary texts rests ultimately on faith, on an intuition that has always seemed probable but can never be proved. Moreover, contextual explanation depends on a certain model of historical process. Between the events that are considered as context and the event they explain there must be a continuity or causal connection. If we are committed, as postmodern historians often are, to models of the real that posit discontinuity between events, contextual explanation becomes logically impossible. And it becomes very much more dubious, in any case, if we emphasize, as postmodern historians do, the extent to which both the "event" and the "context" are constructed by the historian.

Yet postmodern literary historians are generally committed to contextual studies. They use them to dissolve historical generalizations. They show the diverse contexts—regional, local, class, professional, institutional—that were present in the tract of past life they consider, and the different, particular realities shaped by these contexts. Whatever the object of historical inquiry, it breaks down into innumerable, differentiated objects, heterogeneous particulars. Periods, movements, traditions, and other concepts, hitherto used by literary historians to synthesize works, are now usually entertained only as unreal hypotheses. They are generally admitted to be necessary, but are also deplored, and are erected as a background against which we can make visible the multiplicity, difference, and particularity that correspond to our sense of reality. Along with this comes a suspicion of narrative literary history as an imposition of false coherence on the incoherent, for we are beginning to submit narrative literary history to the same questioning scrutiny long since brought to other history. The history of literary history, complete with periodizations, that was briefly suggested in the opening paragraphs of this essay is exactly the kind of thing that invites a dismantling criticism. But there is a very real question whether postmodernist literary history, impressive as it may be in its detail and profound in its vision of the way things are, can serve the purposes for which histories are written if these purposes are still to organize the past, to make it comprehensible, to explain why it had the character and tendency it did, and to bring it to bear on our own concerns.

Thus literary history is in a state of ferment and crisis, not for the first time. On the one hand, it is pursued with eagerness and with new methods and insights. On the other hand, its purposes are unclear, and its traditional forms, procedures, and concepts have been theoretically undermined.

These remarks may indicate not only the timeliness of this volume but the particular relevance of the essays it includes.

Alastair Fowler addresses fundamental problems in the relationship between literature and its historical context and between the disciplines of literary history and history. In analyzing the views of I. A. Richards and of Croce, John Paul Russo goes back to two modern sources of uneasiness with literary history. Croce was for many years its chief philosophical antagonist and I. A. Richards, more than anyone else, gave the New Criticism its antihistorical direction. Mark Parker shows how the inherently problematic character of period concepts has caused a continuing debate among scholars of English Romanticism. Jon Klancher writes about cultural transmission and the ideological discourse that accompanies this process and tries to govern it. In a wide-ranging reflection Ernst Behler takes up the problem of an origin of literary history. Dwelling on the ideas of Friedrich Schlegel, Nietzsche, and Heidegger, he shows that they make the beginning of modernism paradoxically contemporary with that of classicism. Paul Cantor challenges the commonly accepted idea that literary history, in any form we would recognize as such, begins in the eighteenth century. Aristotle, he argues, already had a sophisticated way of thinking about the development of genres. Looking at Third World countries whose literary history is just being written, Michael Valdez Moses reveals functions of the discipline in our society also. Ülker Gökberk studies the representation in contemporary German criticism of literature in German by ethnic minorities. She finds that such criticism often continues its traditional cultural solipsism even in the gestures by which it seeks to escape from it, and she proposes a way out of the dilemma. My article explores the grounds and motives by which, in fact, literary historians have up to now made their classifications. Ronald Bush performs the enfolding gesture of the literary historian. If we now question the possibility of literary history, some portion of our doubt derives from Paul de Man. Yet Bush inscribes de Man within literary history, explaining his thought in relation to precisely that to which de Man denied history—modernism. John Frow explores the paradoxes involved in writing either postmodernist literary history or a literary history of postmodernism. In a closely related

article, Jerome McGann shows that since "facts" in literary
history are "embedded in indeterminate sets of multiple and
overlapping networks," they cannot be adequately represented
in linear narratives. Most of these essays highlight dilemmas
in writing literary history, as is inevitable and necessary in reflection on this subject at present. Ralph Cohen, taking these
dilemmas for granted, argues that a sophisticated concept of
genre and generic change could be the basis of a new literary
history, one that would be more adequate and powerful in its
explanations.

These essays were written specifically for this volume. The
terms of the fund by which the book is financed require that
most of the authors have some connection with Harvard University, present or past, but this restriction does not entail harmony of opinion. Dealing with particular examples or cases,
the authors keep wider implications in mind, illuminating important current issues in the theory of literary history.

ERNST BEHLER

Problems of Origin in Modern Literary History

The most prominent target in contemporary critical thought about history is clearly the assumption that an autonomous human subject is the sovereign master of its own history. Hegel and Marx had already assaulted this concept and characterized it as the mere by-product of much larger forces. Yet only with Nietzsche did the subject undergo the intense questioning and reflection which characterize the contemporary poststructuralist and deconstructive rethinking. Nietzsche taught us to see the notion of the autonomous human subject as a mere desirability, something "human, all too human," a humanization of history and an anthropological interpretation, even falsification, at the root of which was not only desire but also fear. He warned us to be on our guard whenever such an interpretation imposed itself upon us, especially when this appeared to be the most natural interpretation, and to be aware of the ingredient of self-congratulation, self-confirmation, and self-assertion this interpretation conveyed.

From the perspective of history, the critique of the subject assails perhaps its most basic assumption: the individual as the center and goal of history. The subject is losing this privileged position and appears more as a secondary entity at the mercy of superindividual constellations of power, as a predetermined effect in the formation of new orders of things, or as an inci-

dental appearance in the randomness of events and their vicis-
situdes outside of any human-oriented order and finality. At
the least, the notion of the subject has become exposed to
such hypotheses and confronted with options precluded in any
subject-centered interpretation of history. The critical analysis
of the concepts of origin and finality, genealogy and teleology,
beginning and end are the direct outcome of the critique of the
subject in modern historical thought, for these concepts are
inexorably linked to subject-centered thought about history.

A critique of such a fundamental nature has necessarily extended into the field of literary history and shaken some of its
basic assumptions. The rise of cultural and social history or
reception theory within literary history, the critique of ethno-
centricity, the critical analysis of canon, discourse, and institutional power formation, as well as the proclaimed "fall of
literary history" are from a broader consideration all signs of
a departure from the subject-oriented literary history in the
sense of writer and subject matter. The theme of a beginning
of literary history or rather our inability of assigning a true
beginning to literary history can be seen as further evidence
against the subject-centered view. Beginning in this context is
of course not to be understood as a convenient starting point
in the writing of literary history. Rather, it has a foundational
character, a principal significance, and involves the issue of a
true classicism. Although the critical analysis of the beginning
of history corresponds to the critique of any goal-oriented, teleological notion of history, in contemporary thought the notion of a beginning and the critical analysis of it have been
overshadowed by the more dominant discussion of the end of
history. It is my intention to show that the notion of a beginning in literary history in the sense of an ascertainable reference point has been a constant target of critical thought since
the Romantic age, and because of the evasive, receding character of this idea, has been subjected to continued radical reflection and questioning which forms an essential part of our
critical thinking about history.

The three authors chosen to illustrate the point (F. Schlegel,
Nietzsche, and Heidegger) were not themselves directly engaged in this critique. One could even say with good reason

that they were interested in establishing a true classicism and considered classical Greece as the worthiest example. The dissolution of the notion of beginning followed more from their methods than from their arguments themselves. That all three focused on classical Greece as the model for their discussion should be seen not as a tyranny of Greece over their minds, but as a deliberate choice enabling them to raise larger issues such as the cultural unity of the West and our capability of writing about these themes. It is of course questionable whether these three authors can be grouped equally under the heading of literary history. The first, F. Schlegel, is undoubtedly the one who comes closest to this theme. Yet his notion of literature was broader than what one would usually expect and contained a great deal of what is normally ascribed to philosophy. Nietzsche and Heidegger, on the other hand, had their starting points in philosophy and took off from there into literature. All three, however, offer enough similarity and variety with regard to the topic of beginning to permit a diversified exposition of it. After that, Derrida's comments serve to point out the more basic consideration underlying the three contributions: a necessity for a beginning in our thinking about history without our ability, however, of designating a true one.

I

Friedrich Schlegel's innovations in the writing of literary history can best be described by contrasting his work in this domain with the habitual *Literärgeschichte* prevailing in Europe during the previous centuries. That type of literary history had the character of a compendium and presented its material in the form of incoherent aggregates of information, mostly in a chronological sequence, of authors and of all facts known about them. The realm of literature often extended to everything written, and the temporal beginning for these presentations was usually at the creation of the world. Discussions of literary texts consisted of quotations of special instances and were minor in comparison to the huge material data about authors and their lives. Because of the vast extent of such works, their authors often had to deal with subjects of which they had no firsthand knowledge and to which they referred with the greatest amount of material available to them.[1]

In sharp contrast to this tradition, Schlegel shifted the focus of literary historiography from a sequence of authors to literature itself and its course through the centuries.[2] The number of authors diminished because he only wrote about literary figures he actually read. He thus reduced the literary canon to a considerable degree, but augmented it by including authors of his own preference, especially those in the Romantic tradition. The beginning sections of Schlegel's early and sketchy essay on *Epochs of Literature* of 1800 illustrate how poetry appears in his texts as a personified entity capable of infinite mutability and transformations. He reflects about Homer and the school of the Homerids as the source of poetry for Europe: "This was an inexhaustible source of manifold shapes of poetry, a powerful stream of representation in which one wave of life rushes forth after the other, a peaceful sea in which the fullness of the earth and the splendor of the heaven are pleasantly reflected. Just as the sages sought the origin of nature in water, so does the oldest poetry manifest itself in fluid form" (*KFSA* II, 291).

It appears that such a history of literature could not be carried out on the basis of a separate national literature. If the

1. Examples of this type of writing in Germany are Peter Lambeck (Lambecius), *Prodromus historiae literariae* (Hamburg, 1659; 2nd ed. Leipzig, 1710), considered as the first chronologically arranged compendium of literary history; Ludwig Wachler, *Versuch einer allgemeinen Geschichte der Literatur* (Lemgo, 1793); and Johann Gottfried Eichhorn, *Litterärgeschichte: Erste Hälfte* (Göttingen, 1793). Bouterwek's voluminous *Geschichte der Poesie und Beredsamkeit seit dem Ende des 13. Jahrhunderts* (Göttingen, 1810), the most advanced work in literary history of the time, is still arranged according to the scheme of the Literärgeschichte (historia litteraria). See on this subject Hans Eichner's introduction to F. Schlegel's *Geschichte der alten und neuen Literatur,* and for a more comprehensive presentation, Klaus Weimar, *Geschichte der deutschen Literaturwissenschaft* (Munich: W. Fink, 1898).

2. Especially in his *Geschichte der Poesie der Griechen und Römer* of 1798 and his *Geschichte der alten und neuen Literatur* of 1815. Schlegel is quoted from *Kritische Friedrich Schlegel Ausgabe,* ed. Ernst Behler with the collaboration of Jean-Jacques Anstett, Hans Eichner, and other specialists (Paderborn: F. Schöningh, 1958–). References to this edition are henceforth abbreviated as *KFSA.*

spirit of poetry is to be investigated in all its possible expressions, a national literature is too limited for this task. Yet Schlegel's literary history is also not outright a world literature. In spite of cross-cultural ventures into extra-European territories such as Sanscrit literature of ancient India, the range of vision is strictly European. This Eurocentrism, however, is not a matter of momentary limitation and temporary deficiency in the present state of knowledge, but a distinct cultural bias for Europe as the most promising field for such investigations (*KFSA* XI, 15–18). As for the beginning of literary history, classical Greek literature occupies the first place and assumes a position of special importance for the intended research into the nature of literature.

In a more direct way one could say that such a literary history purports to discover what poetry is, what poetry can be, or in which form has poetry shown itself. The intended literary history thereby assumes a cognitive aspect, transcending the historical scope and providing an increased knowledge of the infinite possibilities of literature through its history. This aspect is best expressed by the dictum: "The theory of art is its own history"—a statement that occurs in numerous variations throughout the writings of the Schlegels and can indeed serve as a motto for their endeavors in the field of literary history.[3] This theme of an interrelationship between theory and history has a significant tradition in German thought; it gives the Schlegelian use of the motto its particular twist. Winckelmann and Lessing appear in this tradition as the representatives of the theoretical or systematic approach, whereas Herder usually functions as the advocate of history, of the plenitude of historical life. The systematic approach to history easily assumed a tendency toward rigidity, whereas the historical attitude leaned more toward historicism, toward a contemplation of things, as F. Schlegel said about Herder, "merely according to place, time, and manner and finally leading to no other result than that everything ought to be what it is and what it was"

3. See Ernst Behler, " 'The Theory of Art Is Its Own History': Herder and the Schlegel Brothers," in *Herder Today: An Interdisciplinary Colloquium* ed. Kurt Müller-Vollmer (Berlin: W. de Gruyter, 1990).

(*KFSA* II, 54). A conflict arose between theory and history which foreshadowed the great controversies about history: for instance, one between the Hegelian and the historical schools in the nineteenth century and another about historicism in the twentieth.

At the time F. Schlegel worked on a history of Greek literature, from about 1794 to 1798, the philosophers of transcendental idealism, especially Fichte and Schelling, were the strongest advocates on the side of theory. When Schlegel made Fichte's acquaintance in Jena in the late summer of 1796 and told him about his historical projects, Fichte responded with a "smile" and retorted that he would "rather count peas than study history" (*KFSA* XXIII, 333). When Schlegel later sent him his *Epochs of Poetry,* Fichte answered with the rhetorical question: "Are we supposed to adopt the work of the great artists of previous times? It may be that in our desiccated ages we have nothing better to do. But where did the source for the first artist, who had nothing before himself, come from? Should this original fountain now and for all times be completely dried up? Alas, if only we had yet a pure aesthetics!"[4] For Schelling too at that time history was, at best, a preliminary, elementary, mythological state of knowledge which had to be overcome by "theory a priori." He said: "Only that which has no theory a priori has history." In this sense history had preceded theory in all sciences. Schelling maintained: "The more the boundaries of our knowledge expand, the narrower those of history become." History, in other words, is only a sign of our limitation, or in a different formulation: "The sphere of historical knowledge stands for the human being in an inverse relationship to the sphere of his true knowledge."[5]

Schlegel's proposed synthesis of theory and history, based on the complete understanding of the historical individual and his functioning in the general framework, would constitute the

4. In a letter to Schlegel of August 16, 1800, to be published in vol. XXV of *KFSA*.

5. F. W. J. Schelling, *Sämtliche Werke* (Stuttgart-Augsburg, 1856), I, pp. 471–472.

highest type of knowledge for us, absolute knowledge. In this mood Schlegel had said in 1795: "The perfection of a science is the only key to its history, and its perfection is mostly nothing but the philosophical result of its history" (*KFSA* XVI, 17). In another instance he described this knowledge with the image of a Newton of the history of humanity (*KFSA* VII, 7), and he presented history as "a becoming philosophy" and philosophy as "a perfected history" (*KFSA* II, 221). Although these phrases seem to inspire the expectation of accomplishing the state of absolute knowledge in the future, they are essentially borderline concepts, ironical metaphors circumscribing our actual state of knowledge, which is certainly both, but neither merely historical nor fully theoretical. To apply Schlegel's ideas about a "becoming philosophy" and a "perfected history," we could say that the intended theory will always be in a state of becoming (history), just as our historical knowledge has always been theoretical. As Schlegel said, "One can only become a philosopher, not be one. As soon as one believes oneself to be a philosopher, one stops becoming one" (*KFSA* II, 173). And, as he commented about the desirability of systematic (theoretical) knowledge: "It is equally fatal for the mind to have a system, and to have none. One will simply have to decide to combine the two" (*KFSA* II, 173).

The theme of beginning and origin in literary history is a case in point for this attitude. While working on the first volume of his *History of the Poetry of the Greeks and Romans,* Schlegel had spent some time in Halle in the winter of 1796–97 to discuss the most difficult sections with F. A. Wolf, the great Hellenist of Halle University. After the volume had appeared, he sent one of the first copies to Wolf, who greatly admired the work, but like other readers got stuck at the first sentence and considered it, if one did not let it pass as a "painting of historical obscurity," as entirely incomprehensible (*KFSA* XXV, 136–137). Indeed, by attempting to describe the "night of antiquity" releasing the first visible figures, Schlegel had produced a stylistic monstrosity (*KFSA* I, 397). Other beginning sentences have similar problems. In the Prologue to his Joseph trilogy, Thomas Mann intended to introduce the fath-

omless impenetrability of the mythological realm and came up
with the sentence: "Very deep is the well of the past. Should
we not call it bottomless?"[6] In a more critical but also more
successful fashion, he thematized the beginning in his essay on
Lessing in the context of a national literature as a "stage setting whose shifting scenes lure us from beginnings backward
to earlier beginnings and so into the infinite."[7] Schlegel certainly had something similar in mind when in the first sentence
of his book he wrote about the "darkness surrounding the earliest beginnings of Hellenic poetry" (*KFSA* I, 397).

Schlegel was especially interested in the old Greek tradition
according to which there was "among the Hellenes a special,
assumedly age-old mystical poetry," and which presented
Orpheus as "the father of poetry, the founder of the mysteries"
(*KFSA* I, 399). Excess, orgy, and "solemn madness" had been
essential elements of Orphic poetry, according to Schlegel's
sources. Plato was inclined to trace poetry from this tradition,
which had been the source for the variously formulated opinion of the Greeks that "poetry derived from the Gods, that the
enthusiasm of the holy poet was a true madness and a higher
inspiration" (*KFSA* I, 403). The various Platonic versions of
this hypothesis about the origin of poetry persisted through
Cicero. At that time it had become general opinion "that no-
body could be a good poet without an inflammation of the an-
imal spirits and a certain touch of madness" (*KFSA* I, 405).
Schlegel knew of course that Plato's theory derived from the
old "hostility between poetry and philosophy and corre-
sponded to the Platonic jealousy." Yet he recommended not
taking these assertions of Plato's unambiguously, as one usually did, but reading them in the spirit of "Socratic irony,"
which was capable "of interweaving the most holy with the
joyful and capricious," that is, in the spirit of "that Socratic
mixture of jest and seriousness which for some is more secret
and obscure than all mysteries" (*KFSA* I, 404–405).

6. Thomas Mann, *Joseph and His Brothers,* 3 vols., trans. H. T. Porter
(New York: Knopf, 1939), I, p. 3.
7. Thomas Mann, *Essays of Three Decades,* trans. H. T. Lowe-Porter
(New York: Knopf, 1948), p. 189.

The Platonic assumption of a divine origin of poetry had, in other words, a certain validity for Schlegel as long as one did not construe it as a doctrine and took it with a proper dose of irony. The Orphic "higher madness" of the poet even expressed an important point in Schlegel's own theory of poetry, according to which poetic creation derives from the clash of effervescent enthusiasm and skepticism, of "self-creation" and "self-destruction" (*KFSA* II, 149, no. 28; 151, no. 37; 172, no. 51; 217, no. 305). But the Orphic element was only one point in Schlegel's theory, to be complemented by a counteracting skepticism and disillusionment. It was not correct to date the origin of poetry from this tradition: the early appearance of this tradition revealed the tendency among the Hellenes to move the origin back to a more ancient time, which was of special importance to them (*KFSA* I, 406). Secret societies tended to do that with a special eagerness. After all, it was priests who preserved and promulgated the allegedly age-old mystical poems, and for Schlegel priests have "always and everywhere been great in pious falsifications" (ibid.). Aristotle spoke about "so-called Orphic songs" and maintained that "there had never been a poet with the name of Orpheus." Other authorities of classical antiquity expressed themselves similarly (*KFSA* I, 607). Homeric poetry constituted for Schlegel "the oldest document of Hellenic history," and instead of these "priestly fairy-tales about Orpheus," it ought to serve as the "basis and the guide for all investigations into Hellenic antiquity." This poetry, however, knows "neither orgies nor enthusiasm in the sense of the later priests, poets, and thinkers." The Homeric poet is not "enthusiastically possessed and full of God," but his character is of "quiet self-possession, not of pious intoxication" (*KFSA* I, 408–409).

Schlegel then moved Orphic poetry up to a later, post-Homeric period and tried to justify this by a lack of any "feeling for infinity" or any reference to the Orphic tradition in Homer. In similar manner he rejected the derivation of poetry from the cults honoring Dionysus and relegated the gods who, like Dionysus and Demeter, stood for the infinite life force, to a later period, for he characterized them as profoundly differ-

ent from the Homeric gods.[8] The historical correctness of such
hypotheses is not at issue here and is probably hard to ascertain. Yet it establishes Schlegel as a theoretician of poetry who
stands apart from a prominent German tradition (beginning
with Hölderlin) because he did not set up the origin of poetry
in "mystical" traditions but in the Homeric songs.

With Homer, Schlegel's speculations about a true beginning
of poetry reach firm ground. The *Iliad* and the *Odyssey* appear
as the first credible documents of classical antiquity—the
dawn in the history of Hellenic poetry. A distinct knowlege of
these poems is "an essential need" because Homer was "so to
speak the protopoet of the ancients," who called him *the poet*.
He became the prototype not only of all subsequent epic poetry but also of all other kinds of poetry, especially lyric poetry
(*KFSA* I, 453–455) and tragedy (*KFSA* I, 461–464). An aesthetic appreciation of the particular character of Homeric poetry was therefore not only a matter of historical interest but
also a task for the theory of poetry. However, the more intensely we attempt to occupy ourselves with Homer, the more
he seems to recede and finally to disappear "as the father's
shadow in the embrace by Aeneas" (*KFSA* I, 515). Schlegel is
of course referring to the famous hypothesis advanced by
F. A. Wolf in 1795,[9] according to which the *Iliad* and the *Odyssey* are not the works of a single author, Homer, but orally
transmitted songs, collective products of rhapsodes, which
were brought into the form of the two unified epics only around
540 B.C.

To dissolve an individual author into a collective entity
governed by a "popular spirit" or a "spirit of the age" was
not unusual during the Romantic period: the Song of the
Nibelungen, Shakespeare's dramas, and the fairy tales collected by the Grimm brothers come to mind. Schelling and
other spokesmen for an "unconscious creation" in poetry had
a natural predisposition for such a theory, whereas someone
like F. Schlegel, who insisted on the artistic, conscious, delib-

8. See Ernst Behler, "Die Auffassung des Dionysischen durch die Brüder
Schlegel und Nietzsche," *Nietzsche-Studien* 12 (1983): 335–354.
9. F. A. Wolf, *Prolegomena ad Homerum* (Halle, 1795).

erate, even arbitrary and playful character of poetry, showed a deep skepticism toward any "mystical" inclination in these matters. When Schlegel first discussed this issue with his brother, who was more inclined toward a collective view of Homer, he asked: "Tell me, wouldn't you, with an equal uncertainty of documents, nevertheless consider the *Divina Commedia* as the work of one person?" (*KFSA* XXXIII, 215). Later, under the weight of Wolf's arguments, he modified his opinion, but showed little interest in the disappearance of Homer's authorship and personality. He thought the reception of Wolf's hypothesis had been over-sensationalized in his time. As with Kant, Schlegel claimed, the public had only grasped the negative, skeptical part of the new theory (*KFSA* I, 116). He considered this aspect rather insignificant in comparison to the view Wolf had opened for a genetic, a genealogical understanding of the epic genre, and how it progressively stood out against the fables of bards and priests and became true poetry.[10]

Schlegel thought that in this perspective his own artistic or aesthetic approach and Wolf's hypothesis of a plurality of authors could very well coexist. In his characterization of the Homeric epic, perhaps the most important piece of his classical criticism (*KFSA* I, 447–527), he approached poetry from the point of view of the "epic age," but treated the individual poems as if they were products of one author. As for the beginning of poetry, however, this is lost in a retrogression of beginnings which don't show one conclusively initial step. If one wanted to translate these historical assumptions into theoretical language, one would come very close in the sphere of poetry to what Kant had said in speculative reasoning about art in general, that is, that poetry is autonomous, has a radius of activity of its own, and cannot be derived from, or reduced to, any other source such as religion, mysteries, the state, society, the useful, or labor. Yet we also realize the greater stringency, exclusivity, and thereby fallibility in the elaboration of

10. Most succinctly discussed in Schlegel's essay of 1796, "Über die Homerische Poesie. Mit Rücksicht auf die Wolfischen Untersuchungen," *KFSA* I, 116–132.

theory in contrast to the more flexible character of the historical discourse. In his earliest attempts to formulate a theory of poetry, Schlegel had followed the Kantian and Fichtean model of a speculative, theoretical, systematic exploration of poetry (*KFSA* XVI, 3–31), but soon abandoned this approach. The great diversity in the realm of poetry according to history, imagination, language, and forms of presentation and communication obviously had convinced him that a theory of poetry could not be worked out by speculation alone but was in need of history and could perhaps only be articulated in a historical context.

The relationship between theory and history is even more obvious in Schlegel's essay *On the Study of Greek Poetry* (1795–1797), which has a broader scope than his *History of Poetry of the Greeks and the Romans* and attempts to elucidate the character and validity of modern poetry in the face of the overwhelming impact of classical antiquity upon the early Romantic generation in Germany. The essay can be interpreted as a struggle for self-affirmation against the almost absolute classicism of the Greek world of art, as a new and continued effort in the battle between the ancients and the moderns. The theme of beginning does not arise with regard to classicism, which appears as given, eternally existing, or originating spontaneously "as the goddess of love emerged with ease and at once perfect from the sea" (*KFSA* I, 298). The crucial question of this essay is the beginning of modernism, of modern, non-classical, perfectible, historical poetry. However, once this question has been raised, it necessarily erodes the firm foundations of classicism and establishes modernism in an ever more receding and retrogressive fashion. Modernism stretches far back into antiquity and, with Euripides, looks into its own face. Schlegel said: "In this manner, perhaps already Socrates or even farther back, Pythagoras, who first dared to organize morality and the state according to the ideas of pure reason, stand at the apex of the system of modern history, that is, the system of an infinite perfectibility" (*KFSA* I, 636). Plato's "poetic philosophemata" and "philosophical poemata" are by all means to be considered as literary works in the modern sense

(*KFSA* I, 332). In similar fashion, the "sublime urbanity of the Socratic muse," that is, Socratic irony, can be understood as the language of the modern human being (*KFSA* II, 152, no. 42).

II

Schlegel seems to anticipate a good deal of Nietzsche's writings on classical antiquity, particularly *The Birth of Tragedy*, in which beginning and origin appear in the image of an emergence from a night of barbaric darkness. Like Schlegel, Nietzsche seemed to adore the classical world of the Greeks as absolutely exemplary. Nietzsche emphasized the "indescribable simplicity and dignity of the Hellenic" and thought that the purpose of classical philology with regard to Greek antiquity was "to hold out to the present the mirror of the classical and the eternally valid."[11] Nietzsche's writings on classical antiquity can also be read as a search into the origins of modernity, which in his text clearly gives the impression of a fall from the standards of true classicism, a disintegration of classical purity, and the beginning of the monstrous forms of decadence in the modern age.

In his direct manner of writing, Nietzsche condensed the origin of modernity into one single figure, that of Socrates, who in exemplary fashion showed what the fall from true classicism entails. He opens the world-historical aspect of Socrates in *The Birth of Tragedy*, asking "how the influence of Socrates, down to the present moment and even into all future time, has spread over posterity like a shadow that keeps growing in the evening sun" (*N* I, 67; *BT*, 93).[12] Socrates appears in this presentation as a "type of existence unheard of before him": the "type of the *theoretical man*" whose "profound illusion" con-

11. *Nietzsche in drei Bänden*, 3 vols., ed. Karl Schlechta (Munich: Carl Hauser, 1954), III, pp. 157–159.

12. In *Kritische Studienausgabe*, ed. Giorgio Colli and Mazzino Montinari (Berlin: W. de Gruyter, 1980). References to this edition are henceforth abbreviated as *N*. References to Friedrich Nietzsche, *The Birth of Tragedy and the Wagner Case*, trans. with Commentary by Walter Kaufmann (New York: Random House, 1967) are henceforth abbreviated as *BT*.

sisted in the unshakable faith "that thought, using the thread of causality, can penetrate the deepest abyss of being, and that thought is capable not only of knowing being but even *correcting it*" (*N* I, 99; *BT* 95–96). As the originator of this new attitude, Socrates is, first of all, the prototype of the "theoretical man" inspired by the "instinct of science . . . to make existence appear comprehensible and thus justified." He is the "mystagogue of science," after whom "one philosophical school succeeds another, wave upon wave." Through Socrates, "the hunger for knowledge reached a never-suspected universality." He led science "onto the high seas from which it has never again been driven altogether." In his wake, the "universality" of science for the first time "spread a common net of thought over the whole globe, actually holding out the prospect of the lawfulness of an entire solar system." If we take all this into account, Nietzsche argued, along with the "high pyramid of knowledge in our time," we have to recognize in Socrates "the one turning point and vortex of so-called world-history" (*N* I, 100; *BT,* 96).

But optimism in the realm of science and theory will eventually be shipwrecked, since every honest human being engaged in these fields will come to certain "boundary points" or borderline positions "from which one gazes into what defies illumination" (*N* I, 101; *BT,* 98). Nietzsche even noted this self-critical element in the boundless drive for knowledge represented by Socrates. This self-criticism manifested itself in feigned ignorance, in irony, through the "daimonion of Socrates," the utterances of a divine voice which spoke up at certain moments and opposed conscious knowledge (*N* I, 90; *BT,* 88). Even the consequences of the resistance to absolute knowledge were voiced in this manner. Despite his "hunger for insatiable and optimistic knowledge," Socrates came to realize with horror "how logic coils up at these boundaries and finally bites its own tail" (*N* I, 101; *BT,* 98). At these points the drive for knowledge will "turn over," and a new form of knowledge will originate, "*tragic knowledge,*" which, merely to be endured, Nietzsche adds, "needs art as a protection and remedy" (ibid.). He found references to this dimension in Socrates in allusions by the ancients to a "*music practicing Socrates*"

(*N* I, 102; *BT*, 98), as, for instance, in Alcibiades' speech on Socrates in the *Symposium*.

What interested the West in the figure of Socrates, however, was its aspect of "theoretical optimism." Fascinated, Western humanity took a pathway of thought toward an ideal of absolute knowledge, of an accomplished enlightenment, which will eventually come up against the rock of tragic knowledge and then take a direction toward art similar to that indicated by Socrates. During this long process all the requirements of knowledge and theory will be satisfied, one after the other. Nietzsche's *The Birth of Tragedy* certainly is not a critical history, neither in an intellectual nor a literary sense. Like Schlegel, however, especially in the essay *On the Study of Greek Poetry,* Nietzsche articulates theoretical insights in the context of a historical drama. But in at least two instances he is as detail-oriented as a historian, and both concern the origin of art, of literature in the West. In the first he describes the release of the Greeks from the barbaric night of darkness and terror under the Titans and the rise of the Homeric world in beautiful forms under the guidance of Apollo. The second depicts the moment of a departure from classical beauty and the beginning of modernism in aesthetics, which for Nietzsche is inextricably linked with Euripides. Since the fall from classicism is for him a result of the interference of reason, rationality, theory, and optimism, "Euripidism" is closely connected to "Socratism" and reveals itself in the last analysis as nothing but an "aesthetic Socratism." It is art, poetry, tragedy viewed by the "one great Cyclops eye of Socrates" (*N* I, 92; *BT*, 89).

Nietzsche's main reproach to the new types of tragedy originating with Euripides is a reformulation of the old argument of Aristophanes: instead of the mythical events of the olden times, "the common, familiar, every day life and activities of the people" became the center of the stage (*N* I, 77; *BT*, 78). "Euripides brought the spectator onto the stage and thus qualified him to pass judgment on the drama" (*N* I, 78; *BT*, 79). The old Athenian audience had a special affinity for the glimmer of incomprehensibility at the heart of the Aeschylean-Sophoclean tragedy, and received it with a pre-rationalistic, pre-calculating mentality. The effect of this older tragedy never depended on "epic suspense," on the "fascinating uncertainty as to what is to happen now and afterwards"; it rested not on action but on passion, on the "great rhetorical-lyrical scenes in which the passion and dialectic of the protagonist swelled to a broad and powerful current" (*N* I, 85; *BT,* 84). Euripides' claim that the audience was anxious "to solve the problem of the background history" was therefore mistaken; rather, the anxiety was his own. The audience and object of his aesthetic speculation were in the first place Euripides himself, "Euripides as *thinker,* not as a poet," displaying the "brightness and dexterity of his critical thinking" (*N* I, 80; *BT,* 80). In extension of the Socratic principle "Knowledge is virtue," the supreme law of aesthetic Socratism could be stated as: "To be beautiful everything must be intelligible" (*N* I, 85; *BT,* 83–84). Following this principle, Euripides modified all the separate elements of drama—"language, characters, dramaturgic structure, and choric music." (ibid.). Most important, he eliminated the Dionysiac elements and intended "to reconstruct tragedy purely on the basis of an un-Dionysian art, morality, and world-view" (*N* I, 82; *BT,* 81). Yet Euripides was only a "mask," only the representative of a demonic power speaking through him. The deity that spoke through him was "neither Dionysus nor Apollo, but an altogether newborn demon, called *Socrates*" (*N* I, 83; *BT,* 82). Socrates was that "second spectator," standing behind Euripides, "who did not comprehend and therefore did not esteem the Old Tragedy," and in alliance with him Euripides dared to become "the herald of a new art" (*N* I, 87; *BT,* 86).

The phenomenon of an aesthetic Socratism is another aspect of the world-historical dimensions of Socratism as Nietzsche sensed it, now focused on the destructive tendency in the realm of art rather than on the optimistic view of knowledge. It is a force that singlehandedly dared to negate that "Greek genius which as Homer, Pindar, and Aeschylus, as Phidias, as Pericles, as Pythia and Dionysus, as the deepest abyss and the highest height, is sure of our astonished veneration"—a "demonic power" which "dares to spill this magic potion into dust" (*N* I, 90; *BT,* 88). Nietzsche put great emphasis on "how the enormous driving-wheel of logical Socratism is in motion, as it were, *behind* Socrates, and that it must be viewed through Socrates as through a shadow (*N* I, 91; *BT,* 89). This Socratism behind and before Socrates brings us to the decisive point in Nietzsche's theory about classicism and the beginning of modernity, that is to say, to that point where it begins to deconstruct itself.

Nietzsche makes this point in an early essay on *Socrates and Greek Tragedy* (1870), which articulates for the first time the pernicious influence Socrates had on the development of Greek tragedy and certainly anticipates the basic argument of *The Birth of Tragedy.* Yet in the earlier text he takes a much more sympathetic attitude toward Euripidism and Socratism. Euripides appears in a more human, even comic guise, without the schematized features of the later texts. Nietzsche's tolerance here is probably a consequence of his frequent references to Aristophanes, who lends his conceptualization greater historical directness and proximity. In the earlier text he also presented the "death of tragedy" as more of a tragic and inevitable event. In this context he emphasized the enormous distance between the "old musical drama" that is, the Aeschylean and Sophoclean tragedy, and the Athenian public sitting on the benches for the spectators. What was for Nietzsche "the highest and most difficult for the poet," obviously the tragic pathos and passion in the lyrical scenes, was perceived by the masses as something of no concern to them, whereas many accidental events seized them "with a sudden effect" (*N* I, 537). The principle that "everything has to be understandable in order to be understood" was therefore not invented by Socrates or Euripides and stuck onto the old tragedy, but resulted from a deeper, more general, and also more inevitable decay: from the historical distance between the Athenian public and the classical form of tragedy (ibid.).

This early text reveals not only Nietzsche's assumption that Socratism is older than Socrates, but also that Socratism in this fundamental meaning of self-reflection is an intrinsic element in the development of literature and poetry and furthermore an element inherent and germane to literature itself, not

alien and implanted from outside. The "element of dialectics,"
which formed for Nietzsche the pernicious, "disastrous" component, took its point of departure from dialogue that was originally absent in tragedy and lead to "argument," "contest,"
and "dispute" (*N* I, 545). This process developed into the
"play of intrigues" and culminated in the new comedy (*N* I,
546). Signs of decay, however, began to appear "long before
Euripides." Nietzsche had the "courage" in this early text to
point out "that even the most beautiful figures of Sophoclean
tragedy—an Antigone, an Electra, an Oedipus—at times engage in barely tolerable trains of thoughts, that the dramatic
characters are altogether more beautiful and magnificent than
their articulation in words" (*N* I, 548). Only Aeschylus would
then remain as the true "flowering" and "summit" of the
"Greek musical drama," since its decay, which Euripides
brings to an end "with tempest-like speed," already begins
with Sophocles (*N* I, 549). Yet the processes at work here cannot be designated by historical figures, but result from more
fundamental forces. Nietzsche's friend Heinrich Romundt
summarized *Socrates and Greek Tragedy* aptly. He considered
it "exemplary" how Nietzsche "proceeded from Euripides, investigated and presented his manner without any imposing tendency, then transformed the concept of Euripidism into that of
Socratism, and finally established Socratism as pre-Socratic
and post-Socratic, as an eternal disease."[13] In *The Birth of
Tragedy,* Nietzsche had exposed Socratism as a fundamental
phenomenon of human expression and historical development
"down to the present moment and even into all future time."
In the earlier essay on *Socrates and Greek Tragedy,* he seems
to look back and to realize his inability to pinpoint the beginning of this development.

III

Reflecting upon the beginning of our history, Schlegel and
Nietzsche became entangled in ever earlier stages and the bot-
tomlessness of origin. Heidegger took a slightly different per-

13. *Nietzsche Briefwechsel. Kritische Gesamtausgabe,* 16 vols., ed.
Giorgio Colli and Mazzino Montinari (Berlin: de Gruyter, 1976), II, p. 176.

spective, but came to a similar questioning of what constitutes our history and where its origin lies. The context for Heidegger's approach to this theme is not so much the literature and poetry of classical Greece, but rather the earliest manifestation of philosophical thought among the Greeks, known as pre-Socratic philosophy. This name has a noticeable Nietzschean flavor in Heidegger's usage, since it refers to a period in our history preceding the shadow of Socratism, not yet touched by the decaying process of history, and thereby permits us a glance at, or even an experience of, our true origins. In the early 1870s, Nietzsche had offered a lecture course at Basel University on "The Preplatonic Philosophers, with Interpretation of Selected Fragments." In 1873 he wrote an essay based on these lectures, *Philosophy in the Tragic Age of the Greeks*.[14] The designation "tragic" obviously stands for the pre-Socratic, nonoptimistic, undialectical perception of the world in a pre-rationalistic experience of the tragic. Nietzsche's essay was published in 1903, the same year as Hermann Diels's *Fragments of the Presocratics*. This edition comprised the literary remnants of these early philosophers under the name which today has become a standard designation for them. Heidegger was of course acutely aware of the fine line this designation drew in our intellectual tradition and, through his own reflections upon a pre-Socratic and pre-Platonic philosophy, he widened the gap considerably between these different origins in our intellectual inheritance.

From a broader perspective, Heidegger's study of pre-Socratic philosophy is part of his history of Being, a topic which connects his interpretation of pre-Socratic thought even more with the theme of beginning. The notion of a history of Being, a history of metaphysics, or a history of our interpretation of Being follows directly from the most basic tenet of Heidegger's philosophy, the "ontological difference," the differentiation between Being and beings. At the beginning of Western thought, for example with Parmenides, the anonymous auxiliary verb "to be" (*einai*) gained another form, the

14. This text is omitted from *Kritische Studienausgabe* but can be found in *Nietzsche in drei Bänden*, III, pp. 349–413.

noun "being" (*to einai*), a nonsensuous mental image which
introduced the ontological difference between Being and
beings. The most decisive distinction, however, was Plato's
naming of Being that founds all beings, the "Being of beings"
(*ontos on, Sein des Seienden*). This is precisely the ontological
difference which Heidegger considers crucial for Western
metaphysics and with which the history of metaphysics actually begins. It corresponds to that world-historical turn
which in Nietzsche's scheme was brought about by Socratism.
All the metaphysical implications—a prior and a later, a primary and a secondary, a ground and its surface, and also the
division of being into two realms, two worlds—are already inscribed into this original distinction. Furthermore, Plato had
called the Being of beings an idea and ascribed to it the qualities of the good, the well-born, the high-stationed, the capable,
and thereby introduced a valorization into the ontological difference with all the implied discriminations of spirit versus
matter, soul versus body, speech versus writing, and so on.

Faced with the differentiation of Being and beings, people
focused on the question "*What* is Being?" in the sense of
something present, objectifiable, ascertainable, and manageable, and neglected Being as Being (*to on he on, Sein als Sein*).
The suppression of Being for the sake of something tangible
developed in parallel with the subject as the source of perception, the ground and master for the scientific and technological
domination of Being. The history of Being is for Heidegger
precisely this progressive mastery and domination of Being,
which is simultaneously a progressive loss of Being, a "forgottenness of Being." The history of Being can very well be described as a history of the oblivion of Being, as a process of
oblivion of such boundless nature "that the very forgottenness
is sucked into its own vortex" (*HN* IV, 193).[15] In all his work
since *Being and Time* Heidegger continued to formulate his
bewilderment in the face of this crucial event. "In the history

15. Martin Heidegger, *Nietzsche*. 4 vols., trans. David Farrell Krell and
others (San Francisco: Harper and Row, 1979–1985), henceforth abbreviated as *HN*.

of Western thought," he said in a later instance, "from its inception, the Being of beings has indeed been thought, but the truth of Being as Being remains unthought; not only is such truth denied as possible experience of thinking, but Western thought, as metaphysics, expressly though unwittingly conceals the occurrence of this refusal" (*HN* III, 189–190). Heidegger's own philosophy is not only a nostalgic reflection on this loss of Being, but can also be characterized as an attempt to reinaugurate the question of Being. His occupation with pre-Socratic philosophy is an important expression of this attempt that is also related to his interpretations of Hölderlin and Trakl and his own sibylline use of words—all examples of thought and language which had not been obliterated by the dominion of beings over Being and thereby offering some experience of true origin.

A reflection on one particular stage in the history of Being can perhaps best illustrate Heidegger's double-edged mode of thought about loss and origin. He conducted this exercise himself when he analyzed "the age of the world picture" as a special chapter of the history of Being in an essay with the same title.[16] The age of the world picture is the period of beginning modernism in the seventeenth century, of Descartes and the *cogito,* that is, the age of the "subject of knowledge," in which human self-consciousness became the center of the world and modern sciences began their triumphant conquest of the natural world. Heidegger does not analyze this development from a notion of progressive truth. In his view, the claim that modern understanding of being is more correct than that of the Greeks is even sillier than the claim that Shakespeare's poetry is more advanced than that of Aeschylus (*AWP,* 117). The subject of his investigation is not the evolution of the human mind, but Being. The self-empowering of the human mind in the seventeeth century, in other words, is only a phase in the history of Being, or rather in the history of the oblivion of Being, al-

---

16. Martin Heidegger, "The Age of the World Picture," in *The Question Concerning Technology and Other Essays,* trans. William Lovitt (New York: Harper and Row, 1977), pp. 115–154, henceforth abbreviated as *AWP.*

though the "whole of modern metaphysics taken together, Nietzsche included, maintains itself within the interpretation of what it is to be [being] and of truth that was prepared by Descartes" (*AWP,* 127).

One could interpret this process as an introduction of "subjectivism and individualism," but at the same time, "no age before this one has produced a comparable objectivism and . . . in no age before this one has the nonindividual, in the form of the collective, come to acceptance as worthy" (*AWP,* 128). Heidegger maintains that the essential feature of this age is precisely "the necessary interplay between subjectivism and objectivism" and that this interrelationship between the subject and the object, the human being and the world, is precisely the result of man's becoming the "relational center of that which is as such," of man's becoming "that being upon which all that is, is grounded as regards the manner of its Being and its truth" (ibid.). Nothing depicts this event better for Heidegger than the phrase that the world has become a picture, that is, something represented, or more intensely, something which in its entirety "is now taken in such a way that it first is in being and only in being to the extent that it is set up by man, who sets it up and sets it forth" (*AWP,* 129–130). This observation makes it obvious that with the notion of world picture the whole constitution, the entire perception of Being changes. This does not mean that each age has its particular world picture or that world pictures change in the transition from antiquity into the Middle Ages and into the modern period. World picture and modern age coincide to such a degree that "the world picture of the modern age" and "modern world picture" are the same; in short, "the fact that the world becomes a picture at all is what distinguishes the essence of the modern age" (*AWP,* 130).

All the particular features of the modern age as, for instance, the interpretation of the world as "anthropology" or "humanism," derive from the interweaving of the two events "that the world is transformed into a picture and man into *subjectum*" (*AWP,* 133). For humanism in the strict sense "is nothing but a moral-aesthetic anthropology" and would have been inconceivable in the "great age of the Greeks," just as "anthropology" does not designate "some investigation of man by a natural science," but "that philosophical interpretation of man which explains and evaluates whatever is, in its entirety, from the standpoint of man and in relation to man" (ibid.). Even the more recent developments of our view of the world as "gigantic," quantitatively enormous, having the "American" perspective, result from the basic fact that the world has become a picture and are, in the last analysis, nothing but "pathways upon which the modern age rages toward fulfillment of its essence" (*AWP*, 135). This late image of the world is then confronted with the experience of Being in the great age of the Greeks. Heidegger quotes one of the oldest pronouncements of Greek thinking in this regard, the sentence by Parmenides which, in his interpretation, says: "The apprehending of whatever is belongs to Being because it is demanded and determined by Being" (*AWP*, 130). This refers to the theme of the beginning of Western history, although Heidegger senses in Plato's definition of the Being of beings as idea the "Presupposition, destined far in advance and long ruling indirectly in concealment, for the world's having to become a picture" (*AWP*, 131).

Heidegger deals most directly with this theme in his interpretation of the Anaximander fragment, considered by many the oldest document of Western thinking.[17] In the English translation the fragments reads: "But where things have their origin, there also their passing away occurs, according to necessity; for they pay recompense and penalty to each other for their injustice, according to the assessment of time."[18] Heidegger asks what this fragment from a distance of two-and-a-half thousand years can still say to us and attempts to expound in bold strokes of interpretation Anaximander's experience of the "totality of things present," of their "having arrived to linger a while among one another in unconcealment"

17. Martin Heidegger, "The Anaximander Fragment," in *Early Greek Thinking*, trans. David Farrell Krell and Frank A. Capuzzi (New York: Harper and Row, 1975), pp. 13–58, henceforth abbreviated as *AF*.

18. G. S. Kirk and J. E. Raven, *The Presocratic Philosophers: A Critical History with a Selection of Texts* (Cambridge: Cambridge University Press, 1966), p. 117.

before they depart into concealment (*AF*, 40–41), and all this according to an order of necessity, interpreted by Heidegger as an order of deep-rooted "usage," of an old habit in the structure of Being (*AF*, 55). His main concern is of course Anaximander's experience of the "presencing of Being," and he finds it precisely in this order of necessity (*to chreon*), which he translates as "usage," as the "handing over of what is in each case present into its while in unconcealment" (*AF*, 55). Being, "since the dawn of thinking," names for Heidegger "the presencing of what is present, in the sense of gathering which clears and shelters" (*AF*, 39). He finds an expression of this gathering in Anaximander's particular experience of an inherent necessity.

This fragment does not, however, return us to a state prior to the forgottenness of Being and the history of Being. To grasp the essential nature of Being, one would have to find in language "a single word, the unique word" fully adequate to Being, and this alone illuminates "how daring every thoughtful word addressed to Being is" (*AF*, 52). Even the things Anaximander talks about in this fragment do not have this direct access to Being, but relate to philosophy in the sense of a "thinking of Being," to thinking "when Being presences" (*AF*, 40), that is, they occupy a secondary stage, a derived position, an impending forgottenness of Being. However, this is perhaps our only way of experiencing Being. In this way, the history of Being would be synonymous with the history of the oblivion of the ontological difference, the difference between Being and beings which remains forever forgotten (*AF*, 50–51). Anaximander's fragment speaks of this difference in terms of a relation (*to chreon*). Yet we would deceive ourselves "if we thought we could locate the distinction and get behind its essence merely by etymologically dissecting the meaning of the word *chreon* with enough persistence." The best we can do to make "the early word speak in our contemporary recollection" is to "experience historically what has not been thought—the oblivion of Being—as what is to be thought" (*AF*, 51). In this way we must rethink the beginning, although the beginning will already be on the path of our own destiny, on the path to the

oblivion of Being. Heidegger says: "Then thinking must poe-
tize on the riddle of Being. It brings the dawn of thought into
the neighborhood of what is [being] for thinking" (*AF*, 58).

IV

The common endeavor in Schlegel's, Nietzsche's, and Heidegger's reflections on the beginning of our history is to develop
an intensified sense for our historical experience and to discover what constitutes our history. Such a sense and such
questioning could not develop from within the historical experience itself but arise from the projection of a realm of true
origin, unimpaired by the reality of history; indeed, historical
life is a progressive departure from it. This is obviously the
function of a true classicism for Schlegel, the pre-rationalistic
experience of the tragic for Nietzsche, and the unimpeded
presencing of Being for Heidegger. Conversely, the rise of ra-
tionalistic modernism in the case of Schlegel, of Socratic dialectics for Nietzsche, and of oblivion of Being in Heidegger's
structure of thought mark the step from this pure realm of origin into the world of history. Moreover, as soon as we reflect
on the first moment of this departure or this beginning, the
realm of origin begins to dwindle and to recede into a metaphysical sphere. What remains is the historical world in which
Schlegel's modernism extends into the earliest manifestations
of classicism, Nietzsche's Socratism appears as an enormous
driving-wheel set in motion long before Socrates, and
Heidegger's oblivion of Being is essentially linked with the
first thought about Being, the first word spoken.

We could say about this mode of thought that it embodies
the critical undermining of its own illusions. Yet that would
undercut the metaphysical component that causes it to thrive.
If we were to summarize the critical, deconstructive aspect of
this thought by the term "questioning" or simply "question,"
as Derrida has done in a recent text on Heidegger,[19] we could

19. See Jacques Derrida, *Of Spirit: Heidegger and the Question*, trans.
Geoffrey Bennington and Rachel Bowlby (Chicago: University of Chicago
Press, 1989).

see that it is the most valuable part of thought and be inclined
to equate it with thinking itself. Yet for the sake of this questioning and in the name of it, we could not avoid extending the
question to the question itself, if only to ascertain and remove
the residue of an unquestioned Enlightenment or an uncritical
ideology which might still be hidden in it. From the point of
view of the question, we are also bound to consider that earliest event which is earlier than any other event, that "pré-
archi-originalité" (Derrida) which we, as prisoners of the metaphysical tradition, cannot bring to mind and which seems to
shine up in the deconstruction-free notion of origin. Similar
thoughts arise with regard to the end of history[20] and demonstrate how a type of thinking deeply imbued with the critique
of the subject and the presuppositions implied in the subject's perspective maintains and articulates itself. Schlegel,
Nietzsche, and Heidegger have anticipated a great deal of this
thought and articulated it, if not directly in literary history,
then at least in that intermediate zone of literature and philosophy which is just as much the subject matter of that discipline.

20. See Jacques Derrida, "The Ends of Man," in *Margins of Philosophy,*
trans. Alan Bass (Chicago: University of Chicago Press, 1982), pp. 109–136,
and his *D'un ton apocalyptique adopté naguère en philosophie* (Paris: Editions Galilée, 1983).

RONALD BUSH

Paul de Man, Modernist

A deliberately provocative title, it is enmeshed in the difficulties of approaching literary history at the present time. After
all, not only did de Man challenge our notions of periodization
and question the very "possibility of literary history" itself
(*BI*, 144); he did so in essays that effectively displaced the
cachet of "modernity" from Anglo-American modernism[2] and
forestalled attempts to link his own writings with twentieth-
century politics. Lately critics like Frank Lentricchia and
Terry Eagleton have remarked upon the self-serving function

1. The following abbreviations have been used for works by Paul de Man
cited in the text: *CW, Critical Writings 1953–1978*, ed. and introduced by
Lindsay Waters (Minneapolis: University of Minnesota Press, 1989); *RR,
The Rhetoric of Romanticism* (New York: Columbia University Press,
1984); *BI, Blindness and Insight: Essays in the Rhetoric of Contemporary
Criticism* (1971; rpt. and expanded version, Minneapolis, University of
Minnesota Press, 1983); *AR, Allegories of Reading: Figural Language in
Rousseau, Nietzsche, Rilke, and Proust* (New Haven: Yale University
Press, 1979); *RT, The Resistance to Theory* (Minneapolis: University of
Minnesota Press, 1986); *WJ, Wartime Journalism 1939–1943*, ed. Werner
Hamacher, Neil Hertz, and Thomas Keenan (Lincoln: University of
Nebraska Press, 1988).
2. Lindsay Waters goes so far as to contend that de Man's "most suc-
cessful academic achievement" was "the simultaneous disposal of the New
Critics and the reestablishment [in academic literary history] of the cen-
trality of the romantics" (*CW*, xl).

of de Man's dismissal of history and have tried to resituate de Man's writing in a Marxist context only slightly less hostile to modernism than de Man's own.[3] In what follows I would like to examine and redirect their comments. By linking de Man with modernism, I want to continue the process of contextualizing de Man and then dispute some of the kinds of radical history that have used de Man to simplify our notions of twentieth-century literature.[4]

I

De Man made clear in his apprentice writings of the fifties and sixties his bemusement with the English and American view of twentieth-century writing. For him, only a certain backwardness enabled Anglophone critics to regard the modernist writers as contemporary. Reviewing Ellmann and Feidelson's *The Modern Tradition* for the *New York Review of Books* in 1965, he notes the naive reverence of the thirties and forties for the "generation of considerable inventive power" (*CW,* 138) that preceded them and remarks on how this reverence "mythologize[d] the preceding generation into the absolute embodiment of modernity" despite the reality that "the phenomenon of modernity itself is by no means unique" (*CW,* 138, 137). In his judgment Ellmann and Feidelson were "still partly laboring under the fallacious prewar illusion of modernism" and were using the term "modern" to refer to "the literature of Yeats, Joyce, Eliot, Lawrence, Proust, Valéry, Gide, Mann, Rilke and Kafka" (*CW,* 138).

De Man's judgments here are made not from the ontological perspective he would make his trademark, but from the viewpoint of a historian who claims to see both the distant past and the recent present better than his Anglo-American contempor-

3. See Frank Lentricchia, *After the New Criticism* (Chicago: University of Chicago Press, 1980), pp. 282–317, and *Criticism and Social Change* (Chicago: University of Chicago Press, 1983), *passim.* See also Terry Eagleton, *The Function of Criticism* (London: Verso, 1984), pp. 100–106, and *Against the Grain: Essays 1975–1985* (London: Verso, 1986), pp. 53–56, 136–138, and 156–162.

4. For another essay in this spirit that concentrates on de Man's wartime journalism, see Reed Way Dasenbrock, "Paul de Man, the Modernist as Fascist," *South Central Review* 6 (Summer 1989): 6–18.

aries. Regarding the past, he had written ten years earlier that "if one extends the historical perspective far enough to include romanticism, the present-day state of mind appears in a much clearer light. This awareness of a deep separation between man's inner consciousness and the totality of what is not himself had certainly existed before 1800, but it becomes predominant around that time" (*CW*, 14–15). As he elaborated in the Ellmann/Feidelson review, better than anything written by "Yeats, Joyce, Eliot" et al., "Hegel's famous passage on the unhappy consciousness" represents "the truly central insight of modernity"—"how self-understanding can lay bare the divided structures of consciousness: irony, alienation, conflict of appearance and being, etc." (*CW*, 143).

Concerning recent trends, de Man observes that Yeats, Joyce, and company "are already part of history" (*CW*, 138) and that "later and different developments of Western thought and literature" involve "emphasis on certain themes (such as existential theories of consciousness, neorealist and neo-Marxist writing, negative theologies, etc.)" (*CW*, 138). De Man has in mind the French post-Heideggerian concerns of the forties and fifties, which had given him his own intellectual *point de depart*.[5]

As early as 1955, in his essay "The Inward Generation," de Man began to articulate the central premises of his critical program, intending to make a counterstatement against the canon of twentieth-century writing as the New Criticism had interpreted it. In a move directed against the academic establishment, he described several prestigious modernist writers as essentially superficial—that is, insufficiently aware of the crisis which was their subject. In his opinion, Hemingway and Pound in the United States and Malraux in France were "semipopularizing writers" who had engaged with both politics and aesthetic form as "protection against an anxiety" they dimly but inadequately felt—an anxiety that really had to do with "the defense of being itself" and that was "such a fundamental matter that it could no longer take on the benign aspect of a literary movement or an avant-garde magazine" (*CW*, 14). According to "The Inward Generation," the true subject of mod-

5. See *CW*, pp. xxxii–xxxviii, xl–il, and below.

ern writing since Hegel has been the "ontological crisis" in which "man is thrown back upon himself, in total inwardness, since any existence within the framework of accepted reality can no longer satisfy him" (*CW*, 15). This is the essence of modern history, and yet, affecting an aestheticizing "antihistoricism" (*CW*, 15) and avoiding the "ontological question," all too much of twentieth-century writing has spoken of history without reference to it. With Karl Löwith, it has ignored history's "eschatological aspect," which "constitutes precisely the most profound impulse that stands behind [Heidegger's] philosophy" (*CW*, 17). Against this authentic kind of history, modernism's myth of permanence seeks only "protection from painful consciousness" (*CW*, 17).

For de Man, then, as for Heidegger, the only true history is an ontological history of man's "divisions," and this authentic history is to be located within the "naive" attempts of man to forget those divisions as he narrates his story in the world. Hence it becomes usual for de Man to make an interlocking critique of history and modernism. Following up his remarks in "The Inward Generation" on the "antihistoricism" of recent literature, he writes in a 1964 review of J. Hillis Miller's *The Disappearance of God* and Joseph Frank's *The Widening Gyre* that modernist literature both transforms "the historical imagination into myth" (*CW*, 112) and conceives of form as a "well rounded shape," rather than as "a fragment in the incessant interpretation of Being that makes up our history" (*CW*, 114). In the broad-ranging and ultimately reductive attack de Man was about to make, modern literature would be characterized by a "tendency . . . to regress toward more primitive levels of experience" (*CW*, 142) and to "surrender the autonomy of the conscious mind to the unquestioned hegemony of the physical world" ("What Is Modern," *CW*, 144).

At first, de Man was willing to allow in an unguarded moment that not just modernist but "all modern writers and thinkers have moments during which they give in to such regressive tendencies, especially when they feel tempted to undertake vast, general syntheses" (*CW*, 142). These acknowledgments were never frequent, however, and they became fewer as the years went on. It was more usual for de Man, who never seems to have read Eliot or Pound with pleasure, to caricature the

Anglo-American modernists and their proponents, the New Critics (who had already made his job easier by simplifying modernist writing for their own purposes[6]). As early as 1956, when he wrote "The Dead-End of Formalist Criticism," de Man pointed to bits of Eliot's *Four Quartets* (the only one of Eliot's works he ever cited) and disdainfully included Eliot in the camp of what he called "salvational" critics. Telescoping modernist and New Critical assumptions, and without reference to any examples beyond I. A. Richards' *Principles of Literary Criticism*, Philip Wheelwright's *The Burning Fountain*, and a few lines of the *Quartets*, de Man diagnosed what the modernist-New Critical mix had become ("formalist techniques . . . overlaid with intentions of a mythical and religious order") without acknowledging that modernist practice had ever been more interesting. In his view, "the work of T. S. Eliot" summed up aspirations toward "an ultimate reconciliation on a cosmic scale, cut off from the memories of the past" and veiling a "nostalgia for immediate revelation" (*BI*, 242–243). Nearly thirty years later de Man had not changed his mind. In "The Resistance to Theory" (1982), he remembered the buzzwords of the fifties ("tone, organic form, allusion, tradition, historical situation, etc.") and called "the personality and the ideology of T. S. Eliot" ("a combination of original talent, traditional learning, verbal wit and moral earnestness") "the perfect embodiment of the New Criticism" (*RT*, 6). Little wonder he was eager to redirect critical attention away from the twentieth century, or that he wrote in "The Rhetoric of Temporality" (1969) that "wide areas of European literature of the nineteenth and twentieth centuries appear as regressive with regard to the truths that come to light in the last quarter of the eighteenth century" (*BI*, 208).

During the same years that he was preparing his assault on the modernists and their academic supporters, de Man was also sharpening the philosophical premises that sustained him at least through *Blindness and Insight* (1971) and, in the view

6. In James Breslin's words, they "deradicalized the modernist grandfathers and provided paternal authority at a time when beginning poets were eager to find it." See *From Modern to Contemporary: American Poetry 1945–1965* (Chicago: University of Chicago Press, 1984), p. 17.

of some, until the end of his career.[7] His concern is insistently the negation at the heart of Heidegger's crisis of being, and he is occasionally required to defend *this* Heidegger even against the later Heidegger, who sometimes implied that authenticity has a more positive aspect.[8] Thus in "The Temptation of Permanénce" (published originally in French in 1955), de Man argued that Heidegger's influence has had two "principal merits": it has detached history "from [the] naive forms it had taken in the interior of activisms and political determinisms"; and it has "led the problem of history back onto the ontological level where Hegel had situated it" (and where "it designates the destiny of the division" within being; *CW,* 34). In 1966, in "The Literature of Nihilism," de Man defined Romanticism not as a "pantheistic, irrational unity with nature" but as a withdrawal from nature into a human "inwardness" that "always begins as a negative movement" (*CW,* 167, 168). And in the essays collected in *Blindness and Insight* (1971), he anchored that "negative movement" within the process of reading. In all fiction, he now argued, "the human self" experiences "the void within itself." Fiction, "far from filling the void, asserts itself as pure nothingness, *our* nothingness stated and restated by a subject that is the agent of its own instability." For this reason, literature is "a primary source of knowledge" about ourselves. And not only literature, but language usage in general, which cannot but demonstrate the "duplicity" of the human condition (*BI,* 19, 9).

7. See Stanley Corngold, "Error in Paul de Man," in *The Yale Critics: Deconstruction in America,* ed. Jonathan Arac, Wlad Godzich, and Wallace Martin (Minneapolis: University of Minnesota Press, 1983), pp. 90–108, esp. p. 98ff.

8. De Man deemphasized his debt to Heidegger in a late interview (see *RT,* 118–119), but given his extensive references to the philosopher in *BI,* his remarks are hard to credit. Allan Stoekl in "De Man and the Dialectic of Being" (*Diacritics,* Fall 1985, pp. 36–45), and Lindsay Waters in the introduction to *CW* supply a useful corrective, but neither puts enough stress on de Man's familiarity with *Being and Time* (see, for example, *CW,* 104) and how it helps him resist what *BI* calls (see below) the "recent Heidegger." Thus de Man's critique in "Heidegger's Exegeses of Hölderlin" (*BI,* 246–266) should not be taken as a divergence of paths so much as an affirmation of principles from which the master had departed.

Probably the most refined statement of de Man's themes in *Blindness and Insight* can be found in "Impersonality in the Criticism of Maurice Blanchot," where de Man stakes his claim for the value of critical theory in these words:

"For [Blanchot], as for Heidegger, Being is disclosed in the act of its self-hiding and, as conscious subjects, we are necessarily caught up in this movement of dissolution and forgetting. A critical act of interpretation enables us to see how poetic language always reproduces this negative movement, though it is often not aware of it. Criticism thus becomes a form of demystification on the ontological level that confirms the existence of a fundamental distance at the heart of all human experience. Unlike *the recent* Heidegger, however, Blanchot does not seem to believe that the movement of a poetic consciousness could ever lead us to assert our ontological insight in a positive way." (BI, 76, emphasis mine)

By the time of *Allegories of Reading* (1979), de Man would resituate the negative movement of consciousness within the inevitable "aporia" constituted by "the irrevocable occurrence of at least two mutually exclusive readings" [of any text] and designating "the impossibility of a true understanding" (*AR,* 72). Here "figurative structure" rather than fiction is the mark of our divided humanity, but, as Stanley Corngold puts it, although "the system changes; the void remains the same."[9]

How closely interrelated de Man's philosophical premises were to his powerful reaction against modernism and New Criticism became vividly apparent in the program of *Blindness and Insight,* which in its 1971 version was anything but the "somewhat unsystematic" volume de Man described in his "Foreword" (*BI*, viii). *Blindness and Insight* is all but framed by an attack on the New Critical establishment and its modernist predecessors. The beginning of this frame, "Form and Intent in the American New Criticism," immediately follows an opening essay ("Criticism and Crisis") intended to introduce de Man's ontological imperative. "Criticism and Crisis" builds toward the statement that [texts like Rousseau's consist] "of the presence of a nothingness. Poetic language names this void with ever-renewed understanding. . . . This persistent

9. Corngold, "Error," p. 103.

naming is what we call literature" (*BI*, 18). It is a statement that gains most of its force by means of the comparative analysis that follows. In "Form and Intent," de Man argues that the New Criticism, because it regards literary texts as impersonal objects that deny their divided ontological status, mystifies both literature and the human condition. In fact, the New Critics' notion of the literary object is hopelessly implicated in a mystified "unity that belongs precisely to a living and natural organism." And since de Man insists that the movement grows out of the "larger metaphor of the analogy between language and a living organism" that has shaped so much of modernist thought (*BI*, 27), for him not only the New Critics but the whole Anglo-American notion of modernism is corrupt and backward looking. In the book's final essays, "Literary History and Literary Modernity" and "Lyric and Modernity," de Man argues that the literature that generated the New Criticism is in Hegel's normative sense hardly "modern" at all, and that the inauthentic kind of history we have relied on to construct a story of the modern is radically deficient.

The most polemical essay in *Blindness and Insight* was also the most influential. "Literary History and Literary Modernity" makes an extended critical analysis of Anglo-American modernism and New Criticism the center of de Man's rejection of literary history. "[W]e all speak readily," de Man writes, "about modern literature and even use this term as a device for historical periodization, with the same apparent unawareness that history and modernity may well be even more incompatible than literature and modernity" (*BI*, 142). For him, the issues are clear. Literature, like "man himself," is defined by a capability of putting its own "mode of being into question" (*BI*, 165). Ontologically, that is, literature has to do with an authenticity derived from negation. Therefore the only valid history we can have of literature resembles a Heideggerian history of Being, which is to say a naming of man's unchanging divided mode of being and an "abandoning [of] the pre-assumed concept of history as generative process" (*BI*, 164).

These truths come into focus when we consider the contradictions involved in the notion of the modern, a notion, de Man insists, that has little to do with what century we live in. For

despite "some French and American contemporaries" who
would locate the modern in our time and place, embroiling us
"in qualifications and discriminations that are, in fact, superficial matters of geographical and historical contingency," the
"modern," de Man claims, has more to do with a recurring set
of attitudes Nietzsche connected with "life." A more "authentic spirit of modernity," in this sense, is a recurrent "radical
impulse" to forget the past that belongs to some of what the
deluded call "the moderns" more than others. It is, for example, "the tone of Rimbaud when he declares that he has no
antecedents whatever . . . that all one has to expect from poets
is 'de Nouveau'" (*BI*, 147), and it can be equated with "a desire to wipe out whatever came earlier, in the hope of reaching
at last a point that could be called a true present, a point of
origin that marks a new departure" (*BI* 148). Yet even this notion, which is both divorced from history and opposed to it, de
Man continues, is naive. As Nietzsche demonstrates in "Of the
Use and Misuse of History for Life," it is impossible to con-
ceptualize the new except in historical terms. Thus "modernity and history" must be seen "to relate to each other in a
curiously contradictory way that goes beyond antithesis or opposition. If history is not to become sheer regression or paralysis, it depends on modernity for its duration and renewal; but
modernity cannot assert itself without being at once swallowed
up and reintegrated into a regressive historical process" (BI,
151). True modernity, de Man concludes, involves not just a
recurrent human impulse toward the new, but the dividedness
that this recurrent impulse necessarily reveals. In this sense,
modernity is at one with literature and with the mode of being
of man himself. Thus modernity is "one of the concepts by
means of which the distinctive nature of literature can be revealed in all its intricacy" (*BI*, 161), and "literature has always
been essentially modern" (*BI*, 151). Consequently, literature is
impervious to genetic literary history, which bleaches out dividedness, and literature may put into question "history in
general" (*BI*, 165).

Persuaded by these arguments, a great many of de Man's
students have come to believe that pursuing the literary history
of modernism is doubly silly. For them literary history in gen-

eral is suspect because it precludes the kind of authentically modern existential history that "would be able to maintain the literary aporia throughout [and] account at the same time for the truth and the falsehood of the knowledge literature conveys about itself" (*BI*, 164). The literary history of modernism, however, is even more pernicious since it also obscures the liberating problematic of modernity disclosed by post-Hegelian discourse. Linked to conservative cultural ideology, willing to give only peripheral status to Rimbaud and the writers of the new, modernism as the academy has conceived it associates itself with superficial historical contingencies and ignores the existential complexity of human life.

The irony of de Man's discussion, of course, is that it has reshaped and reinforced the course of the very literary history it opposed. Since *Blindness and Insight,* so many students have followed de Man's exhortation to study the modernity of the late eighteenth and early nineteenth centuries that the profession's emphases have altered. And although "modernity" continues to have some cachet, more and more the modernist writers de Man defined himself against have become objects of condescending philosophical or ideological analysis that regards the modernists' own "mystified" notion of the modern as the mark of an essential benightedness. A salient case in point is Perry Meisel's 1987 *The Myth of the Modern,* which argues that, in lieu of "a dialogical notion of referentiality . . . any claim that literature's self-announced crisis of the modern is rooted directly in the events of the present century is based on a variety of dubious premises." Announcing his own canon of truly modern writers, Meisel announces he will take "the difference between the playful, self-accounting discourses of Hardy, Pater, Joyce, and Bloomsbury, and the rhetorically repressive, incrementally mythmaking work of Arnold, Lawrence, and Eliot as the line that distinguishes what we call art and criticism from the reifications of ideology as such."[10]

10. Perry Meisel, *The Myth of the Modern: A Study in British Literature and Criticism after 1850* (New Haven: Yale University Press, 1987), p. 3.

The mirror image of an argument like Meisel's is one that attempts to illustrate de Man's contention that "literature has always been essentially modern," and these too have become commonplace among de Man's followers. So Howard Felperin argues in *Shakespearean Representation* that "the literary modernity of which Shakespearean tragedy serves as a paradigm" is "not a matter of chronology or period," but rather begins with the fact that "both modernity and mimesis seek ultimately to break through or away from the mediations of art and become spontaneous and unprecedented 'life.' It is in this sense that Shakespearean tragedy can fairly be called 'modern' and 'mimetic' without contradiction, at least as modern and mimetic as literature has ever succeeded in becoming."[11]

But if the "modern" is thus dehistoricized, what are the consequences? One, of course, is that pre-twentieth-century works tend to lose some of their contextual focus, and the concerns of fictions throughout the ages begin to sound more and more alike. A second, no less serious, is that we lose a problematic but still useful way to characterize the literature of the twentieth century, and we give up what has been a difficult fight against that literature's own tendency to dehistoricize itself. Finally, the less we think of the modern as a historical category, the harder it is to come to terms with figures who insist that they transcend their own place and time: to understand, for example, that de Man himself was a man born in 1919, constituted by the rhetoric and some of the procedures of the modernist practice he would deconstruct, and vulnerable to the same kind of opacity that afflicted his antagonist, Eliot, and his master, Heidegger.

II

Although (as I shall discuss in the next section) it has become commonplace to associate de Man with the perceived shortcomings of the New Critics, rather less attention has been paid

11. Howard Felperin, *Shakespearean Representation: Mimesis and Modernity in Elizabethan Tragedy* (Princeton: Princeton University Press, 1977), pp. 6, 7, 8.

to the fact that many of deconstruction's strengths derive from affiliation with the very literature de Man so often took to task. For one thing, as Meisel might have been reminded by Frank Kermode's *The Sense of an Ending,* an analysis of modernism that anticipated some of de Man's political critique five years before *Blindness and Insight,* writers like Eliot, Pound, and Yeats did not blindly or mechanically produce artifacts of totalitarian ideology. True, these authors suffered lapses into authoritarian politics, but their most important work inscribed a critical consciousness of "organicist" and "totalitarian" impulses within modernist literary structure. In Kermode's words, their "mood was eschatological, but scepticism . . . held in check what threatened to be a bad case of literary primitivism."[12] At their best they were self-conscious of their own ideology, and they made that self-consciousness their fundamental subject. One has only to think of recent commentary on *The Waste Land* to realize the truth of his assertion. Although the poem was for years described by admirers and critics alike as celebrating an actual historical break with the past, it has now become a commonplace that *The Waste Land* may allow no such inference. As James Longenbach has recently pointed out, Eliot went out of his way to emphasize the poem's figural status.[13] And as another recent book contends, the structure of *The Waste Land,* far from articulating an organicist totality, might better be described in terms of a series of texts followed by deliberately unreliable explanations of the phenomena they attempt to explain.[14]

Nor is *The Waste Land* an exception. Like it, *Ulysses, Hugh Selwyn Mauberley,* and *Women in Love* among others exhibit a self-consciousness about the partiality of assertions, and this self-consciousness is closely related to what de Man found in Rousseau. Which is no doubt why de Man's characterizations of paradigmatic Romantic texts so often turn out to fit mod-

12. Frank Kermode, *The Sense of an Ending: Studies in the Theory of Fiction* (New York: Oxford University Press, 1966), p. 104.

13. James Longenbach, "Matthew Arnold and the Modern Apocalypse," *PMLA* 104/5 (October 1989): 845–846.

14. See Louis Menand, *Discovering Modernism: T. S. Eliot and His Context* (New York: Oxford University Press, 1987), p. 89.

ernist ones even better. ("[In Hölderlin] poetic language can do nothing but originate anew over and over again; it is always constitutive, able to posit regardless of presence but, by the same token, unable to give a foundation to what it posits except as an intent of consciousness. The word is always a free presence to the mind, the means by which the permanence of natural entities can be put into question and thus negated, time and again, in the endlessly widening spiral of the dialectic" [*RR*, 6].) Or, to quote *Blindness and Insight* against itself, it is true that we cannot "divide the twentieth century into two parts: a 'creative' part that was actually modern, and a 'reflective' or 'critical' part that feeds on this modernity in the manner of a parasite" (*BI*, 143). But it is true not just because "the field of literary theory and criticism" possesses a 'creativity' resembling earlier poetry and fiction (*BI*, 144). The reason also has to do with the 'critical' self-consciousness of modernist work.[15]

Further, it is one of the ironies of recent literary study that while one set of poststructuralist critics begins by assuming the thoroughgoing "organicist" ideology of early twentieth-century writing, another set has accelerated an already well established literary historical tendency to emphasize modernist irony and skepticism. Thus when de Man and his followers maintain that literature "does not fulfill a plenitude but originates in the void that separates intent from reality" (*BI*, 34), they use many of the same phrases with which one school of literary historians has described *Ulysses*.[16] And when de Man, in "The Rhetoric of Temporality," derives a notion of irony related to man's discontinuous being from the discussion of pratfalls in Baudelaire's "De l'essence du rire," he points to a formation of being and language easily associated with the near ubiquitous modernist clown.[17] More strikingly, Jacques Der-

15. On the modernist anticipation of these positions, see Longenbach, "Matthew Arnold," p. 845.

16. See, for example, Michael Groden, *Ulysses in Progress* (Princeton: Princeton University Press, 1977).

17. See, for example, Fred Miller Robinson, *The Comedy of Language: Studies in Modern Comic Literature* (Amherst: University of Massachusetts Press, 1980), especially the chapters on Joyce, Stevens, and Beckett.

rida has recently associated his own project with Joyce, and deconstructionist-minded critics have argued for essential connections between Pound and Nietzsche and Eliot and Heidegger.[18]

But the affiliations between de Man's project and modernism go deeper than the notions of self-consciousness, skepticism, or irony, and the deepest of them align de Man with ethical issues the bulk of his followers have claimed it was his genius to avoid. Consider this passage from "Impersonality in the Criticism of Maurice Blanchot" in which de Man endorses and extends Blanchot's reading of Mallarmé:

The various forms of negation that had been "surmounted" as [Mallarmé's] work progressed—death of the natural object, death of the individual consciousness in *Igitur*, or the destruction of a universal, historical consciousness destroyed in the "storm" of *Un Coup de dés*—turn out to be particular expressions of a persistent negative movement that resides in being. We try to protect ourselves against this negative power by inventing stratagems, ruses of language and of thought that hide an *irrevocable fall*. The existence of these strategies reveals the supremacy of the negative power they are trying to circumvent.   (*BI*, 73, emphasis mine)

Here the phrase "irrevocable fall" alludes (as de Man acknowledges three pages later) to Heidegger. As so often in *Blindness and Insight*, de Man invokes the notion of *Verfall*, one of Heidegger's conceits (in *Being and Time*) for conveying the shape of our being-in-the-world. De Man wants to remind us of our ontological limitations, and he has no more powerful tools than those developed by the philosopher of being-toward-death, the philosopher who renovated Hegel as a "thinker

18. For Derrida's comment ("every time I write, and even in the most academic pieces of work, Joyce's ghost is always coming on board"), see *Post Structuralist Joyce: Essays from the French*, ed. Derek Attridge and Daniel Ferrer (Cambridge: Cambridge University Press, 1984), p. 149. On Pound and Nietzsche, see Kathryne Lindberg, *Reading Pound Reading: Modernism after Nietzsche* (New York: Oxford University Press, 1987). On Eliot and Heidegger, see William V. Spanos, "Hermeneutics and Memory: Destroying T. S. Eliot's *Four Quartets*," *Genre* 11 (Winter 1978): 523–573.

of 'negation' and separation."[19] This pairing of Hegel and
Heidegger was introduced to de Man, as Lindsay Waters recounts in his admirable introduction to *Critical Writings,* by
Heidegger's disciple Alexandre Kojève, and by his colleague
Jean Wahl. In wartime and postwar Paris "de Man had considered writing a thesis on Hegel and Hölderlin under Wahl before
deciding to come to America." In Waters' words, it was intellectual training that prompted de Man to follow out the implications of modernity's principle of negation—a principle adumbrated against "Coleridge and the other exponents of
totality" by Adorno and "the Heidegger not of *Geist* but of
Riss (conflict)." "Convinced that death . . . separates us forever from nature, exponents of negation believe we can do no
better than to try to understand the structure of our failure to
know, to connect with nature, to make word and object coh-
ere" (*CW,* xxxiii–xxxiv).

But as George Steiner reminds us, notions like *Verfall* cannot help but recall Heidegger's theological training, and they
make his critical philosophy difficult to dissociate from the
"lineage of pessimism and admonition in Augustinian Christianity."[20] Emphasizing the admonition, Heidegger uses the notion of loss or negation to generate "a fertile dissatisfaction. It
opens busy, empty *Dasein* to the vertigo of the uncanny. In its
dizziness, *Dasein* hungers and wills beyond itself."[21] In linguistic terms, the notion requires us, aware of our inability to
name our being, to strive to constitute an authentically limited
discourse even as we are necessarily reminded (in de Man's
phrase) of the way our language resorts to "ruses . . . that hide
an irrevocable fall." This is the ethical imperative at the heart
of Heidegger's and de Man's discussions of language. And although in de Man's writing, particularly in the late seventies,
this pessimism and this admonition were translated into a concern with rhetorical aporias, his fundamental concerns were
not with critical procedures but with a view of human existence. No less than Eliot's denomination early in his career of

19. Quoted from Lindsay Waters's Introduction to *CW,* p. xxxiii.
20. George Steiner, *Martin Heidegger* (1976; rpt. Chicago: University of
Chicago Press, 1987), p. 147.
21. Steiner, *Martin Heidegger,* p. 100.

"the natural sin of language,"[22] de Man's aporias point toward
something larger than literature—something that the New Critics who domesticated Eliot liked to call a tragic sense of life.
For better or worse, both Eliot's interest in ambiguity and de
Man's in rhetoric are ethical and ultimately rooted in their
sombre sense of man in the world.

III

I am not the first to point out the connections between de Man
and Eliot, or even with the New Criticism. But so far most of
those who have done so have gone on to include de Man as an
object of his own reductive critique. To take an early and low-
keyed example, Gerald Graff, in *Literature Against Itself*,
points out that that "deconstruction is in many respects old
ambiguity and irony writ large . . . For the New Critic, the true
meaning is invariably an ironic inversion of the apparent or
explicit meaning. And the principle of ambiguity guarantees
that this true meaning will be indeterminate. The deconstructionist reading carries both the irony and the indeterminacy a
step further."[23]

Graff's argument has lately acquired a Marxist twist. Paul
Bové, for example, repeats many of the same points in a less
sympathetic key: "A description of some of the various deconstructive transformations of the New Criticism would be useful
in understanding the [larger socioeconomic contexts] of academic institutions . . . A preliminary sketching of those transformations would reveal how deconstruction has redeployed
the discursive power of the New Criticism's representation of
irony, author, the ideogram, propositional language, etc."[24]

Bové goes on to elaborate among other things the similarities between de Man's and the New Critics' "theoretical . . .
totalization," between New Critical irony and de Man's

22. T. S. Eliot, "The Post-Georgians," *Athenaeum* (April 11, 1919): 171.
23. Gerald Graff, *Literature Against Itself: Literary Ideas in Modern Society* (Chicago: University of Chicago Press, 1979), p. 145.
24. See Paul Bové, "Variations on Authority: Some Deconstructive
Transformations of the New Criticism," in Arac et al., *The Yale Critics*, pp.
8–9.

aporia, and between the deconstructionist "critique of the 'author'" and the "New Critical assault on 'intentionality.'"[25] In doing so he joins W. V. Spanos in tarring de Man's project with de Man's own brush. These are Spanos's words, cited by Bové:

In thus reducing the signifiers emerging from and addressing *different* historical/cultural situations to a timeless intertextual (ironic) text, deconstructive criticism ironically betrays its affiliation with the disinterested—and indifferent "inclusive" formalism of the New Criticism . . . which it is one of its avowed purposes to repudiate. The deconstructive reader, like the New Critic . . . becomes a distanced observer of the "scene of textuality" or, in Kierkegaard's term, an aesthete who perceives the text from the infinitely negative distance of the ironic mode.[26]

But is there any reason, once we recognize the continuities between de Man and his predecessors, to condemn them both and to condemn them in this way? In other words, must we agree with Frank Lentricchia who, sensing that de Man's "mood is all from early T. S. Eliot" ("we are Prufrocks all, all hollow men"), contends that de Man's conclusions constitute "for the literary mind a matrix of despair, resignation, futility, frustration, fatalism, cynicism and hopelessness," and adds that deconstruction is thus "conservatism by default"?[27] And once we acknowledge that there is a peculiarly modernist variety of bad faith at work when de Man asserts from an absolute, transhistorical point of view that "literature has always been essentially modern," must we also accept that this bad faith resides at the heart of the modernist project and is necessarily reactionary? Finally, ought we to affirm Terry Eagleton's explanation that "what for de Man is the irony of the human condition as such" is a displaced version of "the dilemmas of the liberal intellectual under late capitalism"?[28]

These questions might best be considered in light of the

25. Bové, "Variations," pp. 10–11.

26. Bové, "Variations," p. 5, quoting from W. V. Spanos, "Retrieving Heidegger's Destruction," *SCE Reports* 8 (Fall 1980): 30–53.

27. Lentricchia, *Criticism and Social Change*, pp. 49, 51.

28. Eagleton, *The Function of Criticism*, p. 100.

questioning of authority that is central not only to de Man's critique of modernism but also to the Marxists' critique of de Man. Although the core of de Man's message is that authoritative exposition is always blind, Graff, Lentricchia, Corngold, and Eagleton among others have pointed out that de Man consistently and systematically makes use of the tone and syntax of assurance.[29] As Graff writes, some of the deconstructionists' favorite words seem to be *always, never, only, all, must, and necessarily* (for example, "sign and meaning can never coincide"), and de Man shares their habit of declaring "a universal truth that makes no exceptions." Nor is this syntactic habit unrelated to larger issues. In Graff's words, "this self-assurance is more than a matter of tone; it characterizes the entire stance of the critic and determines the method of procedure."[30] For, as Eagleton points out, although de Man has in one sense discredited the authority of the intellectual ("he or she can no longer speak an authentic discourse"), in another sense he has reinforced the intellectual's ability "to deliver an authoritative message. That message, however, is now wholly empty and negative: it consists in the ceaseless act of naming the inauthenticity of all empirical engagements."[31]

These charges can, I think, be particularized and pushed further. For de Man's message is not quite as negative as Eagleton claims—it is related, as I have suggested above, to ethical imperatives that serve to ground action as well as judgment. In the earliest essay included in *Critical Writing* ("Montaigne and Transcendence," 1953), de Man praises Montaigne's resistance to Pyrrhonism and compares the Frenchman's assertion of the positive power of the mind to Husserl's moral phenomenology. In both writers he finds an emphasis on the "fundamental humility of the mind." And, he adds, both recognize that "just as reason's functioning must be preserved as an in-

29. See Gerald Graff, "Deconstruction as Dogma, or, 'Come Back to the Raft Ag'in, Strether-Honey!" *Georgia Review* (1980): 404–421; Lentricchia, *After the New Criticism*, p. 313; Corngold, "Error," 90–91; and Eagleton, *Against the Grain*, pp. 156, 160–161.

30. Graff, "Deconstruction as Dogma," pp. 409, 411, 409.

31. Eagleton, *Against the Grain*, pp. 160–161.

tegral part of our vitality, the ethical sense cannot dissolve into a pluralistic cynicism that would leave us in an impoverishing stagnation. The ethical gesture must continue, and naturally this gesture will begin in the continuity of an authority we can learn . . . it is not *the good* that matters but the formal procedure of ethical exercise" (*CW,* 9).

We can say, of course, that this is an early statement, unconnected to de Man's mature work. But that, I think, would be mistaken. Although the remarks certainly go against the oppositional application de Man and others would later give to his skepticism, the skeptical thrust of the essay as a whole (for example, "the lucid mind can know its own subjectivity, precisely at the point where subjectivity destroys its functioning" [*CW,* 7]) is consistent with his later writing. Also consistent, and perhaps more interesting, is de Man's belief that "the ethical sense cannot dissolve into a pluralistic cynicism." This conviction would cause the later de Man to steer determinedly clear of the nihilistic freedom of postmodernism,[32] and would drive the criticism of his last years toward what, in "Return to Philology," he speaks of as his duty to "respond to structures of language which it is the more or less secret aim of literary teaching to keep hidden" and to allow reading "to transform critical discourse in a manner that would appear deeply subversive to those who think of the teaching of literature as a substitute for the teaching of theology, ethics, psychology, or intellectual history" (*RT,* 24).

There always was, in other words, a deeply evangelistic strain in de Man's work, a strain associated with Heideggerian prophesy and one that requires something firmer from us than the delights of free play. De Man lays claim to the ethical authority of the philosophy underlying deconstruction to justify his techniques, and he calls on us to see his techniques as instruments of his "ethical sense." Is this not another instance of the modernist desire to save us from ourselves, and can it

32. See Christopher Norris, *Paul de Man: Deconstruction and the Critique of Aesthetic Ideology* (New York: Routledge, 1988), pp. 74–78. Norris also comments on de Man and Husserl, pp. 172–174.

be free of that dark underside that led Pound into Italy and
Heidegger into the arms of the Third Reich?

One thing we can say for certain is that the evangelistic
thrust in de Man's writings has intensified in the works of his
disciples, and that its latest manifestations recall the questionable moments of modernism in a distinctive way. After de
Man's death, for example, J. Hillis Miller chose to call a collection of his criticism *The Ethics of Reading,* a title one of his
subsequent essays takes pains to justify. Following de Man's
recommendation at the conclusion of "Return to Philology"
that departments of English be changed from "large organiza-
tions in the service of everything" into "much smaller units"
dedicated to "professional specialization" in rhetorical reading
(*RT,* 26), Miller argues that "the proper ethical decision" incumbent on readers "is that we should give up the attempt to
transfer ethical themes directly from literature to life" and that
"departments of literature should reduce their function to a
kind of linguistic hygiene, that is, to a study of the rhetoric of
literature, what might be called 'literariness'." (For "literariness" in de Man, see *RT,* 9–11.) Miller goes on, "the rest
should be left to departments of history, philosophy, religion,
American studies, Victorian studies" and so on. And he concludes "by saying that the stakes are enormous in keeping the
rhetorical study of literature flourishing." He ends his essay
with his own prophetic volume turned up full blast: "I said
above that it would be beneficial to the health of our society to
have an abundance of good readers. I would go so far as to say
it would bring a millennium, the millennium of good readers,
the end of wars and of class conflict, an eternal reign of justice,
peace and happiness. That this millennium, like others, is ex-
ceedingly unlikely to occur is not incompatible with my conviction that one of the major tasks of higher education in the
next century will be to foster conditions in which good reading
as I have defined it is likely to happen."[33]

33. J. Hillis Miller, "Is There an Ethics of Reading?" in James Phelan,
ed., *Reading Narrative: Form, Ethics, Ideology* (Columbus: Ohio State
University Press, 1989), pp. 98–100.

Miller's claim here is stunning and perhaps a little self-consciously outrageous. Yet it is not entirely out of keeping with the moral fervor of his arguments or de Man's. Nor, I would point out, is it, in emphasis or rhetoric, unfamiliar to readers of modernist literature. Consciously or not, it replicates Ezra Pound's insistence at the beginning of the century that critical reading, practiced first by the artist who uses *le mot juste,* would bring a comparable millennium. Arguing for the importance of James Joyce's fiction, Pound said:

Flaubert pointed out that if France had studied his work they might have been saved a good deal in 1870. If more people had read *The Portrait* and certain stories in Mr. Joyce's *Dubliners* there might have been less recent trouble in Ireland . . . Clear thought and sanity depend on clear prose. They cannot live apart. The former produces the latter. The latter conserves and transmits the former . . . A nation that cannot write clearly cannot be trusted to govern, nor yet to think . . . The terror of clarity is not confined to any one people. The obstructionist and the provincial are everywhere, and in them alone is the permanent danger to civilization. Clear, hard prose is the safeguard and should be valued as such. The mind accustomed to it will not be cheated or stamped by national phrases and public emotionalities.[34]

De Man's followers would no doubt cry foul here, and with some justice. De Man's notion of critical reading is not the same as Pound's, and Pound's politics were very different from de Man's. But, as we may remember, not always. Let us return to "Montaigne and Transcendence," with its recommendation that even in the face of the mind's failures, "the ethical gesture must continue, and naturally this gesture will begin in the continuity of an orthodoxy we can learn" (*CW,* 9). I have suggested the connections between this essay and de Man's later work, but I could just as well have tied it back to his wartime journalism, especially to the notorious piece that recommends us to accept (presumably with our skepticism intact) the cul-

34. From "James Joyce: At Last the Novel Appears," originally published in *The Egoist* for February 1917 and reprinted in Forrest Read, ed., *Pound/Joyce: The Letters of Ezra Pound to James Joyce* (New York: New Directions, 1965), pp. 88–91.

tural hegemony of the Germans and, preserving our ethical
sense, approve "la création d'une colonie juive isolée de
l'Europe" (WJ, 45). Given the sweeping correlations that de
Man, his followers, and his sympathetic critics have made between the totalitarian aesthetics and the totalitarian politics of
modernism, such an association would be entirely in order. (Indeed, unaware of the "Montaigne" essay, Terry Eagleton
comes close to making it on the basis of the journalism alone
when he argues in the TLS that de Man's literary criticism is
continuous with wartime "extreme right-wingism" because of
an untransformed "resolute opposition to emancipatory politics."[35])

IV

Denis Donoghue, Christopher Norris, and Lindsay Waters
have argued that de Man's mature criticism is not an extension
but an extended critique of the wartime journalism he could
not disclose,[36] and despite the above discussion, I would fully
agree. It seems egregious to me to assume that de Man's wartime writings have a necessary connection to his later criticism. Nevertheless, as I have just demonstrated, such conclusions seem the inevitable outcome of recent analyses of
modernist literature and politics. Once we lump the entire
modernist project under the rubric of organicist neofascism, it
seems to me impossible to make distinctions between modernists or to distinguish between modernist writing that may in the
right political circumstances be used to support authoritarian
politics, and writing that is consciously political. To be more
specific, given the bluntness of the present critical fashion, the
scandal of Paul de Man begins to resemble the scandal of Ezra
Pound. True, de Man's antisemitism and collaborationism
were less extensive than Pound's (though one could argue they
did more harm), but they were no less beyond the pale. More
to the point, the pronouncements of de Man's literary criticism

35. *TLS,* May 26-June 1, 1989, p. 574.

36. See Denis Donoghue, "The Strange Case of Paul de Man," *New York
Review of Books,* June 29, 1989, pp. 32–37; Christopher Norris, *Paul de
Man,* pp. 179–180; Lindsay Waters, Introduction to *CW,* lxii.

seem by present standards no more and no less unrelated to
the barbarous totalities with which he rubbed shoulders than
were Pound's. If we are to discriminate between de Man's significant work and his fascist journalism, it will not be because
the two have no ideological affiliations. (Even Miller in this
case is not entirely innocent: even if we overlook the magister-
ial authority with which he links "reading as I have defined it"
with the salvation of the world, his comparison of "the study
of the rhetoric of literature" to "a kind of linguistic hygiene"
is not so unlike either the tenor of Pound's comments on Joyce
or the metaphors of "organic health and disease" that ob-
sessed Pound and slid all too easily into antisemitism.[37])

To conclude, it is difficult to deny de Man's affiliations with
the modernist situation. Whether we regard this in a positive
way (his work is based on a profound existentialist view of life)
or a negative one (his ethical imperatives were more compatible than he was aware with authoritarian politics), his philosophy of the void is implicated in modernism's salvationist
mood. Both are versions of twentieth-century antirationalism,
and both can be traced to the ambiguities of post-Romantic
skepticism that finally connect Heidegger and Husserl with
Hegel, and de Man with Eliot and Pound.[38] The tipoff is the
crusading rhetoric of de Man and his followers, and in using
the term I do not follow de Man's revisionary definition. The
rhetoric that counts here is not "the study of tropes and of
figures" but what de Man slightingly calls "the derived sense
of comment or of eloquence or persuasion" (*AR,* 6). In this
sense, de Man's, Miller's, and Pound's rhetorics admonish
with the inflections of antirationalist conviction.

Nevertheless, if examining de Man's affiliation with modern-

37. See Robert Casillo, *The Genealogy of Demons: Anti-Semitism, Fas-
cism and the Myths of Ezra Pound* (Evanston: Northwestern University
Press, 1988), pp. 53ff.

38. In Terry Eagleton's gloss, "no simple binary opposition can be established between 'ideology'—conceived as relentlessly closed and seamlessly
self-identical—and *écriture.* Deconstruction's failure to dismantle such an
opposition is the surest sign of its own ideological character, and of its col-
lusiveness with the liberal humanism it seeks to embarrass." (*The Function
of Criticism,* p. 102.)

ism tells us anything, it is that assertions about the univocal
political implications of modernist criticism are seriously inadequate. In de Man's career no less than in Pound's or Eliot's
it mattered a great deal whether statements of antirationalist
ideology were made self-consciously or unselfconsciously, and
in the latter case whether they fueled and were fueled by the
discourse of a particular moment of political debate. In esti-
mating the political meaning of writing composed with a high
degree of self-consciousness, it seems perverse to invoke de
Man's *Le Soir* articles or Pound's radio speeches.

On the other hand, it may be too much to argue, as de Man
does in an extremely interesting moment, that there is a strain
of nineteenth- and twentieth-century writing invulnerable to
political appropriation. In "The Literature of Nihilism" (1966),
de Man recalls that when the Nazis had established themselves, they tried "to interpret certain figures of the German
past [including Nietzsche] along hypernationalist and even racist lines," and that some of these attempts still persist among
the historians of German literature. But, de Man claims, "it
should be clear to anyone who follows . . . German critical
writing . . . that the poets themselves, in their own works, provide a very adequate defense against such misrepresentations"
(*CW,* 163).

The problem is that in the interactions of history, the modernist critique of rationalism seems never to be fully defended.
It is *not* a misrepresentation to say there is a side of Nietzsche
that allowed him to be championed by the Nazis. Which brings
us back to contexts, and to the notion that literary history may
sometimes be something other than the totalizing and mystified narrative de Man describes in "Literary History and Literary Modernity." It may, instead, serve to keep not the ontological but the historical and ideological inconsistencies of
literature open. Some of the best recent historical work on
twentieth-century literature, especially textual work, has operated in this spirit—including Michael Levenson's *A Genealogy of Modernism* and Sanford Schwartz's *The Matrix of Modernism* on Pound and Eliot; Sandra Siegal's commentary on
Yeats's *Purgatory*; and Hans Gabler and Jerome McGann on

the text of *Ulysses*.[39] All of these studies demonstrate that
what at first appears to be ideological consistency in one or
another of the modernist writers turns out to be a complex and
sometimes contradictory tissue of ideological connections,
usually unstable and often capable of unexpected change.

In a final irony, one might argue that such studies are following in the footsteps of de Man. For it seems to me that de Man
practices just this kind of literary history in "Genesis and Genealogy," when he avails himself of the textual scholarship
that excavated "lateral material for *The Birth of Tragedy* that
Nietzsche left out" (*AR,* 99). With the aid of this material (and,
according to Stanley Corngold, a convenient mistranslation[40]),
de Man argues that Nietzsche's organicist myths are less powerful than the published text reveals. It is in what de Man himself calls this "historiographical" moment, before he goes on
to assert that such disjunction "turns out to be a recurrent
structural principle of Nietzsche's work from the start" or "a
paradigm of poetic language" (*AR,* 101, 102), that I would locate a critical as opposed to a totalizing form of literary history. With such techniques one can begin to construct suitably
qualified accounts of literature and ideology and perhaps even
perform what J. Hillis Miller maintains is theoretically "non-
negotiable": a negotiation "between the rhetorical study of literature . . . and the now so irresistibly attractive study of the
extrinsic relations of literature."[41]

39. See Michael Levenson, *A Genealogy of Modernism* (Cambridge:
Cambridge University Press, 1984); Sanford Schwartz, *The Matrix of Mod-
ernism* (Princeton: Princeton University Press, 1985); Sandra Siegel, ed.,
Purgatory: Manuscript Materials Including the Author's Final Text (Ithaca:
Cornell University Press, 1986); Jerome McGann, "*Ulysses* as Postmodern
Work," in *Social Values and Poetic Acts: The Historical Judgment of Literary Work* (Cambridge, Mass.: Harvard University Press, 1988), pp. 173–
196; and Hans Walter Gabler, "The Synchrony and Diachrony of Texts:
Practice and Theory of the Critical Edition of James Joyce's *Ulysses,*" *Text*
(1981): 305–327.
40. See Corngold, "Error," p. 104.
41. Miller, "Is There an Ethics of Reading?," p. 81.

PAUL A. CANTOR

Aristotle and the
History of Tragedy

I

To suggest that Aristotle might have something to teach us
about literary history must sound almost as strange as declaring him to be an authority on genetic engineering. Aristotle
wrote long before the concept of literary history was supposedly developed.[1] In fact, today he often serves as an example
of *ahistorical* thinking, a representative of what is sometimes
called essentialist humanism.[2] Whatever Aristotle's differences from Plato may be, he is said to share with his teacher
the illusion that things have eternal natures or essences, a fundamental character which can be separated from the accidents
of history. In literary terms, Aristotle's belief in eternal truths
is supposed to be reflected in his belief in the fixed nature of

1. See D. A. Russell, *Criticism in Antiquity* (Berkeley: University of
California Press, 1981), p. 158: "There can be little doubt that the historical
study of literature in antiquity was very rudimentary by modern standards."
Russell's chapter on "Literary History" (pp. 159–168) goes on to survey
the rudiments of literary history in antiquity, including a brief look at
Aristotle's contribution.
2. For a discussion and a critique of essentialist humanism, see, for ex-
ample, Jonathan Dollimore, *Radical Tragedy: Religion, Ideology and
Power in the Drama of Shakespeare and His Contemporaries* (Chicago:
University of Chicago Press, 1984), pp. 249–271.

genres. In his *Poetics* he appears to be elucidating the nature of tragedy for all time, that is, as a transhistorical possibility, permanently available to all writers.[3] Evidently blind to the historicity of literature, Aristotle is accused of mistaking what are merely Greek literary conventions for the nature of literature itself. It seems to some readers of the *Poetics* that just because Sophocles introduced a third actor on the Athenian stage, Aristotle came to understand tragedy as somehow requiring three actors by nature.

Despite this widespread impression of the *Poetics,* I want to argue that Aristotle's thinking on the problem of history and literature is more sophisticated than is usually acknowledged, and in particular that his "essentialist" notion of genre is precisely what provides him with a powerful analytic tool for understanding literary history. We may recall that Aristotle gives a history of Greek tragedy in the *Poetics,* an account which, brief as it is, remains one of our few sources of historical information on the subject. The presence of a history of poetry in Chapter 4 of the *Poetics* is a good reminder that, however essentialist Aristotle's thinking may have been, he liked to take facts into account in his arguments. Indeed, he seems to have had a passion for facts, which drove him to collect all sorts of data. He is, for example, credited with being the first to compile lists of the winners at the Pythian games,[4] which thus entitles him to the claim of being the earliest known sports statistician. Perhaps, then, we should not assume on the basis of some abstract categorization of classical philosophy as essentialist that Aristotle was utterly lacking in a sense of history,

3. See, for example, Stephen Halliwell, *Aristotle's Poetics* (Chapel Hill: University of North Carolina Press, 1986), pp. 92–96 and 255–256, and also his edition of *The Poetics of Aristotle* (Chapel Hill: University of North Carolina Press, 1987), pp. 79–81. For a contrary view of the *Poetics,* that "the basis of the whole work, indeed, is historical" (p. 63), see R. S. Crane, *The Languages of Criticism and the Structure of Poetry* (Toronto: University of Toronto Press, 1953).

4. See Gerald Else, *Plato and Aristotle on Poetry* (Chapel Hill: University of North Carolina Press, 1986), p. 68 and James Hutton, trans., *Aristotle's Poetics* (New York: Norton, 1982), p. 3. Aristotle was also the first to compile lists of the plays produced in Athens. See Richard Janko, trans., *Aristotle: Poetics* (Indianapolis: Hackett, 1987), p. xiv.

but rather take a look at Chapter 4 of the *Poetics* to see concretely how he approached a historical question.

There are of course many difficulties in dealing with the *Poetics* in general and Chapter 4 in particular. As happens with
all the texts of Aristotle which have come down to us, we do
not know the most basic facts about the *Poetics* with any certainty: what kind of text it is, who it was addressed to, what
function it was supposed to serve.[5] The sketchiness of the discussion has suggested to many readers that the *Poetics* may be
nothing more than Aristotle's lecture notes, or perhaps a kind
of textbook compiled for his students at the Lyceum. It com-
plicates matters that Aristotle's texts have been imperfectly
transmitted to us. The *Poetics* is obviously incomplete, lacking
above all the second book on comedy; moreover, the text we
have displays many signs of corruptions, perhaps of interpo-
lations.[6] Chapter 4 has more than its share of textual problems,
leading editors to propose so many emendations, transposi-
tions, excisions, and additions in this section that translations
of it often diverge significantly. Finally, many analysts have
challenged the historical accuracy of Aristotle's account of the
origins of Greek tragedy.[7] Though they may have a difficult
time finding hard historical facts to cite against Aristotle, these
critics insist that he was not interested in giving an objective
picture of the development of Greek tragedy but rather bent

5. For a brief summary of the status and transmission of Aristotle's texts,
see A. A. Long, "Aristotle," in P. E. Easterling and B. M. W. Knox, eds.,
The Cambridge History of Classical Literature. I: *Greek Literature* (Cambridge: Cambridge University Press, 1985), p. 530. See also Janko, p. xxii.

6. See, for example, Else, *Plato and Aristotle,* pp. 87–88.

7. For a good summary of what is currently thought about the origins of
Greek tragedy, see R. P. Winnington-Ingram, "The Origins of Tragedy," in
Cambridge History, pp. 258–263. For the questioning of Aristotle's historical accuracy and even of his interest in history, see Arthur Pickard-
Cambridge, *Dithyramb, Tragedy and Comedy* (Oxford: Clarendon Press,
1962), 2nd ed., rev. T. B. L. Webster, pp. vi, 95; Else, *Plato and Aristotle,*
p. 89; and Gerald Else, *The Origin and Early Form of Greek Tragedy* (New
York: Norton, 1972), p. 14 (and especially note 14). Before dismissing Aristotle's testimony as a historian of tragedy, we might recall what Webster
says in his revision of Pickard-Cambridge, even after leaving the original
dismissive account of chapter 4 of the *Poetics* intact: "It is perfectly true
that Aristotle was a theorist, as we are, but he was very much nearer the
origin of tragedy than we are and much more intelligent" (p. 97).

the facts to fit his theoretical understanding of the genre. With the text and purpose of Chapter 4 so uncertain, it is hardly surprising that discussions of this section have proven to be highly speculative and controversial.[8]

II

Aristotle's account in Chapter 4 seems at first sight to be confused, if not outright contradictory. He begins in typically Greek fashion by giving all credit to Homer: according to Aristotle, Homer provides the source not only of tragedy but of comedy as well. In order to place him at the fountainhead of comedy, Aristotle must attribute the comic poem the *Margites* to Homer (an attribution rejected by modern scholars). But Aristotle almost immediately appears to reverse himself and to take a more modern, "anthropological" approach. Instead of looking for literary sources, he turns to what we would call popular culture and sees the origin of tragedy and comedy in elementary forms of Greek entertainment: dithyrambs, phallic songs, satyr plays, and other kinds of festivities and rites which had an improvisational character. Aristotle thus appears to end up in the odd position of claiming that tragedy began with the *Iliad* and yet did not purge itself of short or trivial plots and humorous or grotesque diction until late in its history.

Various commentators have proposed emendations of Chapter 4 to try to straighten out Aristotle's history of tragedy, but others have noted that it is only the compression of the account

8. In addition to the Halliwell, Hutton, and Janko editions cited above, I have used the following translations of the *Poetics:* S. H. Butcher in *Aristotle's Poetics* (New York: Hill and Wang, 1961); Ingram Bywater in *The Rhetoric and the Poetics of Aristotle* (New York: Modern Library, 1954); T. S. Dorsch in *Classical Literary Criticism* (Harmondsworth: Penguin Books, 1965); Gerald F. Else, *Aristotle's Poetics: The Argument* (Cambridge: Harvard University Press, 1967); W. Hamilton Fyfe in the Loeb Classical Library (Cambridge: Harvard University Press, 1932); and M. E. Hubbard in D. A. Russell and M. Winterbottom, eds., *Ancient Literary Criticism* (Oxford: Clarendon Press, 1972). I cite first by the standard Bekker numbers for Aristotle's text and then by the name and page numbers of whichever translation I am using at the moment. For helpful comments on a preliminary draft of this essay, I wish to thank Charles Griswold, Jr., Michael Valdez Moses, David Perkins, and Zeph Stewart.

which makes it seem confused. The complexity in the way Aristotle uses the concept of the tragic is at the root of the difficulties. In the *Poetics,* when Aristotle is discussing the tragic he is usually referring to what we think of as Greek tragedy, that is, a certain kind of play produced in Athens in the fifth century B.C. But at times in the *Poetics* the tragic has a broader meaning, referring to a larger literary possibility, of which classic Greek tragedy is only one realization (though perhaps the highest or most perfect one). In Aristotle's view, Homer is the earliest example we have of the tragic in this more general sense, while forms of popular entertainment in Greece provide the origins of tragedy in the first or more restricted sense. Or to be more accurate, what we think of as Greek tragedy results for Aristotle from a fusion of Homeric tragic subjects with popular forms of entertainment, a fusion brought about perhaps as early as Thespis or perhaps not until Aeschylus.[9] What may at first appear to be confusion on Aristotle's part thus in fact reflects the complexity of his analysis of literary history, in particular his ability to sort out content and form in literature, while still being able to see the two as related (with one kind of form being more suited to one kind of content).

To clarify Aristotle's history of tragedy, one must bear in mind that he classifies forms of imitation along three major axes in the *Poetics*: medium, object, and mode of imitation.[10]

9. On the role of Thespis, see Albin Lesky, *Greek Tragedy,* trans. H. A. Frankfort (London: Ernest Benn, 1978), 3rd. ed., pp. 47–50; Pickard-Cambridge, *Dithyramb, Tragedy, and Comedy,* pp. 69–89; and Else, *Origin,* chapter 3, especially pp. 64 and 68 on his relation to Homer: "Thespis felt in Homer the compelling reality of the heroic nature and the heroic fate; he wanted to give this vision and feeling some immediate expression, more direct and pungent than it received in the recitations of Homer . . . Thespis' new creation, therefore, brought together three different things which had never been joined before: the *epic hero, impersonation,* and *iambic verse* . . . Idea and form or inner and outer form came together." Aristotle does · not mention Thespis in the *Poetics,* but the ancient orator Themistius (*Orat.* 26) quotes Aristotle speaking of the legendary dramatist, perhaps in his lost dialogue, *On Poets* (see Pickard-Cambridge, pp. 70, 78, and Else, *Origin,* p. 53). For the view of Aeschylus as the creator of tragedy, see Else, *Origin,* p. 78.

10. On this issue, see Else, *Poetics,* p. 136 and *Plato and Aristotle,* pp. 85–86.

The last two categories are central to Aristotle's attempt to define what is specific to tragedy. In terms of object of imitation, tragedy for Aristotle is the representation of higher types of human beings or the noble (*spoudaios*).[11] In terms of mode of imitation, tragedy involves theatrical representation. Depending on which scheme of classification he has in mind, Aristotle groups authors differently: "Consequently, in one respect Sophocles uses the same mimesis as Homer, for in both cases the objects are good men [*spoudaios*]; while in another respect, Sophocles and Aristophanes are parallel, since both use the mimetic mode of dramatic enactment" (1448a; Halliwell, 33). This consideration explains the otherwise puzzling prominence of Homer in Aristotle's discussion of tragedy in the *Poetics*. For Aristotle both epic and tragedy are realizations of what one might call the tragic idea, since both portray noble characters in the kinds of actions that display their nobility. In the course of the *Poetics* Aristotle investigates which of the two forms is more fully capable of embodying the tragic idea. Though he concludes in favor of the dramatic form of tragedy, he still gives Homer pride of place in the *Poetics* as the discoverer of the tragic idea.[12]

The distinctions Aristotle is making are clearer in the original Greek (though he is not entirely consistent in his usage). The word for "genre" Aristotle usually uses is *eidos*, a word

11. The Greek word *spoudaios* is normally translated as *good* or *serious*. However one chooses to translate the term, the essential point is that Aristotle understands *spoudaios* in contrast to *phaulos*, and that together the two terms reflect the hierarchy of aristocratic society in ancient Greece. *Spoudaios* characterizes the way of life of the Greek hero or warrior or noble; *phaulos* the way of life of the ordinary man, the slave, or the commoner. In short, the Greek terms correspond to the terms *good* and *bad* in master morality as analyzed by Nietzsche in *The Genealogy of Morals* (First Essay). For an excellent and detailed discussion of the meaning of *spoudaios*, see Else, *Poetics*, pp. 73–78. See also Walter Kaufmann, *Tragedy and Philosophy* (Garden City, N.Y.: Anchor Books, 1969), pp. 46–48 and John Jones, *On Aristotle and Greek Tragedy* (Stanford: Stanford University Press, 1980), pp. 56–57. For the purposes of my argument, I will continue to translate *spoudaios* as *noble* in order to keep the focus on the elevated status of the Aristotelian tragic hero.

12. For a good discussion of Homer's importance to Greek tragedy, see the chapter "Homer and the Birth of Tragedy" in Kaufmann, *Tragedy and Philosophy*, pp. 159–190.

which carries the sense of *kinds* or, particularly as developed
by Plato, the sense of things naturally sorting out into classes
or species.[13] But in the *Poetics* Aristotle uses another word
when discussing genre: *schema* or its plural, *schemata*. For
example, in the discussion of comedy in Chapter 4 (1448b–
1449a), he says that Homer was the first to adumbrate the
schemata of comedy. This word gives translators a problem,
and they have come up with a variety of solutions. Butcher
and Fyfe translate it as "main lines of comedy" (56;17),
Bywater as "general forms" (228), Else as "main forms" (143),
Dorsch as "forms" (36), Hutton as "idea" (48), and Hubbard,
Janko, and Halliwell as "form" (95; 5; 35). The translators
tend to gravitate toward some variant of *form* for *schema,* but
the problem with that choice is that *eidos* is also frequently
translated as *form*. If Aristotle is trying to distinguish between
eidos and *schema,* his intention becomes obscured in these
translations. Carnes Lord, who seems to have been the first
to call attention to this issue, explains Aristotle's use of
schemata:

Aristotle does speak of the *schemata* of comedy in the account of
comedy in Chapter 5 . . . "It was only at a late date that the archon
provided a chorus of comedians, while previously they were volun-
teers; and it was only when it already possessed some of its forms
[*schemata*] that the names of the comic poets came to be recorded;
but as to who was responsible for masks or prologues or the number
of actors, it is not known" (49b1–5) . . . In fact, the meaning of *schemata* is relatively clear from its context; Aristotle is thinking . . . of
choruses, masks, prologues and actors. The *schemata* of comedy are
precisely its theatrical externals, the outward "forms" of comedy
understood as theatrical poetry, as a kind of poetry which is acted or
performed. *Schema* must be distinguished from *eidos*. Generally
speaking, *schema* can signify the external form of a thing as distinguished from its inner or constitutive form, its essence or being
[*eidos*].[14]

13. An analogy in English is the Renaissance use of *kind*, with its connotations of naturalness, to refer to *genre*. See Rosalie Colie, *The Resources of Kind: Genre-Theory in the Renaissance* (Berkeley: University of
California Press, 1973).
14. Carnes Lord, "Aristotle's History of Poetry," *Transactions of the*

The way Lord applies the distinction between *eidos* and *schema* to Aristotle's account of comedy in the *Poetics* is very complicated and depends on speculations concerning the *Margites* (which survives only in fragments). Suffice it to say here that Lord concludes that Aristotle views Homer as important to the history of comedy because he turned from composing invectives in his own voice to dramatizing the ludicrous.[15] Without getting involved in Lord's discussion of the details of Aristotle's treatment of comedy, I want to use the distinction he draws between *eidos* and *schema* to reflect on Aristotle's understanding of genre and literary history. In a sense the key to understanding the *Poetics* is to see that for Aristotle every work of literature has, as it were, an "eidetic" and a "schematic" aspect, and the interplay between these two factors is what is involved in literary history and in particular in the development of genres. In this view, *eidos* corresponds roughly to what we think of as content in literature and *schema* to form. But these terms are more properly understood in the context of Aristotle's two axes for analyzing literature, with *eidos* pointing to the object of imitation and *schema* to the mode. The full understanding of a work of literature requires taking into account both *eidos* and *schema*, so that for Aristotle tragedy in the specific sense is the theatrical representation of noble actions.[16] But this does not necessarily mean that *eidos* and *schema* are of equal importance. Judging by the course of the argument in the *Poetics*, the governing principle of tragedy is the aim of representing noble actions, and what Aristotle investigates is which theatrical forms or conventions are best suited to this overarching purpose. In discussing met-

---

American Philological Society, 104 (1974), 200. This learned and careful analysis of one section of the *Poetics* has profound and wide-ranging implications for our understanding of the work as a whole (it has of course proved to be controversial; see, for example, Halliwell, *Aristotle's Poetics*, p. 94 n. 16). I wish to acknowledge that Lord's essay provided the germ of my own; in many respects, I am simply trying to work out the larger implications of his argument.

15. Cf. Else, *Plato and Aristotle*, p. 94.
16. Cf. Else, *Poetics*, p. 150.

rics, for example, he is looking for the meter which will suitably convey the dignity tragedy requires in order to display nobility. In line with Aristotle's general tendency to approach the problem of form in teleological terms, the *Poetics* may be viewed as an investigation of the *schemata* appropriate to the *eidos* of tragedy. To the extent that Aristotle sees an inner essence of tragedy, it is very general and conceived as an end (representing nobility); he views the specific forms that fulfill this function as somehow external to it, though capable of being understood as more or less suited to the function.[17]

III

With these distinctions in mind, let us look once again at Aristotle's history of tragedy. Aristotle views Homer as the first tragic writer because the purpose of the *Iliad* and the *Odyssey* is the representation of noble characters and noble deeds. But writing in the narrative mode of epic poetry, Homer was not able to exploit all the techniques of theatrical representation. Aristotle sees these techniques developing in various modes of Greek popular entertainment, such as the dithyrambs and phallic songs. Because they are staged in one way or another, these popular forms have a more immediate impact and thus a greater potential for affecting an audience than mere narratives or recitations—that in fact is why they are popular. But they are also at first vulgar: they do not deal with elevated subject matter or use elevated diction. In that sense, a step forward in the development of the technical means of representation can mean a step backward in terms of the objects of imitation. Entranced by the novelty of theatrical representation, audiences may desert the noble subjects of Homeric epic for the cheap thrills of dithyrambs and phallic songs.

This development may be what Aristotle has in mind when

17. Cf. Crane's formulation of the aim of the *Poetics* (p. 57): "to distinguish [the] essential artistic principles from the conventions of material or technique through which the principles are realized at any given time."

he says that poets "abandoned epic for tragedy, because the latter's forms were greater than, and superior to, epic's" (1449a; Halliwell, 35). As usually translated, this passage seems in line with Aristotle's general preference for tragedy as a dramatic form over epic, and hence it seems to treat the turn from epic to tragedy as an unequivocal gain from the beginning. But as Lord points out, if one looks at what Aristotle says of these new forms in Greek, "he does not say that they were 'worthy of more esteem,' 'more honorable' or better than Homeric poetry. What he says is that they were 'held in more esteem,' 'more honored' (*entimotera*) than Homeric poetry" (208). This is the sense Hutton conveys in his translation of the passage: they "became tragic poets instead of epic poets because the new types were more important—i.e., got more favorable attention, than the earlier ones" (48). This way of translating the passage suggests that the poets went over to the theatrical modes not because of their intrinsic artistic superiority but because of their greater popularity. This reading gains support from the fact that the Greek word variously translated as *forms* and *types* here is not *eide* but *schemata,* suggesting that in this passage Aristotle's focus is on changes in mode rather than object of representation. That is, at this point Aristotle is not yet speaking of tragedy as a fully mature form, but dwelling upon the development of its *schemata,* the stage devices and techniques which constitute theatrical representation. And, as pleasing to an audience as these may be, they do not necessarily do anything to advance the embodiment of the tragic idea; in fact, given their vulgarity, they may very well run counter to it. Hence the move to tragedy considered solely as theatrical form, that is, without the Homeric subject of noble action, may well involve losses as well as gains.[18]

Thus in Aristotle's account, "tragic form" and "tragic content" are at first at odds: the development of theatrical means

18. For a different view, that Aristotle's reference to the appearance of tragedy and comedy in this passage is to their appearance in *Homer,* see Else, *Poetics,* pp. 146–148 and *Plato and Aristotle,* p. 95, and Lord, "Aristotle's History of Poetry," 208–210.

of representation initially diverts attention from Homer's original success at capturing the "tragic idea" in the form of epic
portrayals of noble deeds. In the specific sense of theater, tragedy has humble beginnings in Aristotle, and only gradually develops into a noble art form.[19] It took poets like Aeschylus and
Sophocles to find the poetic and theatrical means appropriate
to the dignity of tragedy and to purge it of the vulgar survivals
from its origins in forms of popular entertainment. With
Aeschylus and Sophocles poetry recaptured the elevated level
of the Homeric epics, once more portraying noble actions, but
now with all the accumulated force of theatrical representation
at its disposal. This fusion of object and mode of imitation is
evidently what Aristotle has in mind when he says of the development of tragedy, "after going through many changes, it
stopped when it had attained its inherent nature" (1449a; Else,
149). Tragedy reaches its peak of perfection, and hence in
Aristotle's sense realizes its nature,[20] only when it succeeds in
combining the nobility of Homer's vision with the fully developed power of theatrical representation.

IV

This account suggests that Aristotle's view of literary history
is quite sophisticated, especially in his ability to take into ac-

19. Because of the sublime associations which have accumulated around
the word *tragedy* over the centuries, we find it difficult to link the term with
anything low or crude. It is then perhaps well to remember that etymologically *tragedy* means "goat-song." To say that *tragedy* has humble beginnings sounds odd to us; to say that "goat-song" has humble beginnings
sounds more plausible. The origin of the word *tragedy* is a complicated and
much disputed matter, but there is no question that one root of the word is
the Greek name for goat. For the association between tragedy and goats,
see Pickard-Cambridge, *Dithyramb, Tragedy and Comedy*, pp. 112–124. See
also Gerald Else, "The Origin of *Tragôidia*," *Hermes*, 85 (1957): 17–46.
Else argues that the original form of the word was *tragôidos*, coined on the
analogy of *rhapsôidos*, and that as a way of referring to authors such as
Thespis it initially had a "jocose or pejorative connotation" (p. 43). This
interpretation has been much disputed. See, for example, Walter Burkert,
"Greek Tragedy and Sacrificial Ritual," *Greek Roman and Byzantine Studies* 7 (1966): 87–121.
    20. On this point, see, for example, *Politics*, 1252b30–34.

count several variables at once.[21] Indeed, according to this interpretation Aristotle begins to sound quite contemporary in his appreciation of the role of what we call popular culture in the development of the higher forms of art. Our wider perspective on literary history gives us the opportunity of citing many examples which confirm Aristotle's idea that technical advances in the means of representation brought about in the realm of popular entertainment become available to later artists, who are able to adapt them to higher purposes and give them depth. Shakespeare's relation to popular forms of Elizabethan entertainment is only the most obvious analogy to Aristotle's history of Greek tragedy.[22] One can see something similar in the history of the novel, which originally emerged as a subliterary, popular form, basically comic in impulse, but gradually became adapted to higher literary purposes until it eventually became capable of embodying the tragic vision of a Dostoevsky.[23]

The history of cinema provides one of the best analogies to Aristotle's history of tragedy. One aspect of his sophistication is that Aristotle does not view literary history as a simple case of linear progress, but understands that technical advances and seriousness of purpose may not always go hand in hand. The

21. Cf. Else, *Poetics*, p. 162: Aristotle is able "to strike a balance between literary and anthropological factors in the development of tragedy . . . Aristotle lets tragedy be begotten *out of* a matrix of social activity (the improvisations), but *by* individual artistic intuition of a form adumbrated by Homer."

22. See Robert Weimann, *Shakespeare and the Popular Tradition in the Theater*, trans. Robert Schwartz (Baltimore: Johns Hopkins University Press, 1978).

23. On Dostoevsky as a tragic novelist, see Vyacheslav Ivanov, *A Study in Dostoevsky: Freedom and the Tragic Life*, trans. Norman Cameron (New York: Noonday, 1957). As mention of Dostoevsky suggests, one might draw parallels between Aristotle and Bakhtin. As a story of the fusion or hybridization of genres, the development of tragedy as Aristotle presents it resembles the development of the novel in Bakhtin's account. Aristotle's reference to phallic songs and satyr plays seems to reflect an acknowledgment of the role of the Bakhtinian carnivalesque in the progress of art. For Bakhtin's theories of genre, see especially *The Dialogic Imagination*, trans. Caryl Emerson and Michael Holquist (Austin: University of Texas Press, 1981).

impact of the development of sound on the history of motion
pictures illustrates this principle well. Many film historians
have argued that the motion picture reached a kind of peak
with the silent films of the 1920s,[24] the comedies of directors
like Chaplin and Keaton and the serious films of directors like
Griffith, von Stroheim, Murnau, and Lang. But the coming of
sound destroyed this golden age. Audiences were so enthralled
by the new technical possibility of talking pictures that they
switched their allegiance almost immediately to the newly enhanced medium. The new talkies did of course mark a genuine
advance in representational possibilities, but because of the requirements—and limitations—of sound stages, this form of
cinematic progress in fact initially involved a major step backward for filmmakers. The first talking pictures were little more
than filmed stage plays and lost what had been distinctively
cinematic about the great films of the twenties. The spectacle
of audiences forsaking Abel Ganz's *Napoléon* for Al Jolson in
The Jazz Singer[25] is parallel to the switch of allegiance from
Homeric epic to more popular forms of theatrical representation. But like Aristotle's account of Greek tragedy, or for that
matter most stories coming out of Hollywood, the development of the cinema had a happy ending. With silent film directors like Fritz Lang making the transition successfully to sound
and new directors like Orson Welles coming along (out of an
even newer medium, radio), cinematic artists learned to master
sound techniques and motion pictures rose to new heights of
representational power. It is fruitless—though amusing—to
speculate what Aristotle would have thought of the motion picture, but the principles of literary history manifested in his account of Greek tragedy suggest that he could have understood
how the cinema got from *Intolerance* to *Citizen Kane* via *The
Jazz Singer*.

24. See, for example, Kevin Brownlow, *The Parade's Gone By* (Berkeley: University of California Press, 1968), p. 3: "The golden era was the
period from 1916 to 1928."
25. See Brownlow, *The Parade* p. 571: "In 1928, the least impressive
sound film attracted more interest than the finest of the silents." On the
American reception of *Napoléon*, released in 1928 by MGM in a butchered
version, see p. 563.

V

For Aristotle, the "schematic" aspect of literature is largely responsible for its historicity. Because changes in *schemata* may often involve purely technical innovations, they will not always occur for artistic reasons and their aesthetic significance may not even at first be appreciated. Thus literary history cannot be a self-contained subject, but must constantly make reference to nonliterary developments. Authors often feel compelled to respond to changes in the modes or fashions of representation, which may very well be more dependent on what we would call sociological factors than on literary. Far from viewing literature as existing in some kind of timeless realm, Aristotle in fact follows Plato in regarding the majority of poets as time-servers, basically giving audiences what they want or have become accustomed to.[26]

Thus Aristotle's notion of genre is considerably more flexible and open-ended than is usually supposed.[27] As we have seen, the idea of the tragic in the *Poetics* is by no means confined to its realization in tragic drama. For example, nothing in his conceptualization of the tragic would have prevented Aristotle from talking about the tragic novel if he had witnessed developments in nineteenth-century European fiction.[28] As in his discussion of the Homeric epic, Aristotle would have questioned the suitability of the *schemata* of the novel to embody the *eidos* of tragedy fully. He would undoubtedly have raised the issue of whether the length and discursiveness of the novel as a form would tend to dilute the impact, focus, and intensity of any tragedy it attempted to portray.[29] But that only

26. Cf. Else, *Plato and Aristotle*, p. 153, and Crane, *The Languages of Criticism*, pp. 54–55. For this view in Plato, see especially the *Ion*, but see also *Republic*, 605b–606b. For Aristotle's view that the poet is constrained by his desire or need to please his audience, see especially the end of chapter 13 in the *Poetics*: "the poets cater to the spectators, composing plays the way they want them" (1453a; Else, 400).

27. See Mieke Bal, "Mimesis and Genre Theory in Aristotle's *Poetics*," *Poetics Today*, 3 (1982): 179.

28. See Crane, *The Languages of Criticism*, p. 65.

29. This point seems to be implied in the way Aristotle contrasts epic with tragedy. See 1449b and 1459b.

means that the novel, like the epic, cannot be as successful as drama in embodying the tragic idea; it does not mean that the novel cannot be tragic.

Thus the distinction between *eidos* and *schemata* in the *Poetics* functions to discriminate between what is historical and transhistorical in literature. For Aristotle, only the broad purpose of tragedy remains the same over time: representing the *spoudaios,* the noble, in action. The ways of accomplishing this purpose, the modes and fashions of representing nobility, will vary over time, thus introducing a considerable component of diversity into Aristotle's notion of tragedy, though he is willing to argue for the superiority of particular ways of realizing the tragic idea.[30] As is typical of Aristotle, he finds a middle ground between the two extreme views of the nature of genre which have emerged in modern criticism, the formalist and the historicist. The formalist understanding of genre has difficulty accounting for its historical character. If one could give purely formal definitions of genres, one would have to view them as permanently and equally available literary possibilities. For example, if a sonnet can be defined as a fourteen-line poem with a certain meter and a certain rhyme scheme, it is hard to see why any author could not sit down and write a sonnet at any point in history.

But the various genres do not appear to be uniformly available as literary possibilities over time. Genres seem to have histories, to arise at certain points in time, to develop, to reach a peak, to go into decline, and sometimes to disappear. If the genres were simply ahistorical, we would not have studies of the death of tragedy or of the epic. The historicist view of genre therefore tries to correct the formalist: one should not speak of genres divorced from historical context, but rather of the Renaissance sonnet or the Romantic. According to this view, the literary possibilities open to authors are strictly limited by their positions in history. This understanding of genre obviously can account for the timebound aspect of literature,

30. See Hutton translation, p. 86, note 8.

but it cannot allow for any transhistorical element. For example, historicists have a hard time explaining "retrograde" movements in literature, attempts to revive genres thought to be dead. Tragic novels in the nineteenth century, such as Hardy's *The Mayor of Casterbridge,* would be examples of this kind of movement.[31] Historicists tend to treat such literary phenomena as anachronistic or inauthentic, but that is a form of begging the question. Literary history is filled with cases of authors out of sync with their moment in time, either ahead of it or seemingly behind: Milton writing a Renaissance epic well into the Restoration era, or Büchner writing remarkably modern dramas in the 1830s.

In its legitimate concern with correcting the ahistorical character of formalism, historicism falls into the opposite error of turning the *difficulty* of writing in certain genres at certain points in history into an *impossibility.*[32] The fact that a genre has fallen out of fashion or is not in harmony with the spirit of an age will mean that the majority of authors will shun it. But that does not mean that all writers must abandon it. As the place of Aeschylus and Sophocles in Aristotle's history of tragedy shows, authors are not simply the captives of the artistic forms they inherit. The majority of authors may slavishly follow these forms, and all authors may be influenced by them, but the greatest will find a way of mastering them, of adapting them to higher purposes. For Aristotle, the *eidos* of tragedy may become obscured from time to time in literary history, in

31. See Michael Valdez Moses, "Agon in the Marketplace: *The Mayor of Casterbridge* as Bourgois Tragedy," *South Atlantic Quarterly,* 87 (1988); 218–251. Moses's work on the tragic novel, of which this essay constitutes only a part, has been very helpful to me in developing my understanding of the *Poetics.*

32. For a general criticism of historicism on these grounds, see E. D. Hirsch, Jr., "Back to History," in Gerald Graff and Reginald Gibbons, eds., *Criticism in the University* (Evanston: Northwestern University Press, 1985), p. 194. Hirsch derives the point from Karl Popper, "Normal Science and Its Dangers," pp. 56–57, in Imre Lakatos and Alan Musgrave, eds., *Criticism and the Growth of Knowledge* (Cambridge: Cambridge University Press, 1970).

part because poets' fascination with changes in *schemata* may lead them away from a concern with the proper object of imitation. But once a poet like Homer has discovered the tragic idea,[33] it remains available to later writers who have the elevation of vision to attempt to recapture it, albeit in new forms.

Thus Aristotle found a way of accounting for literary change while still preserving a way of speaking about an element enduring through that change. A preliminary formulation of his principle would state that the *schemata* of tragedy alter over time, while the *eidos* remains the same. This of course still leaves Aristotle an essentialist, but this essentialism is more limited than his critics tend to claim. What constitutes the essence of tragedy in Aristotle is much less clearly and strictly defined than is usually supposed. It is true that Aristotle regards tragedy as reaching a kind of peak in the form of Sophocles' drama, which is what he seems to have in mind when he speaks of tragedy having found its natural form and stopped. But it is misleading to read this sentence to mean that tragedy or even tragic drama came to an end with Sophocles; in effect all Aristotle means is that it reached a new (and per-

33. As the discoverer of the tragic idea, Homer more closely resembles the founder of a city (*Politics*, 1253a30–31), who institutes something that did not exist before he made it, than an explorer who stumbles upon an already existing territory. Although tragedy has a nature, according to Aristotle, it does not exist "by nature," but has to be made by human beings (recall that the Greek word for poet means "the maker"). Given Aristotle's view of man as that peculiar being whose nature it is to create conventions, many things in the human world have natures but still have to be made by human beings and thus end up with a large component of convention in their existence. The many commentators who claim that the *Poetics* develops a biological view of the development of poetry as a natural growth have misread Aristotle. He always distinguishes between things which exist independent of human will and things which are the product of human will; only the former exist "by nature," whereas poetry in general and tragedy in particular obviously fall into the latter category (on this point, see especially *Metaphysics*, 1032a–b and *Nicomachean Ethics*, 1140a; see also Lord, "Aristotle's History of Poetry," p. 213). That is why poetry has a "history," according to Aristotle, and why he must name individual human beings to account for its development, as he obviously would not have to do in the case of a biological development.

haps its highest) plateau. Much of the *Poetics* is unintelligible if Aristotle is not considering the possibility that there is life after Sophocles in tragic drama. Admittedly, he appears at times to be wondering whether tragic drama has gone into a decline after Sophocles,[34] but that is to grant that its history as a genre continues, albeit at a lower level. To the extent that the *Poetics* raises the prospect of reforming tragic drama,[35] Aristotle still views tragedy as a living art. In short, Aristotle's conception of the relation of *eidos* and *schemata* in tragedy means that the art will have its successes and its failures, depending in part on the suitability of the *schemata* to the *eidos*.

VI

To understand more fully the transhistorical element in literature, the *eidos*, we must recall that Aristotle sees poetry as fundamentally mimetic or representational in character. Because literature makes reference to a real world outside it, it can derive its generic continuity from the continuity of the phenomena it represents.[36] That is, if there is a continuity in tragedy in Aristotle's view, it must be traced to a continuity in what the poet imitates, the *spoudaios*. In short, if Aristotle sees something transhistorical in the genre, it is rooted in a transhistorical possibility in human life, the fact that human beings always have a conception of the noble, of what is higher in their lives. Once we realize this, Aristotle's merely literary essentialism may begin to pale into insignificance. Anyone ob-

34. See, for example, Aristotle's judgment on Euripides, that "his construction is faulty" (1453a; Else, *Plato and Aristotle*, p. 399), his negative comments on Agathon in chapter 18, or his unfavorable comparison of Euripides with Aeschylus in chapter 22.

35. See, for example, Aristotle's rather daring recommendation: "So one should not try to hang on at all costs to the traditional stories [*mythoi*], around which our tragedies center" (1459b; Else, *Plato and Aristotle*, p. 315).

36. Cf. Halliwell, *Poetics of Aristotle*, p. 82: "tragedy exemplifies the principle that literary genres are firmly tied to the perception of certain aspects of reality, rather than being an autonomous matter of convention and institutionalization."

jecting to the ahistorical character of his thought would shift
the argument from purely literary questions and attack him
at a new point. One could say that the problem is not that
Aristotle misconceives Greek literary conventions as natural
but that he misconceives Greek notions of nobility as natural.
If Aristotle's idea of the transhistorical element in tragedy
turns out to rest on claims to the transhistorical character of
nobility, his essentialism seems at first sight to be more problematic than before.

A full discussion of this issue would obviously lead beyond
the limits of a brief essay and require an examination of virtually the whole of Aristotle's philosophy, and in particular
careful analysis of the *Politics* and the *Nicomachean Ethics* to
see what he means by nobility. I will have to confine myself
here to the merest sketch of this issue. Just because Aristotle
ties tragedy to the representation of noble characters in action
does not mean that he ties it to a particular or limited conception of nobility. Aristotle was quite aware of how human beings
differ in their definitions of such concepts. Much of his *Politics*
is devoted to examining the competing claims as to what constitutes the good life for humanity (and Aristotle even takes
into account non-Greek opinions on the subject, as in his consideration of Carthage as a candidate for the best regime[37]).
The *Nicomachean Ethics* discusses differing ideas of the virtues, and tries to discriminate what is conventionally believed
of them from what is genuinely true. In the discussion of the
great-souled man in Book IV, for example, Aristotle defines
him precisely in terms of his awareness of the distinction between what is conventionally held to be noble and what is truly
noble: "It is characteristic of the [great-souled] man not to aim
at the things commonly held in honour . . . to hold back except

37. See *Politics,* 1272b–1273b. As an example of the range of Aristotle's
thinking, see, for example, *Politics,* 1324b, where, examining an issue, he
takes into account the customs of the Spartans, the Cretans, the Scythians,
the Persians, the Thracians, the Celts, the Macedonians, and the Iberians.
For those who think Aristotle was bound by Athenian notions, it is worth
remembering that he was born in Stagira and lived part of his life in
Macedonia.

where great honour as a great result is at stake, and to be a man of few deeds, but of great and notable ones. He must . . . care more for truth than for what people will think."[38]

Thus the concept of nobility in Aristotle is no more or less essentialist than the concept of tragedy. Like Socrates and Plato, Aristotle is willing to pursue such questions as "what is the noble," but without a sense that one can give a simple answer, and certainly without accepting Greek opinions on the subject as definitive. Consequently, to tie Aristotle's conception of the tragic to his conception of the noble is not to limit the open-endedness of his understanding of genre. In fact we can now begin to see another potential source of the historicity of genre in Aristotle, an eidetic rather than a schematic component. If what remains constant in tragedy is the representation of noble characters and noble deeds, then tragedy will change over time precisely as conceptions of nobility change.[39] This would help explain the great differences between ancient and modern tragedy. For example, given the way Christianity fundamentally reinterpreted the notion of nobility, it is no surprise that tragic heroes in the Renaissance began to look very different from their predecessors in Greek drama.[40] But one could still point to an element of continuity in that modern authors are embodying their view of nobility in their tragic heroes much as the Greeks did in theirs.

One might object that we are getting to a rather attenuated notion of continuity here, but that is just another way of stating the flexibility of Aristotle's notion of genre. And the fact is that authors themselves make much of precisely this continuity. When, as many have, modern authors consciously set out to write tragedy, they want us to be aware of the history of the

38. *Nicomachean Ethics*, 1124b22–27; trans. W. D. Ross, in Jonathan Barnes, ed., *The Complete Works of Aristotle* (Princeton: Princeton University Press, 1984), p. 1775.

39. Consider in this context the fact that Aristotle regards even natural right as changeable (*Nicomachean Ethics*, 1134b–1135a), a remarkable claim for someone who today is often regarded as a naive essentialist.

40. See, for example, my *Shakespeare: Hamlet* (Cambridge: Cambridge University Press, 1989), pp. 3–12.

genre. The polemical thrust of their literary act is to assert: "I can still write tragedy in the modern world; I can do for my age what Sophocles did for his; nobility and tragic heroism are still possible, though in different forms." Hence the history of tragedy as a genre involves progressive attempts to extend what might be called the tragic franchise, to accord the dignity of tragic treatment to hitherto excluded groups. The aim of Wordsworth's tragic poems such as *Michael* and *The Ruined Cottage* is to try to show that the poor and the outcast have their own kind of nobility. In George Eliot's tragic novel, *The Mill on the Floss,* she wishes to show that women are as worthy of being the subject of bourgeois tragedy as men, though she has to redefine the notion of tragedy to make this possible.[41] Writers such as Wordsworth and Eliot have obviously changed the forms tragedy has taken, but without some element of generic continuity their works would lose much of their power. Works like *The Ruined Cottage* and *The Mill on the Floss* gain in meaning precisely because Wordsworth and Eliot think of themselves as working within the genre of tragedy, and want their works to be read with previous tragedies like those of Sophocles and Shakespeare in mind. The case of tragedy is perhaps the best example of how genres actually function in the minds of authors. The decision to write a tragedy may itself be a kind of statement, an attempt to extend our notion of nobility by extending tragic treatment to a new class of characters.

Thus our earlier formulation of the historicity of tragedy must be expanded: tragedy changes not only in terms of its modes of representation, but also in terms of its objects of representation. If a new class of human beings comes to be regarded as possessing its own form of nobility, tragic writers will seek to represent them as heroic in their own way. Aristotle could not have foreseen such literary developments

41. Eliot shows her awareness of Aristotle's notion of tragedy when she actually quotes one of his terms in Greek (*ti megethos*); see George Eliot, *The Mill on the Floss* (Boston: Houghton Mifflin, 1961), p. 90. For her redefinition of tragedy, see especially p. 174: "insignificant people . . . have their tragedy too." For evidence that Eliot had previous tragedies in mind, see her references to Oedipus (p. 117) and Hamlet (p. 351).

as Wordsworth's poems and Eliot's novels, but his broader conception of the tragic idea does not necessarily exclude them. Confronted with such works, he would undoubtedly have quarreled with the conception of nobility they reflect, and with good reason have questioned if they as fully embody the tragic idea as the plays of Sophocles do. But if he regarded them as defective tragedies, he could still have acknowledged some element of generic continuity. Aristotle's notion of tragedy is not limited to a particular notion of nobility, though obviously, given his experience, he is concerned in the *Poetics* with the Greek conception of nobility. Above all, he is not limited to nobility as conventionally defined in social terms (nobility of birth), a definition which he calls into question at many points in his ethical and political writings.[42] To be sure, since Aristotle understood politics as the architectonic human activity, he would have questioned whether nobility in the fullest sense could ever exist without some political dimension. But even this restriction would leave open a wide range of possibilities for nobility, given Aristotle's appreciation of the wide range of political possibilities.

Thus for Aristotle to base the transhistorical possibility of tragedy on the transhistorical possibility of nobility is not to limit tragedy to one form of nobility and hence to one historical form. As long as human beings look up to something, regard one course of life as higher than others, the possibility of nobility exists, and hence the possibility of heroism, and hence the possibility of tragedy. Of course some might question whether nobility, even this broadly defined, is a genuinely transhistorical phenomenon, especially those who dogmatically assert that there can be nothing transhistorical in human life. But at least if one sees that Aristotle is not necessarily tied to a particular form of tragedy or a particular form of no-

42. Consider in this context Aristotle's remark about the goodness of even women and slaves at 1454a in the *Poetics*. Or consider a remark in the *Politics* that has remarkable implications for the conventional Greek notion of nobility: "there is nothing dignified about using a slave as a slave; giving commands concerning necessary things has no share in the noble things" (1325a). Quoted in the translation of Carnes Lord (Chicago: University of Chicago Press, 1984), p. 202.

bility, his essentialism will appear to be less problematic. Moreover, by realizing the connection in Aristotle's view between a form of imitation (tragedy) and an object of imitation (nobility), we begin to see that genre is not a purely literary issue, but often raises political questions. It is no accident that discussions of what constitutes a tragedy tend to become impassioned in a way that discussions of what constitutes, say, a pastoral or a sonnet do not. Critics can easily become offended—*morally* offended it would seem—if a work they regard as a genuine tragedy is excluded from someone else's category of the tragic, largely because they take such an exclusion as an affront to the dignity of characters they admire as heroic. Whether or not one chooses to regard *The Mill on the Floss* as tragic, for example, is likely to have more to do with one's political than one's literary opinions. The way our discussion of Aristotle's view of tragedy has led us from purely formal questions to the kinds of questions he raises in his *Ethics* and *Politics* is a model of what Aristotle can contribute to our understanding of literature. Disputes about the nature of genre, which at first appear to be strictly literary, often turn out to mask more fundamental political disagreements, which Aristotle can help us to bring out into the open.

VII

It may seem strange that a supposedly essentialist thinker like Aristotle turns out to have a sophisticated manner of dealing with problems of literary history. But if one considers the character of classical philosophy in general, it is not surprising that Aristotle found a way of accounting for both a historical and a transhistorical element in literature. The literary problem of relating genre to the history of poetry is only a special case of exactly the sort of question which classical philosophy arose to deal with, the problem of the One and the Many, of how to find points of stability in a world of flux, of how to relate Being and Becoming. Reading the *Poetics* in English translation tends to obscure this insight. Readers familiar with Greek will no doubt already have noticed that the key word in Aristotle's discussion of genre—*eidos*—is not limited to literary criticism in ancient Greece but is in fact one of the central terms of classical philosophical discourse. *Eidos* is the word Plato uses when he is speaking of the Ideas or Forms; perhaps the best way of understanding what Aristotle means by a genre is to realize that from the opening sentence of the *Poetics* as we have it to the last, he tends to refer to genre by the same word Plato uses to refer to the Ideas. The Aristotelian genre is a Platonic idea (in Greek this sentence would be a tautology: the *eidos* is an *eidos*). Hence the idea of the tragic in Aristotle is conceived broadly enough to cover a wide range of embodiments; in Plato's terms, the various forms of tragedy participate in the idea of the tragic. The *eidos* is one; the *schemata* are many.

To explain Aristotle's understanding of genre in terms of Plato's notion of the Ideas is of course to elucidate the relatively clear in terms of the profoundly obscure.[43] By calling attention to the larger significance of the word *eidos,* I do not mean to foreclose enquiry into Aristotle's concept of genre but to suggest directions for future investigation. What I want to emphasize by invoking the Platonic context for the exploration of literary questions in the *Poetics* is the richness and open-endedness of Aristotle's understanding of genre. Whatever one ultimately makes of it, Plato's notion of the Ideas was an attempt not to avoid but to confront the heterogeneity of phenomena: the diversity of things and the fact that they keep changing over time. Plato was searching for a way of understanding how things can be said to endure precisely when they constantly appear to be changing. He was reacting against attempts by Pre-Socratic philosophers to reduce all things to a single substance (as in Thales) or to understand Being as some kind of abstract and homogeneous unity (as in Parmenides). The fundamental thought behind the notion of the Ideas is that

43. I am also well aware that Aristotle is commonly thought to have differed from Plato precisely on the issue of the Ideas. But Aristotle's difference from Plato–his view that the Forms cannot exist apart from their material embodiments—points directly to what we have seen about the relation of *eidos* and *schemata* in literature. Perhaps we might be able to reverse our original perspective, and understand what Plato means by the Ideas better if we are guided by Aristotle's notion of genre.

nature is not a homogeneous whole but articulates itself into natures, into different tribes or classes of things.[44] Today, in our eagerness to reject the essentialism of Plato and Aristotle, we forget that what we call their essentialism was their response precisely to the diversity of phenomena and to what we would call the problem of history, of things changing over time. By analyzing Aristotle's understanding of genre as a special case of Greek essentialism, I hope I have succeeded in showing that classical philosophy in its search for essences amidst the flux of history was not necessarily dogmatic or narrow-minded, but in fact was trying to account for diversity precisely by finding elements of continuity in change.

44. The literature on Plato's Ideas is vast, but for the view I am taking here, see especially three works by Leo Strauss: *Natural Right and History* (Chicago: University of Chicago Press, 1953), pp. 122–123, *The City and Man* (Chicago: Rand McNally, 1964), pp. 119–120, and *The Rebirth of Classical Political Rationalism* (Chicago: University of Chicago Press, 1989), pp. 141–143.

RALPH COHEN

Genre Theory, Literary History, and Historical Change

In the last half of the twentieth century generic theory has reemerged as a critical force, in part owing to discussions of genre by Northrop Frye, R. S. Crane, and Rosalie Colie. More recent genre theory has reexamined the novel (Michael McKeon's *The Origins of the English Novel 1660–1740*), the essay (Alexander J. Butrym's *Essay on the Essay: Redefining the Genre*), the short story (Susan Lohafer and Jo Ellen Clarey's *Short Story Theory at a Crossroads*), satire, elegy, lyric, tragedy, and others. New theories of genre had been advanced by Mikhail Bakhtin in his work on Dostoevsky and in translations of his essays entitled *The Dialogic Imagination* and *Speech Genres and Other Late Essays*. Richard Rorty has practiced genre criticism in an essay dealing with historical explanation in philosophy, "The Historiography of Philosophy: Four Genres." Alastair Fowler's *Kinds of Literature*, Adena Rosmarin's *The Power of Genre*, Arnold Krupal's *The Voice in the Margin: Native American Literature and the Canon*, and numerous feminist discussions of autobiography, journals, novels, memoirs, and other genres have offered examples of generic analysis dealing with theory and practice. So, too, Henry Louis Gates, Jr., Houston Baker, Deborah McDowell, and other African American critics occasionally use generic

analyses when they discuss the works of black authors. Marxist critics like Louis Althusser, Fredric Jameson, Franco Moretti, John Frow, and others use genre as a frame for relating
literature to social formations.[1]

In their reemergence, genre cricitism and theory have
moved from assumptions of genres as fixed to genre as process

1. Mikhail Bakhtin, *The Dialogic Imagination: Four Essays,* ed. Michael
Holquist, trans. Caryl Emerson and Michael Holquist (Austin: University
of Texas Press, 1981), and *Speech Genres and Other Late Essays,* ed. Caryl
Emerson and Michael Holquist, trans. Vern W. McGee (Austin: University
of Texas Press, 1986); *Essay on the Essay: Redefining the Genre,* ed. Alex-
ander J. Butrym (Athens: University of Georgia Press, 1989); Gian Biagio
Conte, *The Rhetoric of Imitation: Genre and Poetic Memory in Virgil and
other Latin Poets* (Ithaca: Cornell University Press, 1986); Stuart Curren,
Poetic Form and British Romanticism (Oxford: Oxford University Press,
1986); Heather Dubrow, *Genre* (London, 1982); Alastair Fowler, *Kinds of
Literature: An Introduction to a Theory of Genres and Modes* (Cambridge,
Mass.: Harvard University Press, 1982); Alastair Fowler, "The Future of
Genre Theory: Functions and Constructional Types," in *The Future of Lit-
erary Theory,* ed. Ralph Cohen (New York: Routledge, 1989), pp. 291–393;
Linda Hutcheon, *A Theory of Parody* (New York: Methuen, 1985); Fredric
Jameson, *The Political Unconscious: Narrative as a Socially Symbolic Act*
(Ithaca: Cornell University Press, 1981); Arnold Krupal, *The Voice in the
Margin: Native American Literature and the Canon* (Berkeley: University
of California Press, 1989); *Short Story Theory at a Crossroads,* ed. Susan
Lohafer and Jo Ellyn Clarey (Baton Rouge: Louisiana State University
Press, 1989); Michael McKeon, *The Origins of the English Novel 1600–1740*
(Baltimore: The Johns Hopkins University Press, 1987); Franco Moretti,
Signs Taken for Wonders: Essays in the Sociology of Literary Forms, trans.
Susan Fischer, David Forgacs, David Miller (London: Verso Editions and
NLB, 1983); Franco Moretti, *The Way of the World: The Bildungsroman in
European Culture* (London: Verso, 1987); Gary Morson, *The Boundaries of
Genre: Dostoevsky's Diary of a Writer and the Traditions of Literary Utopia*
(Austin: University of Texas Press, 1981); Richard Rorty, "The Historiog-
raphy of Philosophy: Four Genres," in *Philosophy in History,* ed. Richard
Rorty, J. B. Schneewind, and Quentin Skinner (Cambridge: Cambridge
University Press, 1984); Adena Rosemarin, *The Power of Genre* (Minne-
apolis: University of Minnesota Press, 1985); Jean-Marie Schaeffer, "Lit-
erary Genres and Textual Genericity," in *The Future of Literary Theory,* ed.
Ralph Cohen (New York: Routledge, 1989), pp. 167–187; J. W. Smeed, *The
Theophrastian 'Character'* (New York: Oxford Clarendon Press, 1986);
Leonard Tennenhouse, *Power on Display: The Politics of Shakespeare's
Genres* (New York: Methuen, 1986).

These few references cannot begin to convey the extent and subtlety of
generic theory and practice at the present time.

of textual change. Indeed, the generic emphasis on change is introduced by examination of the varied texts that compose a single genre, the drafts that lead to a published text that is a member of a genre, and by the ideological implications that result from different genres that combine, contrast, challenge, and oppose one another. The processes of generic change are locatable not merely within written genres but between written and oral genres, verbal and nonverbal genres (art, music, architecture). A definition of genre by a film theorist, Rick Altman, can perhaps provide a beginning for understanding these processes.

In assessing theories of genre, critics have often labeled them according to a particular theory's most salient features or the type of activity to which it devotes its most concentrated attention. Paul Hernadi, for example, recognizes four general classes of genre theory: expressive, pragmatic, structural, and mimetic. In his extremely influential introduction to *The Fantastic,* Tzvetan Todorov opposes historical to theoretical genres, as well as elementary genres to their complex counterparts. Others, like Frederic Jameson, have followed French semiotics in distinguishing between semantic and syntactic approaches to the genre. While there is anything but general agreement on the exact frontier separating semantic from syntactic views, we can as a whole distinguish between generic definitions which depend on a list of common traits, attitudes, characters, shots, locations, sets, and the like—thus stressing the semantic elements which make up the genre—and definitions which play up instead certain constitutive relationships between undesignated and variable placeholders—relationships which might be called the genre's fundamental syntax. The semantic approach thus stresses the genre's building blocks, while the syntactic view privileges the structures into which they are arranged (p. 95)[2]

Such a theory attends to the introduction and change of basic semantic elements, for example, from opera to swing and from folk music to rock. Altman points to the changing relationship between the construction of a film and its implications for viewers of particular communities. In their theories of

2. Rick Altman, *The American Film Musical* (Bloomington: Indiana University Press, 1987). This definition, based on speech act theory and on insights from some of the genre critics mentioned in the quotation, indicates that some types of generic theory can be interdisciplinary.

genre the historian and the theorist are at one in analyzing the "semantic elements and syntactic bonds."

This tentative definition relates constituents of a film to the aim or aims of a generic structure. A further discussion of genre would plot the changes resulting from adding, subtracting, or renaming constituents or ends. For example, the novel develops by drawing upon constituents from eighteenth-century genres such as chapbook narratives, newspapers, religious autobiographies, confessions, histories, and romances. The aims of this genre have been amply discussed and critics have demonstrated the significance of genre study in charting this change in literary history.[3] I note parenthetically that technological inventions such as printing, engraving, and photography can help initiate new genres and alter old ones.

Once a new way of writing produces several examples, a basis exists for writers to identify it further by imitation and for critics by naming and analyzing it. This is done by distinguishing this kind of writing from those from which it has drawn constituents that have combined into a distinct identity or genre. Until some agreements exist about a genre's distinctness, its identity remains in doubt and its denomination puzzling, for example, *Finnegans Wake*. Even when some agreement exists, no text is free from the possibility that it can belong to more than one genre. Members of a genre add, vary, modify, or abandon constituents so that the genre is modified by additional instances. This is especially apparent in the oppositional writings of feminists, Marxists, and African Americans who deliberately seek to oppose patriarchal, bourgeois, or white writings in order to reform the genre system without abandoning a theory of genres.

Altman's theory about writing a history of the American musical emphasizes the shuttling or changes of constituents among the examples of such films, although his reliance upon formal features limits the range of his perspective definition. But he does realize that film genres can become stabilized for

3. J. Paul Hunter, *Occasional Form* (Baltimore: The Johns Hopkins University Press, 1975); Michael McKeon, *The Origins of the English Novel 1660–1740* (Baltimore: The Johns Hopkins University Press, 1987); Lennard J. Davis, *Factual Fictions: The Origins of the English Novel* (New York: Columbia University Press, 1983).

economic and other reasons, and that such genres become governed by predictable formulae. This is the case with written texts as well; the modern romance can of course become governed by a conventionalized relation between constituents and aims. But it is also possible that some romances can initiate significant changes.

Critics and theorists such as Northrop Frye, Alastair Fowler, Rosalie Colie, and Barbara Lewalski have demonstrated that debates about the fixity of literary genre classifications took place in the Renaissance. But it is only recently that genre has been recognized as revealing a historical process that provides a valuable, practical, and theoretical understanding of the changes, gaps, incompletions, and transformations that take place in the writing of literary history and other histories.[4] I wish in this chapter to analyze how some contemporary critics and theorists explain change, continuity, and difference in generic discourses used in the history of philosophy, in the history of ideas, in literary history. Such critics do not uniformly agree on the operation of genres, but they take it for granted in analyzing change.

A genre theory about the writing of history, history of philosophy, or literary history must confront at the very least the question whether genre is discipline-controlled or nation-controlled or both. Is a history of philosophy a history of philosophical problems in Greek, French, German, and English philosophy? If a history of philosophy is situation-based, do the problems change when considered in different language communities? Since medieval romance crosses territorial boundaries and several languages whereas modern romances in English are confined to Britain and the United States, does the romance genre remain historically situated or does it shift when the reading community shifts? These questions only begin to touch the function of genre in literary history; genres are cultural formations and their relation to cultural forces should perhaps begin with an inquiry into their critical and theoretical reemergence.

4. Ralph Cohen, "History and Genre" (203–218) and "Reply to Dominick La Capra and Richard Harvey Brown" (229–233), *New Literary History* 17 (Winter 1986).

Why at this time have generic theories once again become
important? In recent years a huge number of little known texts
written by women, by African Americans, and other minorities have been recovered. They reveal the inadequate "data
bases" for constructing genres in the past. We now know that
critics and theorists have disregarded texts such as slave
narratives, domestic journals, feminist autobiographies, and
confessions and kept them outside the range of literary study.
Such genres did not fit a conception of education aimed at preparing white males for advancing in social and economic hierarchies. The need now is to educate people to understand that
received genres, the so-called mass culture genres such as
Westerns and detective stories and new ones such as advertising or television sitcoms, affect their thinking, feeling, and
knowledge. Reemergence of genre criticism and theory results
from the need for feminist and African American and sympathetic critics to demonstrate the prejudices hidden or obvious
in received texts. Such critics undermine the assumptions of
objectivity of received critical and theoretical genres. Moreover, writings that deal with interrelations between literary and
nonliterary genres or between genres of different disciplines—
literary history and art history, literary criticism and psy-
choanalytical criticism and practice—have led critics and theorists to a reconsideration of genre as a unified kind.

There are other more general reasons for studying the generic history of past writings. A generic history involves the
study of genres that include and exclude constituents; but it
also involves the inclusion and exclusion of genres themselves.
In this respect it makes readers conscious of the functions of
repression and renewal in our society. A generic history
stresses both the need for classification and the need to realize
the limits of any monolithic classification. Classifications are
multidimensional; thus every text within a genre can also be a
member of another genre. This in no way denies identity to a
genre or a text within a genre. It means that such identity requires for its analysis a knowledge of a generic past and its
distinction from related coexistent genres. Such analyses are
characterized in contemporary critical discourse by such
terms as "appropriation," "dominance," "power," "ideology," "politics." The reemergence of genre criticism and the-

ory thus corresponds to the multifaceted study of identity as a
social process. That different readers may disagree about a
text's genre is neither contradictory nor surprising. It merely
indicates that a genre is combinatory, not monolithic.

Terms like "tradition," "discipline," "subject," "self-
awareness" direct the inquiries of genre criticism to the constituents of a text and their multiple relations to political and
social aims. The genre criticism I describe, therefore, focuses
upon problems of change: in studying the genre of tragedy it
seeks to explain the changes in characters, class, economic
authority, and oppositional status, from *The Merchant of Ven-
ice* to *The London Merchant,* from period texts identified as
modernist to those identified as postmodernist. In such cases
genre critics self-consciously question their own practices with
a view to recasting them. When ballads become part of another
genre called ballad opera what consequences ensue? What literary and social practices are altered? And for what end?

Genre criticism, as I propose it, challenges the received view
of historical change. Change remains problematic because we
are only beginning to recognize the importance of genre theory
in formulating its problems. Genre theory provides formulations for change by stipulating constituents of a text within a
genre. Thus it becomes possible to note the particulars of a
change and what these imply in relation to aims. Moreover, by
recognizing the interrelation of texts from different genres, one
can note the shifting directions of texts. This is the case when
feminists introduce autobiographical discourses into theoretical discussions, thus removing claims made about objectivity.
Genres indicate change when they move up or down the hierarchy of genres. They indicate change when they keep the
terms of discourse but change the meaning of the terms. Generic boundaries change when diverse genres such as songs,
narratives, critical essays become collected in a genre like the
miscellany or periodical paper or magazine, and the generic
constituents are changed by further inclusion. I want to argue
that genre theory becomes the enabling basis for discussing
any part-whole relationship.

Semioticians like Maria Corti and Yuri Lotman think of
genre as a cultural classification system in which all written
texts form part of one or more genre systems, and that these

help construct the large system which shapes, characterizes, and defines a culture. My essay is much more restricted. Part I offers examples of genre constructions of the history of philosophy and intellectual history. Part II poses some new alternatives to the generic procedures offered in Part I. Part III discusses cultural change in oppositional literary genres.

I

In his essay "The Historiography of Philosophy: Four Genres," Richard Rorty offers a generic approach to the writing of the history of philosophy as discipline-bound.[5] He begins with the genres "rational reconstruction," "historical reconstruction," *Geistesgeschichte,* and doxography. Each of these has its characteristic aims and procedures. Rorty discusses each genre in terms of the practices that have specific effects upon the modern reader. He writes "the main reason we want historical knowledge of what . . . dead philosophers and scientists would have said to each other is that it helps us to recognize that there have been different forms of intellectual life than ours" (p. 51). As the result of recognizing what is necessary and what merely contingent and dependent on our own arrangements, we as readers have a key to self-awareness. We want also to assure ourselves "that there has been rational progress in the course of recorded history—that we differ from our ancestors on grounds which our ancestors would be led to accept" (51). Rational reconstruction, historical reconstruction, and *Geistesgeschichte* have their self-justifications; doxography, according to Rorty, has no such justification since it

5. Richard Rorty, "The Historiography of Philosophy: Four Genres," in *Philosophy in History,* ed. Rorty, Schneewind, and Skinner. Discussions of Descartes' *Meditations* as a genre can be found in Amelie Oksenburg Rorty, "Experiments in Philosophical Genre: Descartes' *Meditations,*" *Critical Inquiry* 9 (1982–83): 545–564. A revision of this essay entitled "The Structure of Descartes' *Meditations*" appeared in A. O. Rorty, ed., *Essays on Descartes' "Meditations"* (Berkeley, 1986), pp. 1–20. Bradley Rubidge, in "Descartes's *Meditations* and Devotional Meditations," *Journal of the History of Ideas* 51 (Jan.–March, 1990): 27–50, offers a critique of Rorty's views.

assumes that all great philosophers in a history of philosophy were addressing "continuing concerns."

In describing the task of rational reconstruction, historical reconstruction, and *Geistesgeschichte*—as analysis of a past problem in philosophy, a construction of the historical environment that made such problems possible and a study of the history of an idea or ideas as developed by Wilhelm Dilthey and A. O. Lovejoy—Rorty identifies a philosophical genre by a dominant subject matter. It is important to note that Rorty's view of genre does not rest on a body of constituents that undergo change. Genres are discussed as confined to particular tasks and such tasks are treated as though they remain the same. Still, Rorty's procedure is comparative and underlines the way in which histories of philosophy differ from histories of science. In this respect his historical genres quite rightly demonstrate that histories of philosophy require for their practice a comparison with other kinds of historical genres.

Genres are constructions and constructions operate with and against each other. Genres help define each other; they serve Rorty to demonstrate that genres of the history of philosophy are pertinent to establishing our self-awareness. But we must not assume that all genres of the history of philosophy are useful. Doxography,[6] which refers in Rorty's context to the praise of philosophical orthodoxies and illustrates his ironic attitude to them, becomes divorced from an analysis of philosophical problems in terms of current issues. Rorty urges its abandonment because such histories "impose a problematic on a canon drawn up without reference to that problematic, or, conversely, [to] impose a canon on a problematic constructed without reference to that canon" (p. 62). Such histories lack self-justification and the self-awareness such justification produces. A generic text, then, can be identified as adequate or inadequate in relation to its aims and practices.

Rorty writes of the three usable genres that any "given book in the history of philosophy will, of course, be a mixture of these three genres. But usually one or another motive domi-

6. Traditionally, "doxography" refers to compilations of texts from early Greek philosophers.

nates since there are three distinct tasks to be performed. The
distinction of these three tasks is important, and not to be broken down" (p. 68). Nevertheless, each genre can include elements of the others. Such intertextuality leads Rorty to posit
the notion of dominant generic motive—each genre is identified by a dominant motive governed by its aim. Each genre
gives rigor to one or more of the others by keeping in mind the
possibility "that our self-justifying conversation is with creatures of our own phantasy rather than with historical person-
ages" (p. 71).

Rorty does not, however, inquire into the generic problem
posed by identifying Descartes' *Meditations* with religious and
poetic meditations. Does the book belong to two genres? It
could not in Rorty's system. It may, however, fall within a new
useful genre which Rorty names "intellectual history."

I should like to use the term "intellectual history" for a much richer
and more diffuse genre—one which falls outside this triad [rational
reconstruction, historical reconstruction and *Geistesgeschichte*]. In
my sense, intellectual history consists of descriptions of what the intellectuals were up to at a given time, and of their interaction with the
rest of society—descriptions which, for the most part, bracket the
question of what activities which intellectuals were conducting. Intellectual history can ignore certain problems which must be settled
in order to write the history of a discipline—questions about which
people count as scientists, which as poets, which as philosophers, etc.
Descriptions of the sort I have in mind may occur in treatises called
something like "Intellectual life in fifteenth-century Bologna," but
they may also occur in the odd chapter or paragraph of political or
social or economic or diplomatic histories, or indeed in the odd chapter or paragraph of histories of philosophy (of any of the four genres
distinguished above). Such treatises, chapters, and paragraphs produce, when read and pondered by someone interested in a certain
spatio-temporal region, a sense of what it was like to be an intellectual
in that region—what sort of books one read, what sorts of things one
had to worry about, what choices one had of vocabularies, hopes,
friends, enemies, and careers. (p. 68)

This genre opens philosophy to nondisciplinary analyses and
inquiries about the moral tendencies of intellectual life. It re-
vises the notion that history of philosophy must be confined to

purely philosophical texts. It provides, therefore, a puzzling problem in the practice of the history of philosophy. It suggests that the very discipline of philosophy needs to be refigured, that the practice of this genre can lead to a reconception of the discipline to which it refers.

Rorty's essay points to several pertinent generic problems: one is that his useful genres are necessary to define each other and to provide a comprehensive history of philosophy. The second is that though each genre is self-contained, it nevertheless includes intrusions from related genres. The third is that some genres need to be abandoned because they cease to function effectively. Rorty writes about a single discipline and implies that its useful genres are discipline-determined, are ways of formulating the tasks that characterize the history of philosophy.

But the genre of intellectual history is not discipline-determined. Rather, in Rorty's terms it "is the raw material for the historiography of philosophy—or, to vary the metaphor, the ground out of which histories of philosophy grow" (p. 71). It serves as ground for the other three useful genres and at the same time is equal to them because it plays "the same dialectical role with respect to *Geistesgeschichte* as historical reconstruction plays to rational reconstruction" (p. 71). Rorty's intellectual history is thus a genre that applies to history of society or literature as well as to history of philosophy, and thus is not discipline-determined; it can, however, also be considered discipline-determined in relation to *Geistesgeschichte*. "Intellectual history," in Rorty's explanation, functions as a ground for his genres in the history of philosophy and is, itself, one of these genres. It thus undermines the rigidity and self-containedness that Rorty attributed to his useful genres. Several points should be made about the consequences of his use of intellectual history as a genre. The first is that as a "diffuse" genre, it indicates that genres can be more or less diffuse, can contain few or many constituents. Genre can, as intellectual history does, call a "discipline" into question; it can undermine the assumptions that govern philosophy. Genres can function as ground and as constructs derived from the ground. If this creates a conceptual problem concerning genre as pro-

cess and product, it also raises questions about how to define
the task of a genre.

Rorty's intellectual history crosses disciplinary lines and
calls into question the discipline-determined history that his
essay assumes. But some of the generic difficulties that intellectual history raises for him are also discoverable in the uses
that the historian Donald R. Kelley makes of this genre. He
treats it as a revision and extension of Lovejoy's "history of
ideas":

In the first place, I think, the history of ideas should represent itself
as (according to recent convention) "intellectual history," if only to
lay to rest the ghosts of antiquated idealism and to set aside, at least
for historical purposes, the imperialist aspirations and invidious
claims of philosophy to be a "rigorous science" (in the phrase of Husserl). Intellectual history is not "doing philosophy" (any more than it
is doing literary criticism) retrospectively; it is doing a kind, or several
kinds, of historical interpretation, in which philosophy and literature
figure not as controlling methods but as human creations suggesting
the conditions of historical understanding. (p. 18)[7]

For Kelley, intellectual history is a genre or group of genres
that "suggest" the conditions of historical understanding, not
a genre that studies social or political history. Since Kelley is
discussing history, he denies that either philosophy or literature control intellectual history. The kinds of interpretations
that intellectual history produces merely rely upon philosophy
and literature to suggest the conditions of historical interpretations. But whereas Rorty discusses the tasks of the kinds or
genres of interpretation, Kelley is intent on tracing the transition from a history of ideas to intellectual history. What he
undertakes is an explanation of generic change: the transformation of history of ideas. This transformation results from a
criticism of Lovejoy's idealism and an extension of what he
preached rather than practiced. Kelley writes that Lovejoy at-
tended

not only to concepts and rational arguments but also to the other layers of linguistic meaning—and indeed this is the justification for ap-

7. Donald R. Kelley, "What Is Happening to the History of Ideas?"
Journal of the History of Ideas 51 (Jan.–March 1990): 3–26.

plying to the rhetorical as well as to philosophical traditions in historical interpretation, since rhetoric, and its extensions in modern literary criticism, reveals the resources, structures, and perhaps cultural memories preserved by language (topoi, tropes, metaphors, constructions, analogies, connections, etc.), popular as well as literary, beyond, or beneath, the reaches of logical formulation, or at least of narrowly rational argument and "reasoned history." (p. 20)

Lovejoy's history of ideas was a study of change that included varied kinds of philosophical and literary discourses, interpretations of elite and nonelite views of the past. But it neglected any study of the genres with which it dealt. The history of the great chain of being can be found as a topos in philosophical treatises, novels, poems, dramas but Lovejoy does not consider how sermons, lyrics, tragedies, for example, affected the interpretation. Kelley recognizes that intellectual history includes the use of history of philosophy and literary-critical analyses, but he contrasts the practice of this history not with that of history of science or architecture, but with theory of history. "Intellectual history has its own aims, values and questions to pose about the human condition; and these cannot ultimately be honored and pursued on the level of theory, which, distracted by the conversations of neighboring disciplines, tends to neglect the practical problems of its own historical craft" (pp. 24–25).

It is one of the puzzling problems in analyzing the writing of a genre such as intellectual history that thoughtful and careful writers such as Rorty and Kelley insist on making temporary into permanent stability. Although both writers are cognizant of generic boundary crossings, they avoid any generic theory that can buttress the practices they describe.

Without attempting to offer such a theory here, I suggest that a genre theory can deal with temporary stability. To begin with, a genre requires a group of texts that have some trait in common at any one time so that they can be distinguished from other groups. A genre cannot be defined by its own terms. It needs at least one other genre from which it can be distinguished. Call a genre a family of texts, a communal group of texts, a consortium of texts. Whatever they are called, such texts are dynamic. Their semantic elements are *intra*-active within the genre and *inter*active with members of other genres.

Genres can be broad or narrow; they can distinguish literary from nonliterary texts, and parody from irony. When Aristotle distinguished tragedy from epic or when critics distinguish the medieval mystery play from the morality play they indicate the presence of some generic repertoire. Moreover, genre is historical in that its texts exist over time, no matter how short. The stability of a genre is always tentative because different instances or examples within a genre can alter its aim. Thus the novel, for example, has one type of semantic-syntactic construction in *Joseph Andrews* and another in *Pride and Prejudice*.

I mention these practices of genre to stress that genre members, that is, individual texts in a genre, cannot be identical and that subgenres are initiated or combined to tie groups of texts more closely together to achieve more precise stability. Thus tragedy includes tragicomedy or domestic tragedy. The genre "history" in the seventeenth century is distinguished from types of romance. In the eighteenth century the terms "life history," "biography," and "confession" become connected with the novel.

II

The introduction of a genre like intellectual history is obviously combinatorial—a combination of varied discourses that cross generic boundaries. It is an ad hoc effort to make historical writing pertinent to the aims with which we identify our lives. But the combinatorial relations are evident not merely in constructions of "intellectual history" but in the multiple discourses of all writing and speaking, and in the varied contexts of socialization that characterize human experience—no identity without some difference, no change without some continuity. These clichés need to be replaced by what might be called a combinatory consciousness—a theory of genre in which identity is not unity but groups of constituents that can reject unity or coherence as readily as affirm it.

Italo Calvino in *Six Memos for the Next Millenium* offers a statement of the combinatory situation as an aspect of human experience:

I have come to the end of this apologia for the novel as a vast net. Someone might object that the more the work tends toward the multiplication of possibilities, the further it departs from that unicum which is the *self* of the writer, his inner sincerity and the discovery of his own truth. But I would answer: Who are we, who is each one of us, if not combinatoria of experiences, information, books we have read, things imagined? Each life is an encyclopedia, a library, an inventory of objects, a series of styles, and everything can be constantly shuffled and reordered in every way conceivable. (p. 127)[8]

Novels are combinations of varied features that include "a multiplicity of subjects, voices, and views of the world, upon the model of what Mikhail Bakhtin has called 'dialogic' or 'polyphonic' or 'carnivalesque,' tracing its antecedents from Plato through Rabelais to Dostoevsky" (p. 117). Calvino notes that novels like Robert Musil's *The Man without Qualities* seek to include all possible relations and thus remain incomplete by their very nature. And he refers to another type of novel that corresponds to "what in philosophy is nonsystematic thought which proceeds by aphorisms, by sudden, discontinuous flashes of light" (p. 118). These varied genres of the novel are for him instances of combinations that lead the reader to possibilities beyond the text. One might say of genre that its aim ought to be, in Calvino's view, to move beyond known relationships, to move beyond any established boundary to the challenge of the unknown.

The very notion that "everything can be constantly shuffled and reordered in every way conceivable" would seem to argue for far more fluidity than a genre theory can accommodate. But Calvino's image of selves as combinatoria of experiences indicates that this genre is constructed by relations within its encyclopedia and by its *inter*relation with other genres at any one time.

Calvino makes reference to Bakhtin's genre theory of multiple discourses in the novel. Such discourses are examples of the different levels within a novel and of the contradictory ideologies that result from them. It is important to note, too, that

8. Italo Calvino, *Six Memos for the Next Millennium* (Cambridge, Mass.: Harvard University Press, 1988).

Calvino's description of contemporary identity is exactly that. Implicit in his description is a historical dimension of what a life was and what it is. Genre makes it possible to contrast what representations of a society were and what they are. But it also indicates that members of the genre novel, for example, can be defined at the same time in terms of national identity in one society and in terms of generic change that crosses national boundaries.

Every boundary crossing inevitably substitutes another boundary. The issue is whether the premise of combinatorial genres offers a more comprehensive explanation than the addition of a genre such as "intellectual history." An example of a combinatorial genre that supports Calvino's views is Hélène Cixous's essay "From the Scene of the Unconscious to the Scene of History," for it is an autobiographical essay and a study of generic differentiation in the writing of her fiction and drama. The essay is not written as a theoretical inquiry into genre or literary history; it is a description of two kinds of writing which she has practiced. But it posits a conception of genre that is based on her combinatory experiences as a woman. Her fictions are controlled by her feminine absorption of language, rhythms, family, and historical experiences. Her writing of drama, however, is different in kind because it depends upon actors—male and female—to complete her play.

What she implies is that her fictions are so controlled by her personal experience in writing that they cannot be generalized, whereas her dramas are collaborative, requiring men and women to complete them. Her essay suggests the possibility that genre can be understood in terms of subjectivity and otherness. Genres thus become forms of otherness in which constituents of prior texts—dialogue, bodily representations, scene and characters—intrude upon the writer's subjectivity and invoke collaboration with others. In this respect genre would explain why some writers like Joyce experiment with many genres and others, like Cixous, restrict themselves to very few. Since such generic limitations occur in writers living at the same time, it is apparent that generic selection becomes an act of mediating between one's self-awareness and the historical otherness that one wishes to resist, affirm, transform, or explore.

I have never dared create a real male character in fiction. Why? Because I write with the body, and I am a woman, and a man is a man, and I know nothing of his *jouissance*. And a man without body and without pleasure, I can't do that. So what about men in drama?

The theater is not the scene of sexual pleasure. Romeo and Juliet love each other but do not make love. They sing love. In the theater it's the heart that sings, the breast that opens up, one sees the heart rend. The human heart has no sex. The heart feels in the same way in a man's breast as in a woman's. That does not mean that characters are demi-creatures who stop at the belt. No, our creatures lack nothing, not penises, not breasts, not kidneys, not bellies. But I don't have to write all that. The actor, the actress give us the whole body that we don't have to invent. And everything is lived and everything is true. This is the present that theater makes to the author: incarnation. It permits the male author to create women who will not be feigned, and the woman author is granted the chance to create perfectly constituted men!

The discovery of theatrical time is essential for someone who, like me, has written fiction during a long period of time. My texts are tapestries, and they weave themselves in a horizontal manner: what is given to these texts is the chance to take their time to make sense, and sometimes to send meaning quite far off in an afterthought. The Book has all its time and even eternity. The reader can drop the book, come back to it, close it forever, read it in one night or in a year, there is an absolute liberty which is also a limit, in the reading of the text.

In the theater, impossible. Drama writes itself out in a "vertical" manner. Enter Hamlet: and you don't have a minute, you have ten seconds, thirty seconds for everything to write itself out and make itself understood. The theater is impatience. The theater shouts: Hurry! Hurry. Shakespeare's plays are so great because they are carried away by impatience. Cleopatra is impatience incarnated. . . .

The theater is an eternal yet extremely mortal genre. Those who live it know that it is *going to end*. One lives its life its death immediately. Passion and ethics come from this. The author also must accept his mortality, more than ever, in several ways. First, the author encounters his limits: he is not God, he is only a demi-god. That means that he writes a demi-oeuvre. He writes something and then he awaits his other as a soul awaits its body. He waits for the other part of the theater to come to him, the part that will be given by the actors. (pp. 15–16)[9]

9. Hélène Cixous, "From the Scene of the Unconscious to the Scene of History," in *The Future of Literary Theory,* ed. Ralph Cohen (New York:

In this passage, Cixous begins with an autobiographical statement of how she writes and what her exclusions are. She then goes on to make generalizations about theatrical performance, and establishes a philosophical distinction between fictional time and dramatic time. Her fictional writing becomes "horizontal." It is linear and leisurely. To this she opposes her "vertical" writing: abrupt, imperative, hasty, bustling. The last section is in the third person, a statement about the ontology of theatrical performance.

Cixous's description of the differences between the two genres is personal not theoretical: "in the domain of women nothing can be theorized" (p. 11). But it does represent an analysis of two genres that can apply to Lispector and other women writers. One view of drama and fiction is that these can be divided into more specific genres such as comedy and tragedy, epic and novel, these into still more refined genres (or subgenres) like tragicomedy or domestic tragedy. Cixous is not interested in charting the relation between the frequent social changes and generic transformations. Her concern is with the relation of her female subjectivity as it requires or denies the need of collaborators for artistic (generic) expression. Fiction for her derives from her womanly self, but drama means giving birth to the other—to men and history. In the theater, "the actor, the actress give us the whole body that we don't have to invent" (p. 15).

In her play about Cambodia, she writes about others than herself who are of herself: "Because it is not me, because it is me, because it is the world different from myself that teaches me myself, my difference, that makes me feel my/its difference" (p. 17). The two genres of fiction and drama become forms of self-exploration. But not only of self-exploration. For the writing about Cambodia makes it possible to realize that

---

Routledge, 1989). Critiques of Cixous's feminist positions but not the genre views that she published in 1989 are found in Toril Moi, *Sexual/Textual Politics: Feminist Literary Theory* (London; Methuen, 1985), pp. 102–127, and in Janet Todd, *Feminist Literary History* (New York: Routledge, 1988), pp. 55–59.

there are forces of religion that resist history's capture of the self despite life in refugee camps and in exile where the children "who were born in the camps and have never known anything but the fences of the camp, learn eternal dance" (p. 17).

I began by noting the reemergence of genre theory in recent times and provided literary and social reasons for this generic change. I offered a tentative definition of genre as used in film criticism, indicating its relation to literary study, especially to historical study. I then indicated the social formations involved in genre and their relation to historical change. And to illustrate the extensive use of genre theory, I used one example from the history of philosophy and another from the history of ideas. In both examples I sought to inquire into generic explanations of change in a genre called "intellectual history" that was employed by both writers. Here I argued that the two versions of a genre raised questions that a comprehensive genre theory would have to answer. I then offered my suggestions for a comprehensive literary history based on genres and used examples from Calvino's criticism to support my combinatorial theory. Last, I used Cixous's explanation of two genres to illustrate the innovative possibilities of a combinatorial history. My aims have been to demonstrate the inevitability of some type of generic distinctions in the writing of history and to examine some representative generic practices as they enhance or ignore our understanding of historical change.

Genre criticism and theory undergo change in terms of their aims and practices. But all generic practices deal with wholes, with entities, and genre thus remains a basis for analyzing identities and differences. Entities, after all, need not be unified or centered or fixed. (I use the term "entity" to avoid the holism implicit in the term "wholes.") Critics who seek specificity, but claim that they do not find it in genre criticism rely on conceptions of genre that are no longer practiced or defended. If one considers the current practices I have described, then it is apparent that genres are collections of texts each of which has specificities that relate it intertextually to other genres.

Cixous's text is both private and public. Fiction written from the gendered body and drama written from this same body do not produce the same effects. Drama requires other bodies to

fulfill it and thus leads to a different kind of fulfillment for the
writer, the actor, and the audience. Genre practice, therefore,
can be related to the self and to combinations that relate history to conscious and unconscious constituents of autobiography and criticism.

III

Combinations in no way imply harmony. The constituents of a
genre can come in conflict, as Hamlet's discourse of revenge
conflicts with his later discourse of peace and fate. Such
clashes are only one of the generic interrelations that can occur
in a text. One can observe the elevation or domination of one
genre by another when, for example, ballads become part of
the ballad opera or when, in *A Portrait of the Artist,* a dialogue
on aesthetics provides the grounds for understanding the narrative structure.

If we grant that a genre is a construction by writer and
reader, then it follows that readers interpret the genre differently at the same time or at different times. What genre theory
contributes to this phenomenon in literary history is that at any
one time in any one country there are genres that have longer
durability than others and that prevent any chronological period from being generically unified.

The genre of literary history is an embracing name for those
genres that construct approaches to works identified as literary, whatever "literary" may include at any particular time. A
"history" includes many ways of thinking about the past out-
lined in my discussion of Rorty's and Kelley's essays. But I
should note that Rorty's rejection of the historical genre he
calls doxography indicates that one can be against certain
kinds of historical genres. I wish in this section to concentrate
on those genres of literary history that can be identified as oppositional. That is, they work within the framework of received
genres, but invert the constituents and the aims.

Before turning to such oppositional genres, however, I wish
briefly to comment on one type of generic histories, namely,
histories of a genre like the elegy, satire, novel, criticism. Such
histories assume that the genre's constituents and aims change

over time. But such changes are always contingent on some constituents remaining unchanged. This conception of genre is governed by Wittgenstein's family resemblance hypothesis or by the assumed contractual relation between writer and reader. This history is often challenged on the ground that a genre like "romance" or "novel" has no continuity other than the name. One reply to this criticism occurs in Jean Radford's introduction to her volume, *The Progress of Romance: The Politics of Popular Fiction* (1986).[10] She writes: "In so far as genres are contracts between a writer and his/her readers, these contracts, and the conventions which go with them, obviously differ according to the conditions of class, ideology and literacy in different social formations" (p. 8). Radford is fully aware of Raymond Williams's claim that genres such as "tragedy" have no historical relations other than the name. She defends the validity of "romance" as a generically pertinent inquiry by arguing that historical transformations provide an understanding of the interaction between literary and social history. Such transformations, when theorized, provide the continuity that Williams denies.

These theoretical arguments about the continuities or discontinuities of romance or tragedy (indeed of history itself) are necessary but not perhaps sufficient. It is in the detailed historical accounts of the *transformations* of codes and conventions that these questions will be clarified. For if generic forms are, as I argued earlier, signals in a *social* contract between writers and readers, changes in these conventions will be regulated by transformations at other levels of social relationships. Thus for cultural historians, the study of genres may provide a mediation between literary history and social history—one which enables us to break out of the "splendid isolation" in which traditional histories of literature are confined.

Put another way, to see modern romances as genealogical upstarts, or the bastardised offspring of originally noble forbears, is to reproduce a fantasy of the decline-and-fall type, but does *not* help to explain the evolution of cultural forms. But we can instead ask why the romance has moved from being about a male subject to being about a feminine one; or in what way the tests and trials faced by the hero of

10. Jean Radford, *The Progress of Romance: The Politics of Popular Fiction* (New York: Routledge, 1986).

medieval romance differ from the obstacles and trials through which
the heroine of contemporary romance must typically pass to achieve
her object; or how it is that the "magic" which in earlier romances
rescues the hero from false Grails becomes in *Jane Eyre* a superna-
tural voice which unites her with her "true" destiny; and why that
magic/supernatural/Providential force is in today's romance represented as coming from *within:* as the magic and omnipotent power of
sexual desire. A structural and semantic reading of these changing
codes necessarily engages with questions of gender, ideology and
change. (pp. 9–10)

Radford states that changes in the individual examples of a
genre "regulated by transformations at other levels of social
relationships" lead her to look to the writings of cultural historians for whom "the study of genres may provide a mediation between literary history and social history—one which enables us to break out of the 'splendid isolation' in which
traditional histories of literature are confined" (pp. 9–10). Radford's point is that the two genres, literary history and intellectual history, are, in respect to dealing with popular and canonical texts as transformations, intertwined. Each prioritizes
its own discipline and thus can be named as belonging to either
genre. It is with particular jointures such as these that an interdisciplinary genre develops. Radford's generic procedures
constitute a challenge to Kelley's insistence that intellectual
history confronts historical, not literary problems. The problems that Radford poses are indeed historical problems, but
they are also literary.

Radford notes that since generic forms are "signals in a *social* contract between writers and readers, changes in these
conventions will be regulated by transformations at other levels of social relationships" (p. 9). Other Marxists have found
genre theory immensely useful in drawing attention to changes
in the constituents in literary forms. They convert the
Wordsworthian premise of a contract between author and
reader, in which the author agrees to answer given expectations of a form, to a "social" contract governed by class or by
a relation between producer and consumer. The contract theory is generic because it claims that readers of a particular

genre assume that a novel or poem that they are reading will resemble previous instances of the genre. But such views of reader-text relationships tend to refer to texts of the same time; they have little support in assuming that the text of a medieval romance creates contractual relations for a Barbara Cortland romance. Radford is aware of this; still, she overlooks the difficulties in a generic hypothesis based on the contractual metaphor. Her reliance on textual transformations, however, shows genre as a dynamic and changing phenomenon.

Obviously, texts conceal as well as reveal to readers aspects relevant to their constituents or aims. These may be ideological exclusions governed by class or social prejudice or some larger category such as "late capitalism." Such exclusions are deconstructed or exposed in other genres that focus upon the concealed constituents. The literary history of a genre like romance draws attention to its status as a high literary form at one time and as object of mass cultural consumption at another. These shifts in social level are interwoven with changes in what is called literature, in the audiences to which works are addressed, and in the aims of such writing.

This phenomenon of change in an oppositional genre is apparent in the history of feminist autobiography. Sidonie Smith in *Poetics of Women's Autobiography*[11] argues for generic practices that refigure patriarchal autobiography. She finds that the feminist autobiographer needs "to liberate herself from the ideology of traditional autobiography and to liberate autobiography from the ideology of essentialist selfhood through which it has historically been constituted" (p. 58). If feminists are to write their own autobiographies rather than try to fit them to the male-dominated genre, they must write

11. Sidonie Smith, *Poetics of Women's Autobiography: Marginality and the Fictions of Self-Representation* (Bloomington: Indiana University Press, 1987). Recent studies of autobiography are very numerous. Bibliographies can be found in the notes to Smith's text and in the notes to the essays in *Life/Lines: Theorizing Women's Autobiography,* ed. Bella Brodzki and Celeste Schenck (Ithaca: Cornell University Press, 1988). Earlier bibliographies can be found in *Autobiography: Essays Theoretical and Critical,* ed. James Olney (Princeton: Princeton University Press, 1980).

against the genre "by shifting generic boundaries so that there
is neither margin nor center. For as she [the autobiographer]
experiments with alternative languages of self and storytelling,
she testifies to the collapse of the myth of presence with its
conviction of a unitary self" (p. 59).

Smith indicts the autobiographical genre for its construction
of male boundaries, and her revisionary procedure is to recast
the constituents of the genre so that they become decentered,
fragmentary, polyphonic, and feminine. This imaginative vision rests on the transformation of some of the constituents of
the genre. Smith reconstitutes the features of the genre in order
to have it represent the pursuit of the female autobiographer's
own desires. Her aim is to shatter the portrait of herself she
sees hanging in the textual frames of patriarchy, and to create
the conscious and unconscious of her sex by claiming the le-
gitimacy and authority of another subjectivity. With that subjectivity, says Smith, may come a new "system of values, a
new kind of language and narrative form, perhaps even a new
discourse, an alternative to the ideology of gender." One
hopes that this is the case, but one misses the procedures that
would, as in the work of Radford, provide a theory of transformation leading to a new system of values, language, discourse, and genre. This view of the future history of a genre is
an expression of utopian desire. It should be contrasted with
other feminist views of autobiography that focus on the historicity of generic change. For example, Rita Felski writes:

The autobiographical writing inspired by the women's movement
differs, however, from the traditional autobiography of bourgeois
individualism, which presents itself as the record of an unusual but
exemplary life. Precisely because of this uniqueness, the eighteenth-
century autobiography claims a universal significance. Feminist
confession, by contrast, is less concerned with unique individuality
or notions of essential humanity than with delineating the specific
problems and experiences which bind women together. It thus tends
to emphasize the ordinary events of a protagonist's life, their typical-
ity in relation to a notion of communal identity. (p. 94)[12]

12. Rita Felski, *Beyond Feminist Aesthetics: Feminist Literature and Social Change* (Cambridge, Mass.: Harvard University Press, 1989).

Felski shares with Smith the need for a different language and prefers the name "confession" to that of autobiography. She does so because she wishes to stress the historical differences she attributes to feminist genres. Felski is aware that in the writing of confessions women do not abandon all the constituents of a genre that men use, but they combine them to express the notion of communal identity.

I do not wish to discuss the agreements or disagreements that occur among feminist critics and between feminist and nonfeminist critics. Rather I wish to note that feminists engage in refiguring autobiography as a genre. Such refiguring is connected with inquiries into "communal identity" through combinatory events and discourses.

This type of generic history plays a minor role, if any, in literary histories of a period or some other slice of time. Such histories are often entitled *The Age of . . .* or are named after movements such as romanticism or modernism. These literary histories discuss common themes or ideas within a country or in several countries; they attempt to locate common traits that are not genre-bound. Such works can study styles in different countries and disciplines such as history of the baroque or rococo, but they ignore genres in order to emphasize similarities among the diverse kinds of writing.

There are other literary histories that are not generic and that are allied to histories of movements and periods. These are histories of ideas such as the great chain of being or imagination or organic unity or histories of rhetorical features such as irony or allegory. All such histories, whether by a single author or groups of authors, are characterized by an absence of generic contextualization. Themes and ideas in such histories are extracted from their genres and become idealized objects. They lose their particularity, which is embedded in the genres in which they appear.

A generic history of a period or movement would discuss the varied constituents of the different genres and the procedures by which they set forth the divisive aspects of a period as well as its continuities. It would relate received genres to new ones. It would point to the literary and social changes implied in the phenomenon that certain genres cease to be written but start up again at a later date. An example is sonnet sequences, absent in the eighteenth century and resumed by Wordsworth at the beginning of the next century. Generic histories can deal with particular genres—the drama is one example—that come to be prohibited by educational institutions, government, church, or patron. Generic histories would consider the literary and social implications of the return to and revision of older forms, for example, biographies of the nineteenth century or translations from older works that are incorporated in newly written poems by later poets, as for example Pound's *Cantos*. Such procedures raise questions about generic inclusions that involve what we call plagiarism and provide examples of legal problems in literary history.

Histories of movements are all too often written without an awareness of how they move. By seeking to achieve coherence, critics neglect both the procedures by which movements begin or conclude and the generically varied texts that compose a movement. So, too, the attempts to relate the practices of a period to its critical premises overlook the fact that a chronological period combines texts produced much earlier, such as those of Homer, Virgil, Shakespeare, and Milton. A period is not a unified time. The works of Shakespeare and Milton, for example, live as effective presences in later periods. However much their presences are reinterpreted, they create problems in the assimilation to and identification with later examples of their genres.

It should also be noted that to attempt to connect literary history with theory of the period is to assume that theory and practice are synchronic. But works innovated in a period often have no theory to explain them. Theories that exist—whether mimetic or contemplative—are applicable to texts and genres previously written, not to innovations.

In an attempt to write a theory applicable to contemporary black writings, Henry Louis Gates, Jr., one of the most astute of our African American critics, outlines a project for a genre called black literary theory. He knows that such a project cannot ignore the problems set by literary theory regardless of who proposes them. He therefore suggests restating "white" principles of criticism in the language of black critics to create a black theory genre that will address the "integrity" of the black tradition. But the very notion of a tradition implies that the genres of poetry, novel, criticism, and theory form its constituents. Such a generic theory addressed to an interpretation of the black language of black texts would still be distinguished only by comparison to white critical genres. White generic criticism would, therefore, propose the very basis for what a literary theory might be. And this is self-evident in Gates's plan to translate white theory into black idiom:

renaming principles of criticism where appropriate, but especially *naming* indigenous black principles of criticism and applying these to explicate our own texts. It is incumbent upon us to protect the integrity of our tradition by bringing to bear upon its criticism any tool of sensitivity to language that is appropriate. And what do I mean by "appropriate"? Simply this: *any* tool that enables the critic to explain the complex workings of the language of a text is an "appropriate" tool. For it is language, the black language of black texts, which expresses the distinctive quality of our literary tradition. (p. 335)[13]

Gates is aware that renaming is one of the procedures of change. It is understandable that he should wish to dissociate his theory from that of critics who belong to and represent—consciously or not—the attitudes of societies that oppressed his people. To transform the theoretical genre by changing the language in which it is expressed is one way to redraw theory so that it applies to a specific group of texts. In this procedure, genre prompts black writers and critics to analyze the social and political transformations resulting from special language uses.

But Edouard Glissant, the Caribbean critic, declares that genre theory cannot accommodate the needs of newly independent countries because it is too rigid; he proposes instead a criticism that he identifies as nongeneric because it is uncentered, disordered, and replete with diverse styles and dis-

13. Henry Louis Gates, Jr., "Authority, (White) Power, and the (Black) Critic; or, it's all Greek to me," in *The Future of Literary Theory,* ed. Ralph Cohen (New York: Routledge, 1989).

courses.[14] Glissant desires texts that provide an insight into the
uncertainties and dislocations as well as the pleasures of the
newly won independence. His text is not merely opposed to
earlier genres. It is an effort at constructing genres that represent not a racial but a national and social identity.

For him, genres that appear in Caribbean countries and in
Western countries do not function in the same way. In the West
genre criticism based on multiplicity, combinatory aspects of
experience, its complexities, contradictions, and fragmentari-
ness is identified with the break-up of unified identity. In Glissant's view, the combinatory procedures make a new national
identity possible, though he might very well deny that this procedure is generic. In my argument for a combinatory genre
concept, I find that Glissant argues for the kind of criticism I
have been urging: the theory of combinatory genres is itself an
oppositional view of previous generic theories.

In my concentration on generic change in literary history, I
have deliberately ignored questions of method. The particular
kind of literary history is often identified by the method of the
discipline it relies on—psychoanalysis, phenomenology, Marxism, formalism, reader response, and so on. Such history can
also be identified by its dialectical, pluralistic, or organic hypotheses in organizing the constituents of the texts in studies.
Generic constraints, however, impose historical changes on
the methods employed. The dialectical method of dialogue differs from dialectical method in tragedy of different periods. In
this respect the ideological implications a Marxist criticism imposes on the novel *Lord Jim* are constrained by the received
implications of a biographical narrative. A psychoanalytic
study of a novel, for example, is itself a member of a genre. In
its narration of psychoanalytic assumptions, in its analysis of
rhetorical constituents including varied discourses, it remains
tied to the cultural implications of some of the cultural continuities that belong to its recent generic past.

I have been arguing that genres and their members are combinatory procedures that provide the most effective procedure

14. Edouard Glissant, *Caribbean Discourse: Selected Essays* (Charlottesville: University Press of Virginia, 1989).

for dealing with change in literary history. I have described three examples of literary history that oppose received generic practice and that offer revisionary procedures. These procedures are generic even when they deny the usefulness of genre. I have sought to show that a theory of genre can account for literary change more adequately than histories based on themes, ideas, periods, and movements. This theory accepts the assumption of a combinatory consciousness. It argues that texts, especially those by experimental authors, are combinatory entities that challenge us to grasp our multitudinous experiences with their possibilities of irreconcilable values. We need a new literary history, and I believe that a genre theory can provide it.

ALASTAIR FOWLER

The Two Histories

Literary theorizing may not continue at its current flood level
for ever. Those who find theory boring may regain the upper
hand (if not by argument, then by sales resistance); or else the
cadres theory valorizes may become established enough to do
without it. If metahistory then lapses, will literary history continue? It may. Before meteorology, west winds blew; and a
searching, small rain of gentle explorations stands a good
chance of stimulating growth in the readership of old literature,
even after the deconstruction of clouds of mystification. It is
less clear, though, whether, if literary history were to lose its
interest, literature would long survive it. True, there was probably little vernacular history of literature in the dark ages; but
then, there may not have been much literature either. The
Anglo-Saxon Chronicle is a document of considerable interest;
however, it is not the *Divina Commedia*. And as for Dante, his
works already argue the existence of literary history: "Nor,
reader, must you be surprised at our calling to memory so
many poets; for we cannot point out that construction which
we call the highest except by examples of this kind. And it
would possibly be very useful in order to the full acquirement
of this construction if we had surveyed the regular poets, I
mean Virgil, Ovid in his *Metamorphoses*, Statius, and Lu-

114

can."[1] Dante makes Virgil his guide in the *Inferno* because of historical connections between cultures—for example a tradition linking the pagan epicist's *nekuia* and the Christian poet's descent into hell. At the same time, it should not be forgotten that relatively little medieval writing was meant to be literary.

In the early Christian centuries, a writer's aim was generally didactic, and much effort went into subverting, converting, displacing, and capturing pagan tradition: into transforming, if not renouncing, cultural inheritances. St. Augustine's *Civitas Dei* and the preface to St. Jerome's Latin bible are typical in this regard, even if both contain more than a little literary history. Occasionally, the transformation was even carried *à outrance*, to the eschatological fiction of pretending to do without the past altogether. And this is a pretense, or delusion, that has recurred from time to time in more recent centuries. A new beginning. A clean, blank sheet. One can discern instances of such attempts at total cultural renewal in Descartes and certain Puritans of the seventeenth century, and, within living memory, in the radical politics of the late sixties.[2] The latter period saw formal literary history largely abandoned, because of a loss of consensus. And, not coincidentally, it was also a time in universities when much old literature came to be sequestered from the main curriculum—not all of it restored since. What is not studied may not be understood, and not understood is easily disliked. Significantly, the attack on literature has subsequently been directed mainly against its earlier periods.[3] New Historicists and cultural materialists alike dwell on reprehensibly powerful representations in Renaissance and Romantic literature. Although, in their view, literature of all

1. *De Vulgari Eloquentia,* vi.

2. On Descartes' dismissal of tradition, see William Kerrigan and Gordon Braden, *The Idea of the Renaissance* (Baltimore: The Johns Hopkins University Press, 1989), ch. 8. On modern stances, see *New Literary History* (hereafter *NLH*) 2/1 (1970) issue, devoted to the question "Is Literary History Obsolete?"

3. For surveys of new historicist writings on Renaissance literature, see James Holstun, "Ranting at the New Historicism," *English Literary Review* (hereafter *ELR*), 19/2 (1989): 189–225, with full documentation; and Louis Adrian Montrose, "Renaissance Literary Studies and the Subject of History," *ELR* 16/1 (1986): 5–12.

periods must seem more or less equally culpable, they seldom express hatred of contemporary literature to the same degree.

If there had been more, or better, literary history in the sixties and seventies—if it had challenged more critical engagement, then older literature might have been kept more accessible. Literary history might have presented some old works as still valuable; and either made sense of the currently existing canon, or argued for its revision. But as it was, literary history became "impossible," and the old canon appeared to some to constitute an oppressive representation of capitalistic or bourgeois hegemony. There has since been talk of replacing the traditional canon (that is, replacing literature itself) by new canons representative of other hegemonies. In one sense this is an eminently traditional idea. There can be no question, for example, but that the humanists and their inheritors from the fifteenth to the twentieth century have used canons purposefully, if not aggressively: "Reviving a great past is a deliberate attempt to generate fame; traditions, as the humanists understood them, were instructions for the correct dispensation of fame—a knowledge of who was great, and why. Because an intellectual of this kind was a producer of fame, he felt wholly justified in seeking this public amplification, during his life and during aftertimes . . . the mainspring of tradition was this calculus of veneration."[4] And now that humanism itself is under attack, its established traditions, its famous greats, in turn incur obloquy. It has proved harder to dispute the humanist preferences individually, however, than to insist that the existing canon be totally replaced. The historical changes of our time are so great (the argument goes) that new bases for fame and study, a new *paideia,* new traditions, are required.

The sixties' criticisms of literature as bourgeois are readily answered—as they have been, for example, by René Wellek (whose steam hammer, however, besides cracking many nuts, has possibly flattened a useful gadfly or two). But subsequent attacks on literature have become more serious and have gained some credence, particularly as regards its sexist and

4. Kerrigan and Braden, *The Idea,* p. 141.

racist oppressions. Clearly there has been something of a shift in attitudes, when the advertisers of a literary review like *Granta* feel it necessary to offer the groveling assurance that it, too, is "against literature." To many would-be avant-garde readers, literature is distinctly a sacred cow, and one by no means of the color purple. These new attitudes, I shall argue, depend on a particular myth of the origin of literary history, and on misconceptions about how it relates to history itself. For the dislike is of imperialistic, English literary history, rather than of literary history *per se*—of "literature," not literature.

Some critics, indeed, write as if literary history—if not the idea of literature itself—originated with late Victorian and Edwardian patriots of the R. W. Chambers stamp, as a mystification calculated to support British, if not English, imperialism. (The English element in criticism of that period sticks in quite a few throats, not all of them Scottish or Irish.) Now the teaching of English literature was indeed institutionalized in the late nineteenth century at several new British universities (although not yet fully at Oxford or Cambridge).[5] But it is myopic to see literary history as having no earlier origin than that. In the eighteenth century Thomas Warton and others pursued the study indefatigably; and it already then formed part of the *cursus* at the University of Edinburgh, where Hugh Blair (a divine not given to expressions of nationalistic sentiments like R. W. Chambers's) became Regius Professor of Rhetoric and *Belles Lettres* in 1762.[6] Moreover, literary history had made an earlier appearance in grammar and rhetoric courses, particularly in the form of parallels between phases of ancient and modern literature. Seventeenth-century writers, such as Dryden, Edward Phillips, and even popular grammarians, essayed literary historical essays implying considerable applica-

5. On the imperialistic bias of R. W. Chambers's literary history, see John A. Burrow, "The Sinking Island and the Dying Author: R. W. Chambers Fifty Years On," *Essays in Criticism* (hereafter *EC*) 40/1 (1990): 1–23.
6. On this early stage, see René Wellek's forgotten but important *The Rise of English Literary History* (Chapel Hill: University of North Carolina Press, 1941). This needs supplementation at various points: for example, Blair's lectures were partly anticipated by Adam Smith's Glasgow lectures.

tion on their part.[7] And earlier still, among the Italian literary theorists of the *cinquecento,* the history of *litterae* or of *poesia* (fiction; imaginative literature; poesy) was a standard, although limited, topic.[8] Renaissance literature itself, indeed, may be said to have begun with ideas of literary history. And a not dissimilar sense of tradition can be seen at work in the ancient world, in Aristotle's survey of the historical development of tragedy, for example, or Horace's remarks on the satirist Lucillus.[9]

As for the relation between history and literary history, the latter is commonly regarded as but a part of the former—a special branch, merely, albeit one of special interest.[10] Thus historians have sometimes chosen to specialize in literature, considering it a part of their own proper study—sometimes to admirable effect, as with Perry Miller or David Daiches. But this notion of the inclusion of literature within history, however widely received, has proved problematic—to the extent, even, that its converse has been asserted. Is not history, like philosophy, a form of literature?[11] That counterquestion is in line with a current tendency (in E. D. Hirsch and others) to equate literature with letters, or writing in general. In Britain that tendency was long anticipated, and institutionalized, by the inclusion of moral, historical, and philosophical writers in the literary curriculum. And one should not forget such longstanding British programs as American Studies, taught jointly by historians and Americanists.

7. John Dryden, *A Discourse Concerning the Original and Progress of Satire* (1693); Edward Phillips, *Theatrum Poetarum* (1675); J. D.'s Preface to Joshua Poole, *The English Parnassus* (1656).

8. For example, J. C. Scaliger, *Poetice* (Lyons, 1561), bk. VI, "Hypercriticus." For many other examples, see Bernard Weinberg, *A History of Literary Criticism in the Italian Renaissance,* 2 vols. (Chicago: University of Chicago Press, 1961).

9. *Satires* II. i. 62ff.

10. See, for example, Claus Uhlig, "Literature as Textual Palingenesis: On Some Principles of Literary History," *NLH* 16/3 (1985): 481–514.

11. See, for example, *NLH* 16/1 (1983), "Literature and/as Moral Philosophy"; and compare several issues on literature and history, for example, 6/3 (1975) and 19/3 (1988).

Perhaps the subtlest exposition I have seen of the idea of literary history as a part of history is Hans Ulrich Gumbrecht's, in his "History of Literature—Fragment of a Vanished Totality?"[12] But even Gumbrecht implicitly acknowledges the problematic character of the inclusive relation, when he introduces the notion of "fragment"; for "'Fragments' are objects of experience which we identify as parts of a whole, without seeing in their shape a constitutive part of this whole (a part which is bounded by a function). More radically, they are objects of experience, the shape of whose whole is unknown to us" (p. 468). In effect this concedes that an adequate account of literature would not be possible on the basis of its simple inclusion within history. Indeed, the relation of exclusion would provide a basis almost as good—or as bad. Gumbrecht thinks that literary history could not be conceived until "the collective singular 'history'" appeared in the early Enlightenment. Long before that, however, literary history was practiced, and literature's relation to other forms of discourse discussed.

Significantly, literature was then sometimes treated not as a part of history, but in opposition to it. In a familiar passage of *A Defence of Poetry,* Sir Philip Sidney cites Aristotle to the effect that poetry "is more philosophical and more studiously serious than history. His reason is, because poesy dealeth with *katholou,* that is to say, with the universal consideration, and the history with *kathekaston,* the particular: now, saith he, the universal weighs what is fit to be said or done, either in likelihood or necessity (which the poesy considereth in his imposed names), and the particular only marks whether Alcibiades did, or suffered, this or that."[13]

Of course, literary history of the earliest period (and even in its more recent phases) sometimes reads much like ordinary history—aping, perhaps, the older discipline's proper rigor. Thus contextual or factual chronicle has been indispensable in establishing the subject's annals. But no one would hold that

12. *NLH* 16/3 (1985): 467–480.
13. *Miscellaneous Prose of Sir Philip Sidney,* ed. Katherine Duncan-Jones and Jan van Dorsten (Oxford: Oxford University Press, 1973), p. 88.

chronicle is all literary history has to offer. Indeed, many literary historians have a positive distaste for annalistic entanglements, and some manage to avoid it more or less completely. Their interests, methods, even their rhetoric, can then be markedly special. And in general, almost, one may say that literary history has a distinctive form of discourse. Think, for example, of the organization George Saintsbury devised for *The Peace of the Augustans:* it is hardly one that would have suited a historian of his period.

Not that the distinctiveness of literary history consists in innocence of factual knowledge. Like criticism itself, literary history has both chronicling and analytic elements in its own right. And this resembles a division into external and internal found in history too. In each discipline there is an "outside" of superficial facts, more or less certain, and an "inside" of patterns, myths, themes, and laws, more or less interpretable and debatable. The external aspects of both have to be ordered chronologically, spatially, and in other ways: a preliminary job involving many determinations that are, in principle at least, falsifiable. And in each discipline the internal procedures (narrative, comparative, generalizing, and the like) are more concerned with causes or values—more philosophical, moral, or aesthetic. Nevertheless, the "outside" restricts what can reasonably be said "inside" it. Thus certain Marxist views about parliamentary majorities in the seventeenth century had to be abandoned when revisionists scrutinized the Commons votes, just as opinions about Abraham Cowley as an epic poet were modified (or ought to have been) when the manuscript of *The Civil War* was rediscovered. In practice, of course, the division into external and internal is not always neat, for facts may be selected in a manner biased by theories or prejudices or simple misconceptions. My present point, however, is only that literary history does not differ from ordinary history in respect of having both an external infrastructural element and an internal superstructural element.

It is necessary to make this point, since in recent decades many critics have lost interest in the external parts of their subject. At first they were impatient with irrelevant biography and merely verifiable information. And then, dismissing the referential world of contextualism altogether, they retired to an inner fastness of still purer textuality. But this extreme internalism provoked in turn an extreme reassertion of historical contexts. In part this reassertion can be regarded as a proper compensation of the internal emphasis by a corresponding external one. It was high time *some* facts were remembered, *some* mystifications dispelled. New Historicists may oversimplify, or be confused about humanism and hierarchy; but they are surely right to reintroduce such neglected actualities into critical discourse as authorial motivations, political representations, and sociological implications. It was time to reconsider the important (if not all-important) boundary of literature and history.

This is not to say, however, that the boundary can now be safely ignored—that the outside of literature is identical in composition to that of ordinary history, and that it relates to literature's inside in the same way as history's outside relates to its inside. For literature is not simply a section of reality like any other (even if historians sometimes treat it as such). And literary history is in consequence not simply another special history like diplomatic, or the history of technology. The difference arises not from the privileging of literature by literary historians, but from the way literature functions. Literature (and to some extent other arts too) are distinguished in their way of working from most other cultural objects. The objects and events outside literature constitute processes—and together constitute larger processes—that can be analyzed systematically in terms of interrelated causes and effects. True, some ordinary events may at one level seem random; but even these are generally attributable to causes at another level. Now it is not at all clear that literary events form a system in this sense, or that, if they do, this is their most important aspect. Writing of technological improvements, Fernand Braudel asserts that "no innovation has any value except in relation to the social pressure which maintains and imposes it."[14] Could the same be said, with the same force, of literature?

14. Fernand Braudel, *Civilization and Capitalism: 15th–18th Century. Vol. I. The Structures of Everyday Life* (New York: Harper and Row, 1985), p. 431.

In particular, literary events primarily relate to ordinary events not through causation, but rather by reflection, assimilation, representation, and the like.[15] Representations may of course have pervasively ramifying social consequences, perhaps even political effects. But that is not usually the main thing about them. There is an obvious sense in which Auden is right in his view that poetry makes nothing happen. When *The Satanic Verses* is said to have caused many deaths, the charge is framed carelessly. These disastrous afterevents follow not from readings of the book, but from its misapplication. They are not even consequences of misprision of Rushdie's meaning, but of misconceptions about the nature of fiction, or else, less ingenuously, of opportunism among British Muslim leaders.

In fact, literary events—great works, formal innovations, new motifs, beautiful effects, and the like—often relate more closely to each other than to events in the contemporary outside world. In this regard, admittedly, different genres differ somewhat. There is more topical reference in satire, epigram, georgic, and some kinds of novel; less in lyric, elegy, pastoral, romance, and other kinds of novel. And, in a more general sense, some accessible referential content is necessary for any successful communication of meaning. Unless sentences are related by a recipient to more or less appropriate shared domains of association, their meanings are unlikely to be taken up. But the appropriate associations are not always propinquitous or contemporaneous with the literary event. For writers are often involved with events of their childhood; and often (particularly where literary diction or conventions are involved) the associations may be of even longer duration. In the novel, for example, apparently immediate realistic representations may in fact be antiquated or mediated through literature—as is notoriously the case with Dickens's prisons and Fielding's Spenserian characters. Yet it may also come about,

15. Cf. the argument of Virgil Nemoianu, *A Theory of the Secondary: Literature, Progress, and Reaction* (Baltimore: The Johns Hopkins University Press, 1989).

paradoxically, that writers communicate most about their immediate social environment when they are least concerned to do so directly.[16]

Moreover, literary-historical events relate to each other differently from events in history at large. Proximate and distant causes, for example, press with very different relative weights in the two disciplines. In history, although political institutions may have long trains of gradually transmitted consequences— to the third and fourth generations and beyond—it remains true that very remote events—in other civilizations, for example—have usually no present effects worth discussing. "The boundaries of cultural time" may be elusive;[17] but we can be fairly sure that a famine in ancient Sumeria has no immediate bearing on modern life. True, Athenian democracy has had continuing impact, for example in eighteenth-century America; but this apparent exception proves the rule, since it was only possible through the mediating effects of ancient literature and (to a lesser extent) visual art. Similarly, ancient Roman engineering would not have been a factor in Renaissance achievement, without the intermediation of Vitruvius and of architectural remains.

Turning to literature, however, one finds processes of a very different sort. As if on a distinct time-scale, and even time-sequence, literary classics may have direct effects after many centuries. To be sure, where an intervening tradition of renewed transmissions is lacking, these long-distance effects diminish, until eventually even a classic may become irrelevant, drastically "accommodated," or unintelligible. Nevertheless examples abound of authors and works literally rediscovered after a lapse of centuries, and subsequently capable of generating cultural response (Manilius, the Ptolemy of *Tetrabiblos*, and Thomas Traherne come to mind).

Consider, for example, the impact of Virgil's *Georgics* on English literature. I pass over Virgil's astonishing place in the

16. Cf. Nemoianu, *A Theory of the Secondary*, p. 129.
17. Simon Schama, *The Embarrassment of Riches* (New York: Knopf, 1987), p. 597.

cursus of the early Christian centuries, his influence on medieval representations of landscape and of work, and his fuller
reassimilation in the Renaissance, to focus on the 'imitations'
described in John Chalker's *English Georgic*. Of this immensely productive phase of georgic, as Chalker explains,
there was a proximate foregoer, in the shape of Dryden's
Virgil, with Addison's influential preface. The 1697 publication
of this seminal work is a relevant external-world date: an effective *terminus a quo* for reading and response to the *Georgics* for many readers. Again, there were other historical prep-
arations for the vogue of English georgic, among them
alteration in the role of landowners with the greater size of
viable estates; efflorescence of new arts and sciences; a literary tradition stemming from Chapman's *Hesiod's Georgics*
(1618); attempts at georgic throughout the seventeenth century, such as Michael Drayton's *Poly-Olbion,* Nicholas Bre-
ton's *Fantastics,* and John Denham's *Coopers Hill;* and the
many sociopolitical causes Anthony Low has grouped as the
"georgic revolution."[18] For, just as georgic became a political
instrument, so it had political motivations, more or less recognized. For example, Whigs and others might wish to bring
Virgil's authority to bear in order to dignify landowning and
agriculture, or even specifically to promote the values of
peace.[19]

Nevertheless, it is incontrovertible that a main cause of the
English georgics was Virgil's *Georgics* itself: a work seventeen
hundred years old and still effective. Virgil's authority was no
empty idea of politicians, but emanated from his strength and
integrity as a poet. Outweighing all other more recent causes
was the sheer quality of his poem. More than any other, it was
this model of finish and internal organization ("herein consists
Virgil's masterpiece, who has not only excelled all other poets,

18. Anthony Low, *The Georgic Revolution* (Princeton: Princeton University Press, 1985). See also Annabel Patterson, *Pastoral and Ideology:
Virgil to Valéry* (Berkeley: University of California Press, 1987).

19. See, for example, Robert Cummings, "Addison's 'Inexpressible
Chagrin' and Pope's Poem on the Peace," *Yearbook of English Studies* 18
(1988): 143–158.

but even himself in the language of his *Georgics*"[20]) that challenged the transformation of English Augustan style and made possible a new sort of literature, characterized formally by a high degree of local decorum. From imitation of Virgil, for example, stemmed the introduction of detailed accordance between content and rhythmic realizations. And this resource, in turn, was eventually to be generalized and transmitted to the poetry of our own time. In such ways, the argument of literary time moves at a distinct pace: great writing slides over centuries, and flies "in motion of no less celerity / Than that of thought." To take history seriously in the case of literature involves cognizance of this distinct train of causation.

The mention of great literature brings up another difference between history and literary history—at least as they have been understood and practiced until recently. For in selecting and organizing their material, literary historians have typically considered aesthetic quality in a way that historians have not. In history, weight of numbers is commonly decisive: "number is a first-class pointer. It provides an index of success and failure. In itself it outlines a differential geography of the globe. . . . It indicates the decisive relationships between the diverse human masses."[21] In literature, by contrast, statistics have very limited application. The sociology of reading is only a partial exception: its findings have not prevented evaluative critics from continuing to think the fiction of Djuna Barnes worth attention. Similarly, numbers show that in the Renaissance there was a sonnet vogue. But what makes this of literary-historical interest is not merely the quantitative information that a great many *epigoni* used the form (that is almost a negative consideration), but the aesthetic qualities of the uses to which it was put by Petrarch and Shakespeare, Spencer and Drayton. Minor writers and conventional forms have also been studied, but generally with the ultimate intention of illuminating departures from convention, or summations of it, in the

20. Joseph Addison, "Essay on the *Georgics*," *The Works of John Dryden,* vol. V. *Poems: The Works of Virgil in English,* ed. W. Frost and V. A. Dearing (Berkeley: University of California Press, 1987), p. 149.

21. Braudel, *Civilization and Capitalism,* p. 31.

better work. Literary history has everywhere been guided by considerations of quality. History can work on whatever wretched stuff it finds convenient: the writings of minnows are representations of power, quite as much as great literature—perhaps more so. But the literary historian is not content unless he can make sense of the operations and sequences and interrelations of great writing. The aesthetic organization of literature has proved a recalcitrant difference from the world of political concerns.[22]

Attempts to conflate the two histories have encountered many insuperable problems. For example, there is the typical case of a writer's moral failure. Fine writers notoriously often lead coarse lives. Georges Simenon's detective stories, which many consider literature, were written by a man who claimed to have had ten thousand sexual partners, and probably in fact (for he was also a liar) had over a thousand. Similarly, there is not a mean thought in Dylan Thomas's poetry, but he himself stole shirts. Ben Jonson committed manslaughter twice. And Byron—but the point is an obvious one. Throughout history there have been good or even great writers who wrote like angels and behaved like devils, or like mortal sinners. A few writers, to be sure, have apparently led exemplary lives. But it seems fairly clear that in moral respects the histories of literature and of life need to be configured differently. To some extent, indeed, it is convenient to think of different histories, different worlds altogether. Many will not wish to rate Simenon's or Jonson's literary work lower because of their irregular lives. This appearance of a dual standard makes others uneasy, however, and may have been a factor in recent dismissals of aesthetic quality as irrelevant to responsible literary criticism.[23] If reading literature does not make the readers better people, why value it? Aesthetic quality has also been associated with falsely elitist refinement—as if popular literature did

22. See, for example, Terry Eagleton, *The Ideology of the Aesthetic* (Oxford: Basil Blackwell, 1990).

23. Frank Kermode, *An Appetite for Poetry* (Cambridge, Mass.: Harvard University Press, 1989), p. 26.

not also have its aesthetic features, its elitist aspirations, its dual morality.

Conflating the two histories also gives rise to problems of an ideological nature. Within the assumptions of Romantic theorizing, and still in modernism, writers were free to express or convey their ideas, regardless of ideology. They inhabited, as it were, a social heterocosm. But an increasingly thorough politicization of literature, together with its more and more direct engagement with ephemeral mundanity, have removed much of the magic circle once woven round the poet, so that ideological offense now becomes more likely. Hence the case of *The Satanic Verses*—which is alleged to have caused damage to community relations—is instructive. On the one hand Michael Dummett, the Oxford philosopher, appears to hold that Salman Rushdie bears partial responsibility for the damage: "To claim he bears none is to accord to writers immunity from ordinary requirements of human decency; whether they are really so immune is important for us to decide."[24] On the other hand, many signatories have testified to Rushdie's right to free expression. It seems the old heterocosmic freedoms of the writer no longer command the unquestioning endorsement of all intellectuals. The freedoms are now to be conditional, some argue, on the writer's behaving as a decent citizen. But is this not to forget writing's involvement with unconscious creativity in all its indecency? Moreover, when Dummett treats Rushdie as a citizen, not a writer, he seems to forget that long ago (when charges of blasphemy were common in Christian countries) Sir Philip Sidney explained how the poet "nothing affirmeth." Has our centuries-old acceptance of the radical distinction between fiction and nonfiction been on the wrong track all along?

Apparently ignoring the difference between the two histories will not work. I do not wish to be thought a defender of irresponsible bohemianism, or silly anarchism, or hypocrisy. Nor do I regard moral inconsistency as unimportant. Writers have responsibilities as citizens and as spouses. But there is no point

24. *The Independent on Sunday,* 25 February 1990, p. 32.

in pretending that their lives are just like other peoples'. A great part of a writer's time and effort necessarily goes into writing about life, rather than living it. Besides, if we are realistic about the extent of mankind's enthusiasm for virtuous behavior, we shall not expect people to order all parts of their lives equally well. In the case of writers, writing may be the most virtuous part—a selectivity of effort resulting less from choice than from an involuntary involvement that has often been likened to possession. Yet in this one sphere they may achieve works of a special value, even a superior integrity of insight or aspiration. We must take goodness where we find it (even if we subsequently decide to call it badness).

Of this limited authenticity, good writing constitutes an indicator, almost a guarantee. For, even if the writer is not himself a true poem, complex formal resonances necessarily imply creative work, whether from a long-prepared mental set or from a series of *ad hoc* meditations, reconsiderations, corrections, and honest modifications. Not that, morally speaking, all fine writing is exemplary. Even great works need not be that. But one can be sure that great works present, in a sense broader than Lucács's,[25] specially illuminating exemplification of their society and situation. At the very least, we are likely to meet in good writing the challenge of values fully entertained and realized. That is ultimately why aesthetic criteria have been upheld, and why the literary historian's main (although not exclusive) attention may intelligibly be concentrated on what is well written.

To some aesthetically minded critics, the idea of exemplification, even exemplification of "the totality of a historical situation"[26] relates literary history too immediately to history itself—whether in the subservience of ancillary convenience (as spectacles for the historian) or in the superior relation of qualitative arbiter, determining what ordinary histories have left out. Recognizing that certain of the values in literature had little to do with the concerns of external history—this was be-

25. See Hans Ulrich Gumbrecht, "History of Literature—Fragment of a Vanished Totality?" *NLH*, 16/3 (1985): 470.
26. Ibid.

fore the annalists and the history of private life—they insisted on absolute autonomy for the literary heterocosm. When the literary historian George Saintsbury was asked what he believed about literature, he is said to have recited the Apostles' Creed before firmly propelling the questioner out of his office by the shoulders. Few would now wish to posit so total a severance of literary and cotidian worlds. We have learned the need of another lesson: "only connect!" But the current swing towards identifying the two histories has proved just as untenable as their disjunction.[27] What degree of interaction should be postulated, then? What relation between the two histories?

To ask such a question is already to go astray. For there can be no question of boundaries, still less of regular demarcation of responsibilities, between history and literary history. Nothing seals them off from one another, so that there can be no question of a fixed trade agreement. Mundane conditions or events may always turn out to have impinged (and be impinging still) on literary production. How, then, can one know when to invoke mundane causes and political considerations? What parts of history are not parts also of literary history?

The appropriate criterion, I should like to suggest, is simple although difficult: namely, relevance. Relevance, after all, may well be the criterion whereby the associations of meaning itself are selected.[28] External causes must be introduced where they are relevant. "Ah, but," someone will object, "whose relevance? Whose sense of relevance is to decide?" This will depend on circumstances, but commonly, I believe, the literary historian should be concerned with what is relevant to the needs of readers and teachers of literature, rather than to the furtherance of ideological aims. The criterion is relevance to literature as such. But is not literature itself ideological? Is not everything, indeed, political? Certainly; but this only means that everything has a political dimension, not that everything is about politics: " 'Everything is political' only means that to

27. See, for example, Peter Washington, *Fraud: Literary Theory and the End of English* (London: Fontana, 1989).

28. See Dan Sperber and Deirdre Wilson, *Relevance: Communication and Cognition* (Cambridge, Mass.: Harvard University Press, 1986).

do an adequate political analysis you can not neglect anything . . . a framework of analysis is not defined by the kind of
material it looks at, but by the kind of concerns it has; the same
phenomena are of interest to many different kinds of analysis.
Everything is psychological, or economic, or ecological too."[29]
For the literary critic, the political dimension may be much
less important than others.

About nursery rhymes or ballads, political history sometimes has much to tell the literary historian; but on many love
songs, for example, it has little bearing at all, not even when it
takes the form of sexual politics. If the criterion of relevance
is to apply, it seems to follow that no uniform critical method
of political analysis will be adequate.[30] For, while politics may
always be relevant, it also may always be irrelevant. The literary historian needs to maintain a flexible stance of cool judgment. The recent return to political contexts has at times
greatly enriched literary history and criticism, by introducing
associations necessary to the full recognition of meaning. As a
regular method, however, New Historicism must fail, through
aprioristic prejudgment about what is relevant in individual
cases.

This is not to say that one should privilege writers' own
views of their works, as against political demystifications; nor
even that one should privilege literature, as against criticism.
At the same time, I do not mean to go along with Gary Saul
Morson in rejecting Stanley Fish's sort of literary history as
"internalist." If Fish goes wrong, it is rather by putting literary
theory first. In its place, autonomous literary theory is a legitimate special interest, just as radical politics is. But in the
classroom, and in literary history, what is privileged is the literary historical explanation or comment that happens to be relevant to the particular works under consideration. This may,
or may not, be "external" or "internal." And it should not be
ideological conviction that decides.

29. John Ellis, "Radical Literary Theory," *London Review of Books* 8
February 1990, p. 8.
30. Cf. Stanley Fish, *Doing What Comes Naturally,* (Durham: Duke
University Press, 1989), ch. 19.

JOHN FROW

Postmodernism and
Literary History

"To be modern—is this not really to know that one cannot begin again?"[1] Literary modernism is entirely a response to this
dilemma. It confronts at once the imperative to produce difference (to begin again, to make it new) and the apparent satura-
tion of the field of production, which makes difference inconceivable. To define its problematic in this way is to indicate the
exceptional, even impossible status of modernist writing. But
the definition may serve as well as a metaphor for the paradigm
of a modernist literary history, by which I mean any history—
not restricted to the period of modernity—of the series of such
impasses and of the breakthroughs by which the field of the
same, of an established normativity, is ruptured.

The adjudication of value is central to any such literary-historical practice. Its working principle is that those texts, and
only those texts, that manage against all the odds to achieve
difference are truly historical, or rather that history is the dynamic of this play between innovation (the displacement of re-
gularized aesthetic norms) and consolidation. Historical description thus involves a practice of discrimination based on a

1. Roland Barthes, *The Rustle of Language*, trans. Richard Howard
(London: Basil Blackwell, 1986), p. 64.

critical judgment of what constitutes difference within a complex intertextual set. Conversely, however, this means that history need not have the form of a chronicle, since the practice of literary criticism (that is, of reading) is itself inherently historical. It is in this sense that de Man writes, "To become good literary historians, we must remember that what we usually call literary history has little or nothing to do with literature and that what we call literary interpretation—provided only it is good interpretation—is in fact literary history."[2]

Immediately a modernist literary history becomes self-reflexive, however, it renders itself vulnerable to the critical force of its own logic. Indeed, it is possible to suggest that the deeply problematic concept of postmodernism has no other justification or necessity than that of responding to a crisis in the self-understanding of a modernism, and a modernist practice of literary history, that has gone on too long. For the temporality of modernism requires its own obsolescence: a modernism that failed to age, that did not demand to be superseded, would be a contradiction in terms. Hence the necessity of a successor, but hence also its definition solely in a chronological form ("post") which refuses all indications of content. The paradoxical result is that since this "post" must be a real *alternative* to modernism, it must be based upon a different temporality: not novation but stasis. It must be the end of history (hence the postmodern preoccupation with apocalypse). In its determination to *succeed* modernism, however, it corresponds entirely to a modernist logic. According to Habermas, since the nineteenth century, "the distinguishing mark of works which count as modern is 'the new' which will be overcome and made absolute through the novelty of the next style."[3] In this sense postmodernism is precisely a moment of the modern, a "next style." Its founding gesture is a

2. Paul de Man, *Blindness and Insight: Essays in the Rhetoric of Contemporary Criticism*, 2nd ed. (1971; rpt. Minneapolis: Minnesota University Press, 1983), p. 165.

3. Jürgen Habermas, "Modernity—An Incomplete Project," in Hal Foster, ed., *The Anti-Aesthetic: Essays on Postmodern Culture* (Port Townsend: Bay Press, 1983), p. 4.

modernist destruction of the modern, a destruction which is logically entailed by the modernist program itself.[4] As Lyotard notes, we may suspect today that this "break" is more like a repression (that is, a repetition) of the past than it is an overcoming of it.[5]

Another way of putting this would be to say that the concept of the postmodern responds to a *narrative* necessity. This is what modernist artistic production looks like in Lyotard's heroic formulation: it is "a sort of long, persistent, and deeply responsible labour directed towards enquiry into the presuppositions implicit in modernity": a salvational project.[6] Modernism, that is to say, is a *rigorous* program which leads to a predetermined end; it has the pathos of a necessary trajectory. The modernist artist (Duchamp, Mies and Corbusier, Schoenberg and Webern, Mallarmé, Joyce, Kafka, Stein) is the one who explores the given material with absolute commitment and to the point of silence or madness. But this narrative continues, not with a simple succession but with a dialectical reversal: having reached the point of absolute aporia, having taken the exploration of the material to its end, the modernist project becomes both complete and irrelevant. The intervention of postmodernism at this point would involve not a linear succession but a change of ground. Losing faith in both the purity and the futility of modernist practice, postmodernism takes up the discarded or marginalized materials of modernism (figure and representation, for example, or humor and directness of enunciation), and exploits them with a quite different kind of rigor. In particular, it ceases to structure its project on the opposition between high and low culture.

The problem with any such historical model is that it continues to reduce the heterogeneity of modernism to a paradigm of closed epochal unity. Positing a marked break between epochs,

4. Cf. Stanley Rosen, "Post-Modernism and the End of Philosophy," *Canadian Journal of Political and Social Theory,* 9/3 (Fall, 1985), p. 92: "Modernity arises as a 'project' . . . The subsequent rejection of modernity is then simply a re-enactment of the institution of modernity."

5. Jean-François Lyotard, "Note sur les sens de 'post-'," in *Le Postmoderne expliqué aux enfants* (Paris: Galilée, 1986), p. 121.

6. Lyotard, in *Le Postmoderne,* pp. 124–125.

it reinforces the ideal-typical opposition between noncontingent historical unities, and thus cannot deal with the possibility that so-called postmodernist texts remain centrally within the "sentimental" aesthetic of modernism. Following Paz's definition of modernism as a "tradition against itself," Calinescu argues that postmodernism therefore *by definition* cannot escape this paradigm: "Even the 'post' in postmodernism appears to be an unconscious tribute to modernism and to its dialectic of transitoriness and negativity. Insofar as modernism always aspires toward its own dissolution, postmodernism should be seen as one of the most typical products of the modernist imagination."[7] Were it to be qualitatively different, postmodernism would have to be grounded in a quite different temporality, and would thus have to be the paradoxical reversal of its own act of rupture. Rather than initiate, it would have to find itself within a stasis which would perhaps be that of a neoclassicism (and in this case its most representative form would be the advertisement, the genre which is most fully reconciled to the order of things and reads it as utopia), or else that of a frenzied renewal which, in a parody of modernist *ostranenie,* occurs in such short waves that it negates itself. Such a temporality would require a quite different model of literary history from that of modernism, and one which—caught between the conflicting imperatives to change and to stasis—could only be internally contradictory.

However dubious the idea of a radical break with modernism, however incoherent and empty the concept of the postmodern, nevertheless the very existence of the concept (like the irreducibly nondisprovable concept of the unconscious in Freudian psychoanalysis) acts as a provocation to the forms of historical thinking which have accompanied or been derived from modernism. It is not just the concept of novelty or rupture (the dynamic of perpetual change) which becomes problematic, but the political force attached to it—the sense that to break with ossified formal structures is at the same time to

7. Matei Calinescu, "Ways of Looking at Fiction," in Harry Garvin, ed., *Romanticism, Modernism, Postmodernism* (Lewisburg: Bucknell University Press, 1980), p. 168.

challenge or disrupt a broader normative structure of social authority.

The extent of the problem is made clear in Meaghan Morris's careful exposition of the recuperative strategy developed in Lyotard's writings on postmodernism. She identifies two versions of the concept. The first posits a roughly consecutive relationship between modernism and postmodernism (so that the latter is paradoxically understood in terms of a model of progressive rupture derived entirely from the former). In the second version, however, Lyotard "predicates a postmodernity which, as a recurring moment of rupture, actually *institutes* the modern: 'Postmodernism . . . is not modernism at its end, but rather modernism at its very beginning—and that beginning is always recurrent.'"[8] It's a brilliant move, which, in conceding the institutionalization of modernism, posits the moment of critique of (this) institutionalization as the very core of modernist practice; it is only of secondary importance, then, that the critique should occur "afterwards," since it is structurally the *founding* moment of modernism.

The logic of this moment is what Morris calls the "injunction to formal eventfulness (the invention of new rules)," and it is an inherently self-undermining logic because "the very structure of the obligation to 'event' (to coin a phrase), *as well as* the logic of the art market, soon drain any event of its eventfulness." Indeed the history of modernism is the history of the ever-increasing speed of this "draining." Lyotard's response is to insist both upon the untenability of this dynamic (there must be a moment *beyond* it) and upon its ineluctable necessity (to abandon the impulse to make it constantly new would be to give up on whatever critical function is possible for modernist art). But this hypothesis, says Morris, is, for all its theoretical adroitness, quite strictly banal, "because it restores us to the paradox of a history driven by the sole, and *traditional,* imperative to break with tradition." It seems to be driven by its

8. Jean-François Lyotard, "Answering the Question: What is Postmodernism," cited in Meaghan Morris, "Postmodernity and Lyotard's Sublime," in *The Pirate's Fiancée: Feminism, Reading, Postmodernism* (London: Verso, 1988), p. 234.

opposition to the automatizing and deadening power of institutionalization; but "Surely an entire history of modern art institutions (including criticism, the gallery, the museum, and the
relations of all three to the market) could be written precisely
in terms of a strict rhythm of alternation between advance and
arrest, pure event and mere innovation. The transformation of
the former into the latter is vital to the art 'system'—indeed,
as Lyotard's own version of the modern/postmodern relation
suggests, it may actually be a rule that defines the game."[9]

Fredric Jameson has for some years now been making a similar argument about the untenability of a modernist account of
aesthetic change. The paradox he identifies is that the very
opposition to commodification has in fact enhanced the market
value of modernist art, and has furthered the integration of
high art into commodity production: "The dynamic of perpetual change is, as Marx showed in the *Manifesto,* not some
alien rhythm within capital—a rhythm specific to those non-
instrumental activities that are art and science—but rather is
the very 'permanent revolution' of capitalist production itself:
at which point the exhilaration with such revolutionary dyna-
mism is a feature of the bonus of pleasure and the reward of
the social reproduction of the system itself."[10]

The imperatives of capitalist production assign "an increasingly essential structural function and position to aesthetic innovation and experimentation,"[11] and modernism has thus become absorbed into "an economy functionally dependent on it
for its indispensable fashion changes and for the perpetual re-
supplying of a media culture."[12] One might feel that Jameson
reduces a complex process of aesthetic opposition too neatly
to a functionalist vision of social totality, but there is surely no

9. Morris, "Postmodernity," pp. 235–236.

10. Fredric Jameson, Foreword to Jean-François Lyotard, *The Post-
Modern Condition: A Report on Knowledge,* trans. Geoff Bennington and
Bryan Massumi (Minneapolis: University of Minnesota Press, 1984), p. xx.

11. Fredric Jameson, "Postmodernism, or the Cultural Logic of Late
Capitalism," *New Left Review* 146 (July-August, 1984): 56.

12. Fredric Jameson, "The Ideology of the Text," *Salmagundi* 31–32
(1975–76): 246.

doubt that he is right about the extent to which modernism has been bound into the workings of the art market.

The implication of all this is that if we are properly to understand the rhythms of contemporary aesthetic production (but can we still speak of a self-contained aesthetic domain?) we must think in terms of a quite different model of literary history: one in which the moment of innovation immediately gives rise to, and indeed requires, its own subsumption into the aesthetic norm; and in which the dynamic of change is so rapid as to resemble a vertiginous stasis. Let us follow Jameson (but also Baudelaire, who had already in "Le Peintre de la vie moderne" identified the close connection between *mode,* the fugitive and transitory, and modernity)[13] in calling this the temporality of fashion.

Within a postmodernist paradigm time is a closed circle. It leads nowhere, it cannot be broken. The novelty that seems to puncture it is a pointless movement of change which merely reinforces its closure. This is how Chambers puts it: "With electronic reproduction offering the spectacle of gestures, images, styles and cultures in a perpetual collage of disintegration and reintegration, the 'new' disappears into a permanent present. And with the end of the 'new'—a concept connected to linearity, to the serial prospects of 'progress,' to 'modernism'—we move into a perpetual recycling of quotations, styles and fashions; an uninterrupted montage of the 'now.' "[14]

The argument takes "fashion" and "style" on their own terms, as the end of history—and these are terms which are thoroughly ideological in their generalization of a restricted temporality. Indeed, Chambers fails to think through at all the consequences of this state of pastness, which is built around a series of contradictions: such a temporality is either tensely structured on paradox or it is flat and empty—or, to push the logic of the argument further, it will be both at the same time.

13. Charles Baudelaire, "Le Peintre de la vie moderne," in *Curiosités esthétiques, L'Art romantique, et autres oeuvres critiques,* ed. H. Lemaitre (Paris: Garnier, 1962), pp. 453–512.

14. Iain Chambers, *Popular Culture: The Metropolitan Experience* (London: Methuen, 1986), p. 190.

It seems to project a moral imperative to abandon the quest for novelty, but insofar as novelty is fully functional for the system it is never possible to dispense with it, nor even, perhaps, with the illusion that novelty is the same as genuine newness. The time of postmodernism looks something like the stability and closure of neoclassicism, but it rests on a knowing sense of the abyss that is utterly foreign to a neoclassical aesthetic. It seems to presume a cynical acceptance of the commodity status of art, at the same time as it seeks to resist the fetish of the new, the original, the unique, through a parodic imitation of fashion, of advertising, of commodified novelty which is in its turn commodified, and which can never break through into some politically transcendental alterity.[15] It casually junks a whole tradition of radical negativity, the gamble on an absolute and rigorous commitment to critique that was at stake in the dynamic of modernist change. And it makes a queer virtue of the cognitive triviality implied by the word "fashion" (to such an extent that one might be forced to note, with de Man and against our commonsense reaction, that "when it becomes fashionable to dismiss fashion, clearly something interesting is going on, and what is being discarded as *mere* fashion must also be more insistent, and more threatening, than its frivolity and transience would seem to indicate.")[16]

It is in relation to the rhetoric of fashion that Richard speaks of "the critical de-energizing of many postmodernist works that renounce, unlike those which preceded them, the contestation of the cultural institutionality (museums-galleries-markets) which welcomes them and protects them."[17] At the same time, however, she refuses to set up the historical avant-garde as a model of good cultural-political praxis. Instead she sets out the terms of the critique which a later generation (if I may

15. David Bennett, "Wrapping up Postmodernism," *Textual Practice*, 1/3 (1987): 246.

16. Paul de Man, Introduction to H. R. Jauss, *Toward an Aesthetic of Reception*, trans. Timothy Bahti (Minneapolis: University of Minnesota Press, 1982), p. xx.

17. Nelly Richard, "Notes Towards a (Critical) Re-Evaluation of the Critique of the Avant-Garde," *Art and Text* 16 (Summer, 1984): 16.

use that figure) would make of the modernist avant-garde for its "tendency to believe, ingenuously, in the radicality of its desire for rupture and in the irreversibility of the gesture which manifests it": a stance which ignores the historical fact of recuperation, "the ease with which history turns the meaning of the gesture of rupture *back on itself,* reintroducing this movement into the continuity of the principle which founds it as History."[18] To formulate this critique is at the same time to be wary of the classic avant-gardist claim to be able to extend the moment of rupture to the realm of political praxis.

What has changed since the time of the modernist avant-garde is an intensification and an acceleration of the assimilative power of the art system.[19] This is the historical and institutional ground of the postmodernist dilemma: that "the History of Art has now learned to absorb Novelty simply as a variation on Tradition, and to exercise control over the periodicity of forms that *regularizes* any alternating or rotating play between the movements, thus rendering this play predictable."[20] And this has then meant that it has—for historical and institutional reasons—become ever more difficult for artists working today to break through *and remain* "at the limit of what is unacceptable"[21] by working against the grain of the art system.

This is not to say that there can be any position which is outside the system (on the contrary, the system is what makes any production of art, even and perhaps especially the most deviant, possible), nor that postmodernist aesthetic texts should be thought of in the modernist terms of a linear and progressive historicity; I think it is true to suggest that most

18. Richard, "Notes," p. 10.

19. Cf. Andreas Huyssen, "The Search for Tradition: Avant-Garde and Postmodernism in the 1970s," *New German Critique* 22 (1981): 32. "The earlier avant-garde was confronted with the culture industry in its stage of inception while postmodernism had to face a technologically and economically fully developed media culture which had mastered the high art of integrating, diffusing, and marketing even the most serious challenges," making the "shock of the new" much harder to sustain.

20. Richard, "Notes," p. 10.

21. Richard, "Notes," p. 10.

political criticism of the postmodern has taken at face value
the avant-garde project of subverting the art institution, rather
than seeing this project as a move within the institution (I am
thinking of Peter Bürger's work in particular). Rather, it is to
suggest that the concept of the postmodern should force us to
recognize the historicality of the modernist paradigm of literary history, and require us to search for an alternative which
is as yet—and in a classically modernist sense—unthinkable.

Unthinkable, because the concept of the postmodern poses
a fundamental challenge to the whole contemporary critical
project, undermining the very possibility of the modernist paradigm of literary history and the interpretive practice associated with it. This paradigm is dominated by the mutual determination of event and value, such that the event is constituted
by its differential aesthetic value, and value is in turn derived
from the structure of the event. Underlying both of these moments is the principle of the critique of the cliché.

In Lotman's terms,[22] the postmodern is founded on an aesthetic of repetition rather than an aesthetic of originality.
Rather than deviation, it is sameness (imitation, formulaic return) that enables writing to take place. This move allows the
dead end of the modernist striving for novelty within a saturated field to be overcome: it becomes possible to begin again.
Moreover, this displacement of the entire aesthetic problematic of the modern was perhaps the only way in which the crip-
pling burden of the tradition of the new could be shifted. It
does, however, exact a price: the abandonment of critique as
the constitutive principle of literary-historical progression.
Thus Foster writes,

the adventures of the aesthetic make up one of the great narratives of
modernity: from the time of its autonomy through art for art's sake to
its status as a necessary negative category, a critique of the world as
it is. It is this last moment (figured brilliantly in the writings of Theodor Adorno) that it is hard to relinquish: the notion of the aesthetic as
subversive, a critical interstice in an otherwise instrumental world.

22. Jurij Lotman, *The Structure of the Artistic Text*, trans. R. Vroon (Ann
Arbor: University of Michigan Press, 1977), pp. 289–291.

Now, however, we have to consider that this aesthetic space too is eclipsed—or rather, that its criticality is now largely illusory (and so instrumental).[23]

The conditions of postmodern textuality are that writing be indefinitely repeatable, and that it be integrated into the regularities of commodity production. In retrospect, however, it now seems apparent that these conditions held equally for all of the modernist period; and it would be misleading to assume that the integration of writing into commodity production automatically deprives it of all value. The ideology of modernism, and of the literary history that spoke for it, posited the freedom of the modernist text from commodity relations, in direct opposition to the unfree texts of mass (commodity) culture; and it tied this freedom, as critique and self-reflexivity, to the originary figure of the author. This is to say that modernist textuality was not thought of in terms of the complex mix of repetition and deviation that makes up any intertextual system, and that modernist literary histories have constructed their narratives around the figures of rupture and originality rather than in terms of the social conditions of possibility of these figures.

If, by contrast, we were to take iteration as the basis of all textuality, and if we were to agree that integration into commodity production has been the condition of all literary production for at least the last hundred years, then it might be possible to start theorizing the limits of the currently dominant paradigm of literary history. This is not a question of preferring a postmodernist (or even a "modestly postmodern")[24] to a modernist account of literary history, but of generalizing from the critique of this paradigm. Repetition and citation would thus be seen as integral to all forms of writing, and, as Wollen puts it, "reproduction, pastiche and quotation, instead of being forms of textual parasitism, become constitutive of textual-

23. Hal Foster, "Postmodernism: A Preface," in *The Anti-Aesthetic,* p. xv.
24. Preface to the *Columbia Literary History of the United States,* ed. Emory Elliott (New York: Columbia University Press, 1988), p. xiii.

ity."[25] Wollen thus argues for the uselessness for current purposes of "the polarized distinction between avant-garde and
kitsch, high and low art; the doctrine of the purity of genres;
the cluster of aesthetic concepts around the ideal of artistic
originality," and concludes that "the whole apparatus of levels, standards, hierarchies, boundaries, limits, centres and
sources needs to be re-thought."[26]

If this argument is correct it means that literary history in
any of the forms in which it is now usually practiced has lost
much of its force. It is no longer possible to think in terms of
a pregiven field of the literary which would form its proper and
unproblematically constituted object; and there is no consen-
sual structure of value which would provide the ground for an
assured practice of interpretation. At the same time, however,
other possibilities become available: for an opening of the
practice of *textual* history to new configurations drawn from
the whole domain of writing; for an opening of the question of
value to an analysis of the differential social bases of valuation;
and for an analysis of the institutional formations through
which literature, the literary event, and literary value are constructed. If the demand for a new literary history is the wrong
one, there is still the chance to begin again with the writing of
the multiple histories of textuality.

25. Peter Wollen, "Ways of Thinking about Music Video (and Post-Modernism)," *Critical Quarterly* 28/1&2 (Spring, Summer 1986), p. 169.
    26. Wollen, "Ways," p. 169.

ÜLKER GÖKBERK

Understanding Alterity:
Ausländerliteratur between
Relativism and Universalism

In his essay "On Ethnographic Self-Fashioning," James Clifford alludes to the "postcultural" situation from which he or any contemporary author writes, as a "condition of uncertainty." The reason for this uncertainty is that "the privilege given to natural languages and, as it were, natural cultures, is dissolving. These objects and epistemological grounds are now appearing as constructs, achieved fictions, containing and domesticating heteroglossia. In a world with too many voices speaking all at once, a world where syncretism and parodic invention are becoming the rule, not the exception, an urban, multinational world of institutional transience . . . in such a world it becomes increasingly difficult to attach human identity and meaning to a coherent 'culture' or 'language'."[1]

Increased awareness of the questionable validity of meaning and identity, of categories which belong to the traditional understanding of culture, dominates the greater part of Western (self)reflection on culture today. The phenomenon of cultural diversity as such is consequently not the issue at stake, but rather the question of how to speak about cultural diversities.

---

1. James Clifford, *The Predicament of Culture* (Cambridge, Mass.: Harvard University Press, 1988), p. 95.

The critical Western mind, long aware of its off-center position, now problematizes the possibility of "ethnographic authority" in general: "How, precisely, is a garrulous, overdetermined cross-cultural encounter shot through with power relations and personal cross-purposes circumscribed as an adequate version of a more or less discrete 'other world' composed by an individual author?"[2]

This questioning defines the Western critiques of culture today; its aim is the remedy of the representational—and actual—injustices done to the non-Western Other. The postcolonialist age is well aware of the dangers of the neocolonialist mentality in which the non-Western is either absorbed once again in the hegemonic structures of the Western or excluded as the remote exotic. Thus the critical discourse which presently prevails in European and North American cultural studies culminates in a crisis of narration. The binary opposition of the self and the other, a less than productive and often prejudiced construct of Western authorship, has been dismantled in many recent critical studies. Jeffrey Peck applies this approach to the question of minority discourse in the context of German studies: "My attention to the situation of those who address such issues is meant to lead us to think about positioning, both 'inside' and 'outside' the topic. I may, in fact, have to claim that even this opposition is arbitrary and misdirected, since it leads us to separate our position from the discourse we create. Still, any discussion of minority culture or discourse has traditionally assumed a majority against which it is defined. Without making explicit the epistemological dimensions of a subject-object split, such a discussion presupposes a notion of majority grounded in a dubious binary opposition."[3]

Alternative cultural phenomena serve institutionalized studies of culture in the West as an impetus to questioning its position and the categories used to define a particular field of study. It is interesting that this iconoclasm of stereotypes is

2. Clifford,*Predicament,* p. 25.
3. Jeffrey M. Peck, "Methodological Postscript: What's the Difference? Minority Discourse in German Studies," *New German Critique: Special Issue on Minorities in German Culture* 46 (1989): 203–204.

grounded in the discipline of Germanics—as it is in the broader context of cultural anthropology—on an abiding focus on the other and at the same time on its rejection as a Western construct. Thus Peck sees the possibility of liberating the cultural critic from existing prejudices and traditional boundaries of his field in the acknowledgment of diversity and difference. He suggests to his fellow-critics how *not* to talk about diversity; but leaves open the question of how to *talk* about alternative forms of culture. This indeterminacy is intentional and runs parallel to the general direction that cultural studies have taken: cultural discourse, as is well known, is now a discourse on the possibility (or impossibility) of the adequacy of its narrative. Peck's approach to minority discourse is a paradigm of the increasing tendency in humanistic disciplines toward the dissolution of the discipline into a meta-reflection on the discipline itself.

In this chapter I will attempt to discuss critically this recent focus on cultural diversity and on its representation as it manifests itself in German literary studies in the Federal Republic of Germany and in the United States. My concern is to illustrate the productive impulses of certain critical directions dealing with issues of cultural diversity; these impulses not only facilitate an understanding of cultural differences, but also provoke a rethinking of the premises of the discipline of German studies, its canonized interpretive modes and its self-understanding. The occasion for such a critical study can be traced to the unprecedented influx of culturally diverse elements into the West German society since the 1960s.[4] Ethnic

4. By such a lack of precedents I do not mean to suggest that the Germans were never confronted with the penetration of cultural minorities into their society. But the historical precedents did not entail a variety of ethnic groups settling down simultaneously in the German society. In an interview with the Yugoslavian author Zvonko Plepelić, Carmine Chiellino alludes to the previous migrations as follows: "There are two great examples for the power of integration and assimilation of the German culture, the Huguenots and the Poles immigrating into the Ruhr area. While the Huguenots were able to leave traces in the German culture, there is nothing left of the culture of Poles in the Ruhr area. Only the Polish names remain today, after eighty years since their immigration." Carmine Chiellino, ed., *Die Reise hält an* (Munich: Beck, 1988), p. 55. My translation.

minorities, primarily from Southern and Eastern European
countries and from the Middle East, have migrated to the Federal Republic for various reasons: to work, to seek asylum, or
simply to obtain a better education and standard of living than
in their homelands. Recent work in German studies takes as
its target the often superficial and unreflective representation
of the cultural other in the West German mediation of cultural
differences. This unreflective mediation will be a significant
object of my critical approach. At the same time, it is my contention that the critique of the stereotypical image of the other
contains, in spite of all its enlightening and liberating effects,
certain problems that bear scrutiny. I would suggest at the outset that these problems stem from the self-reproachful attitude
of much of Western critical thinking, concentrated on the existence of differences and yet undecided about how to talk
about these differences, and ironically, ending up in a reflection yet again about itself.

The literature of minorities as a collective phenomenon is a
relatively recent development in contemporary German literature. The literary critic Harald Weinrich has called the initi-
ators of this development "the grandchildren of Chamisso," a
designation he invented because he could not think of a better
one.[5] The Romantic Adalbert Chamisso, who abandoned his
native French and his native France, made the German language the linguistic homeland of his poems and novellas. He
thus becomes the predecessor of the minority writers in the
Federal Republic of Germany. The diverse literary productions, primarily in German, of the ethnic minorities entered the
public sphere in the 1970s under the rubric *Gastarbeiterliteratur* (guest workers' literature). This ambiguous and confusing
term has been supplanted in the 1980s by the more neutral label *Ausländerliteratur* (literature of the foreigners).[6] The new
rubric subsumes the literature of non-Germans within the West

5. Irmgard Ackermann and Harald Weinrich, eds., *Eine nicht nur
deutsche Literatur* (Munich: Piper, 1986), p. 99.
    6. The most extensive study on *Ausländerliteratur* published in English
is, to my knowledge, Heidrun Suhr's "*Ausländerliteratur*: Minority Literature in the Federal Republic of Germany," *New German Critique: Special
Issue* (1989): 71–104. Suhr's essay addresses the history of the recent mi-

German society by referring precisely to the non-Germanness
of its originators; it is a literature written by foreigners,
émigrés of some sort, who chose or were compelled to choose
the Federal Republic, at least temporarily, as their home. The
term *Ausländerliteratur,* however, does not eliminate the ambiguities inherent in the earlier label *Gastarbeiterliteratur.* Although "foreigner" liberates the authors from being defined by
the oxymoron "guest worker"—a label that offends many of
the foreign authors who have university degrees and do not
want to be confused with the foreign workers[7]—the com-
pound noun *Ausländerliteratur* leaves its referent unclear.
Does it signify the authors themselves, or a group of texts
distinguished by the fact that they are written in a language
other than the authors' native languages? Are they set apart by
their use of common themes, or defined by a specific mode

gration and focuses on the literature of minorities as a side effect of this
migration. She examines the development of this literature, focusing on the
main trends and the representation of these trends through the publishing
houses founded by foreigners. Suhr also dedicates a special section to the
works of the women minority writers. Her study includes a broad range of
bibliographical references on the issue, particularly of publications in the
Federal Republic. For Suhr's discussion of the problems emerging from various labels given to the literature of the minorities, see pp. 74–75.

7. Suhr comments on this problem as follows: "Some authors deny any
relation between their writings and their background and just want to be
accepted as authors. This is true, for example, of Aysel Özakin, who was
an established writer in Turkey before she came to Berlin in 1981. Although
almost all of her texts published since then address issues of the Turkish
minority in the Federal Republic, the difficulties of Turkish women, or more
general questions of the Self and the Other, she absolutely denies that she
should be considered a Turkish writer" (Suhr, p. 99). The Czech author Ota
Filip rejects in a similarly radical way the classification of his works under
the rubrics *Gastarbeiterliteratur* or *Ausländerliteratur.* He maintains that
"bad books and texts will not become better when they are written by an
émigré or by an author who has learned German as a foreign language. Exile
is, in literature and art, as little an aesthetic category as Eastern dissidence
or any other ideologically colored messianism . . . A German publisher or
another cultural mediator helps neither us nor art when he publishes out of
compassion with the émigrés and the émigre-writers, or for any other reason
which is totally irrelevant to literature and its quality, bad texts written by
non-Germans in German." Ota Filip, "Keine Wehleidigkeit, bitte" (No la-
ments, please), in *Eine nicht nur deutsche Literatur,* pp. 85–86. My translation.

of writing, different from the rest of literary production in German?[8]

The difficulties of circumscribing a group of literary writings based on common premises lead to a series of questions concerning literary history and established norms designating genres, styles, and themes and ending with judgments of aesthetic quality. How is the topos of *Ausländerliteratur* to be determined within the literatures of those countries where German is the native language? What kind of criteria are applied to the foreigners' literature in the present literary-critical discourse? What kind of criteria should be used by literary critics and historians to situate the texts in the broader context of German literature?[9] The current tendency among West German critics is to emphasize either the sociological or the linguistic aspects of the literary texts produced by the minorities. Both trends remain rather superficial, since the sociological approach is limited to a concern with themes, and the linguistic one simply repeats that the texts were written in a second language without going further to reveal their characteristic narrative aspects. Nevertheless, the relevance of these approaches for the literature of minorities is obvious. In the framework of a sociology of literature, *Ausländerliteratur* could be explored in more theoretical terms as a mirror of the cultural confrontation the ethnic minorities experience in their daily lives in West German society. For this approach, the first and foremost question would be to determine the representative nature of *Ausländerliteratur* for the minority groups in the Federal Republic. As the term implies, its representative quality can be seen both in the common—non-German—origin of its authors, and in the experience of a foreign milieu, which

8. The ambiguity in terminology increases if we consider the works written by West German authors specifically on the lives of the ethnic minorities. Günter Wallraff's controversial bestseller *Ganz unten* (At the Bottom) is the best known of these works.

9. A further question is whether *Ausländerliteratur* could be considered a subgenre and new form of exile literature. The term designates in German literary history the works of a particular period, namely 1933–1945, written by prominent authors who had fled Hitler's regime. In spite of certain common premises I see the differences between these two categories as immense; the most important of these differences is that exile literature was written in the native language of its authors.

the authors, as voices and representatives of non-German ethnic groups, thematize in their works. The sociological approach could be transcended or complemented by exploring
the formal aspects of *Ausländerliteratur*. Does the use of language, literary devices, genres, and themes reveal the beginning of a new literary program, of a poetics that might situate
Ausländerliteratur in a significant place in the broader context
of contemporary German literature and the German literary
tradition? How can this topological depiction be adequate if
the categories applied are the same as those used for describing institutionalized literature? It is clear that any critical attempt to define the literature of minorities in West Germany
has to deal with the problem of the applicability of the categories generated by canonized literary-historical studies to a
phenomenon whose nature seems to resist these categories.

While the questions I have raised above have yet to be addressed in any extended treatment of *Ausländerliteratur*, the
problems inherent in its reception have drawn critical attention. A recent issue of *New German Critique* is primarily concerned with the stereotypical image of the foreigner in the German media, as manifest in the works and commentaries of
West German authors, publishers, and editors.[10] Most of the
criticisms in this special issue are directed toward the clichéed
reception of the foreigner, toward the condescending Eurocentric attitude of the Germans evident even in their well-meaning
humanistic attempts to understand and speak for the minorities.[11] The reception of the literary works written by the for-

10. See also a pioneer work on this issue in American Germanics: Arlene
Akiko Teraoka, "*Gastarbeiterliteratur*: The Other Speaks Back," *Cultural
Critique* 7 (1987): 77–101.

11. See Anna K. Kuhn, "Bourgeois Ideology and the (Mis)Reading of
Günter Wallraff's *Ganz unten,*" *New German Critique: Special Issue*
(1989): 191–202. Kuhn states: "*Ganz unten* illustrates the pitfalls confront-
ing even sympathetic members of a hegemonic culture when they try to
(re)present and/or plead a minority cause. In order to test the tolerance of
his compatriots. Wallraff consciously pandered to prevalent clichés about
foreigners. His Ali is a naive, somewhat slow-witted soul, whose bastard-
ized *Ausländerdeutsch* (foreigner's German) conforms to prejudicial notions that Turks are basically stupid and/or uneducated and cannot speak
anything approximating cultivated German. Thus, instead of exposing a
system of representations that generate and support negative images of the
other, *Ganz unten* helps perpetuate them" (Kuhn, p. 192).

eigners is a secondary concern, although it could easily be shown how the same stereotypical notions that determine the reception of the literary works determine the reception of the foreigners themselves by the West German cultural mediators. The contributors to the special issue of *New German Critique* demonstrate that the representation of ethnic minorities in West Germany constitutes a model for a cultural confrontation of the Western mind with the non-Western.[12]

From this premise I will argue that the literary reception of *Ausländerliteratur* reflects the German mediators' image of the other. Tzvetan Todorov's critique of Eurocentrism in his study of Renaissance discoveries provides an excellent framework for exploring this problem, although the discovery of America and the emergence of *Ausländerliteratur* may at first seem unrelated issues.[13] Todorov begins by extending the meaning of "discovery" beyond its commonly accepted geographical connotations. While he agrees with the canonical view that the year 1492 marks a turning point in European history, initiating the modern era, he defines this turning point as a changed mode of consciousness. In this new mode Todorov traces the beginning of Eurocentrism. It is in this sense that "we are all the direct descendants of Columbus, it is with him that our genealogy begins, insofar as the word *beginning* has a meaning."[14] Todorov's narrative of Renaissance history is an ex-

---

12. I am using here the expression "non-Western other" despite the large number of Italian and Spanish minorities living in the Federal Republic. In the framework I am discussing, Westernness designates a certain mode of thinking rather than a mere geographical reference. Nevertheless, I should also point to the fact that there are degrees of otherness in the perception of the Germans. An illuminating study of the point is to be found in Dietrich Thränhardt's article "Patterns of Organization among Different Ethnic Minorities," *New German Critique: Special Issue* (1989): 10–26. Thränhardt distinguishes four categories which describe the Germans' perception of foreigners: 1. Noble foreigners (British, French, Americans, Swedes), 2. Foreigners (Spaniards, Yugoslavs, Greeks), 3. Strange foreigners (Portuguese, Italians, Vietnamese), 4. Rejected foreigners (North Africans, Black Africans, Pakistani, Persians, Turks); p. 13.

13. Tzvetan Todorov, *The Conquest of America* (New York: Harper, 1987).

14. Todorov, *The Conquest*, p. 5.

emplary story responding to the question of "how to deal with the other."[15] His purpose is embodied in the link between the title and the subtitle of his book: *The Conquest of America: The Question of the Other.* The concepts of discovery and conquest become in Todorov's cultural-anthropological critique the paradigms of a mode of behavior characteristic for the European's encounter with new cultures. It is in this paradigmatic sense that "we," as members of Western societies, are direct descendants of Columbus. In Todorov's model, paradigm coincides with history, for it is through Columbus's treatment of the inhabitants of the new continent that the precedent is set for a certain perception of the other in European modernity.

With this critical approach to Renaissance conquests Todorov offers a model that unveils the mechanisms of similar cultural confrontations, past and present. Todorov investigates the encounter of the self with the other from a typological point of view. The category of the other is produced by the concept of the self, through which the "I" posits an identity as autonomous subject. The other designates an otherness only with regard to this "I"—to myself or to a group—with which I identify myself.[16] It is decisive here that the self-definition of the "I"-group establishes the norms of the other. The stories of Columbus, Cortés, Las Casas, Sahagún, Durán, and many other protagonists, witnesses, and historiographers of the conquests—the stories of the *conquistadores*—obtain their exemplary quality in that they imply the dichotomy between the self and the other. But the exemplary does not necessarily mean that the Renaissance paradigm can be applied unreflectedly to any other context. Todorov points to differences, even within this paradigm, as much as he does to parallels. Thus the stories of the fifteenth- and sixteenth-century conquerors do not provide a mirror-image of *our own* relationship to the other. As

---

15. Todorov, *The Conquest,* p. 4.

16. Todorov not only distinguishes between the exterior and the interior other, but alludes to the psychological split of a self and an other within oneself. The discovery of the other within the self is illustrated by Rimbaud's motto *Je est un autre* (see Todorov, p. 3).

Todorov emphasizes, the age of colonialism is behind us, and "not only is Cortés not like Columbus, but we are no longer like Cortés."[17] But the exemplary aspect of these stories and histories still persists because, according to Todorov, we have to learn from differences as much as from resemblances.

The relevance of Todorov's categories for the cultural clash which has been taking place for the last three decades between the ethnic minorities and the Germans in the Federal Republic is almost too obvious. Less obvious and untested is the validity of Todorov's model on the plane of representation, on which *Ausländerliteratur* is situated. However, both on the social and the representational levels, it is important to emphasize the differences as well as the resemblances. In the cultural confrontation in West Germany no massacres take place, as they were then instigated by the Spanish conquerors; neither are here minorities actually enslaved or colonialized. The direction of the occupation is indeed inverse: the 4.5 million foreigners intruded into the German society, and not vice versa; their authors began gradually occupying the realm of German literature, even if marginally. But in spite of the temporal and categorical distance between the Renaissance discoveries and contemporary West German culture, the mode of perception, which defines the other in the latter context, is not so very different from the mode of the former.

It is true that within the West German cultural milieu there is an increasing interest in the literary works of the minorities residing in the country. But these works are hardly considered a part of the "actual" literature of the Germans, Austrians, and the German-speaking Swiss (of what is called in German *deutschsprachige Literatur*). The increasing number of anthologies, and of individual works by the foreign writers, is related above all to the immediate interests of the West-German publishers who clearly have discovered in the exotic of the foreigner new dimensions for book-marketing. "They don't expect the foreign authors to offer literary texts, but '*Gastarbeiterliteratur*' like cookbook recipes or instructions for using

17. Todorov, *The Conquest,* p. 254.

machines," remarks the Turkish author Yüksel Pazarkaya.[18] Jusuf Naoum, another representative of *Ausländerliteratur*, states that "in the image created by Germans the foreign culture is reduced to folklore and exotics. 'Belly dance and kebab, those should be left to them.' "[19] Through the institutional mediation of the texts according to the prevailing images of the minorities, the texts are packaged and posed as genuine self-representations of the other expressly for the consumption of the German host. The German editors select the texts, often as the result of competition; they separate them into thematic units, edit them, or even leave them pointedly unedited.[20] To collect the texts of minority writers in anthologies and to characterize them in the uncriticized and finally superficial frame of themes is to render these literary products little more than a curious side-show or subspecies, even less than a subgenre, of "true" or "genuine" German literature.

The tendency of the German publishers to present *Ausländerliteratur* in the public sphere as an exotic novelty corresponds in Todorov's analysis to two seemingly contradictory myths or notions through which Columbus perceived the Indians: as the "noble savage" when seen from a distance, and as the "dirty dog," the potential slave, close to. It is precisely this distance of the exotic alien that constitutes the characteristics of *Ausländerliteratur* in the image presented by the German publishers. Decisive is the fact that these two ways of perception ("noble savage"/"dirty dog") are corollary. According to Todorov, Columbus is incapable of recognizing the Indians, therefore he refuses to admit that they are subjects having the same rights as he does although they are different from himself. For Columbus being different and being a subject exclude one another. Todorov comes to the conclusion that "Columbus has discovered America but not the Americans."[21]

18. Yüksel Pazarkaya, "Literatur ist Literatur" in *Eine nicht nur deutsche Literatur,* p. 62. My translation.

19. Jusuf Naoum, "Aus dem Getto heraus" (Out of the Ghetto) in *Eine nicht nur deutsche Literatur,* p. 79. My translation.

20. See Suhr, "Ausländerliteratur," pp. 89–92.

21. Todorov, *The Conquest,* p. 49.

The inability of a group, defined as the "self," to recognize a different group of individuals as autonomous, even if different, subjects, stems primarily from a hermeneutic problem which is related to making one's own cultural system an absolute. An example of the problem is to be found in the self's perception of language. In 1984, Deutscher Taschenbuch Verlag, a publishing house which has played a leading role in the introduction of *Ausländerliteratur* to the West German readership, published the anthology *Türken deutscher Sprache* (Turks of the German Language).[22] In the editors' attempt to present the texts of minorities to the German public, a well-intentioned humanism—beyond the above-mentioned market interests—clearly manifests itself. In a brief introduction the good intentions that underlie this publication are contrasted with the "current prejudice" (*das gängige Vorurteil*) of the Germans vis-à-vis the other, here, the Turk. This "current prejudice" concerns language and is articulated in the condescending motto *Du nix sprechen Deutsch* (You no speaking German). The anthology *Türken deutscher Sprache* undertakes to correct this bias: "Many people are not yet aware that there is, in the meantime, *already* a literature of the Turks of the German language, that many Turks who live and work with *us,* also write poems and stories in *our* language. The texts in this volume give the occasion to get acquainted with this new literature, and with the manifold possibilities in it. The experiences expressed in these works are oftentimes bitter, sometimes amusing. But in no case do they leave us indifferent."[23]

The striking point of this humanitarian statement is the degree of the astonishment implied in the use of the adverbs and pronouns I have underscored. They emphasize that the "guests" have come a long way to express themselves in German. At the same time, the genitive construction "Turks of the German language" marks the first step toward the integration of the other into the host culture, the criterion of this

22. Irmgard Ackermann, ed., *Türken deutscher Sprache* (Munich: Deutscher Taschenbuch Verlag, 1984).

23. "Über dieses Buch," in *Türken deutscher Sprache*. My translation: emphasis mine.

acceptance being obviously the more or less evidenced competence of the foreign writers in German. One could argue here that a common linguistic basis is the indispensable presupposition of any communication. But the above introductory statement implies more than an appeal for communication.

In his analysis of Columbus's confrontation with the Indians Todorov alludes to a problem which sheds light on such editorial commentary. Columbus's lack of linguistic awareness, his inability to understand the difference between language traditions, leaves him with the following alternative when he confronts a new language: he either recognizes it as a new language but rejects the idea that this language could be different from his own; or he accepts the difference but refuses to believe that it is a language. Undoubtedly, these two modes of perception are complementary. The former is evident in Columbus's statement following his first encounter with the Indians: "If it please Our Lord, at the moment of my departure I shall take from this place six of them to Your Highnesses, *so that they may learn to speak.*"[24] (Todorov adds here that this statement shocked the French translators of Columbus to such a degree that they felt compelled to correct the statement to "so that they may learn our language.") In this vein, are the German publishers and editors of *Türken deutscher Sprache* pleasantly surprised that the Turks have finally learned to speak, or that they have learned to speak "our" language? It seems that these two possibilities are used interchangeably in the introductory statement. In any case, the humanitarian attempt proves insufficient to challenge the clichéd image of the Turk in whom the German citizen sees the negation of a civilized human identity. The frequent use of the first-person plural pronoun "we" in the introduction implies a vaguely determined sense of a "them," the non-Westerners, whose function it is to consolidate and complement the identity of the self, the European. Thus the image of the Turk is once again presented in the binary opposition of self and other.

It is likely that the problems surrounding *Ausländerliteratur* stem to a great extent from the ambiguities that the term "in-

24. Todorov, *The Conquest*, p. 30. Emphasis mine.

tegration" implies. Many of the foreign authors share with
West German intellectuals the belief that the ethnic minorities
in the Federal Republic and their literary productions can only
be liberated from their isolated stance through integration. But
as the introductory paragraph to *Türken deutscher Sprache* exemplifies, integration itself is a problematic concept. For if the
attempt at integration is initiated by the Germans, as is the
case in the anthology discussed, what often takes place is a
process of *assimilation* of foreign elements into one's own culture, literary tradition, and so forth, instead of the *integration*
of autonomous subjects, individual authors. The German cultural mediator indeed acknowledges the same human rights for
the other that he himself possesses, but he forgets too easily
the specific character of the foreigner. Conversely, if he starts
with the difference, he ends up very often with hierarchical
assessments of superiority-inferiority. For the perception of
differences implies the danger of a normative comparison. The
Turkish author Aras Ören, who has been living in Berlin for
almost thirty years, rejects precisely this mode of comparison:
"The Germans should not think that what they [the foreign
authors] write is inferior culture, but it's o.k. for the foreigners. And they should not tap on our shoulders well-
meaningly."[25] Both the assimilationist attitude and the normative evaluation of cultural differences (in favor of one's own
culture) are grounded in "egocentrism, in the identification of
our own values with values in general, of our I with the universe—in the conviction that the world is one."[26] In both
modes of the experience of alterity, it is the self who establishes the authoritative tone, who determines the categories for
describing the other. Even in the most well-meaning encounter
with cultural differences the self preserves its position of authority.[27]

25. *Die Reise hält an,* p. 168. My translation.
26. Todorov, *The Conquest,* pp. 42–43.
27. Günter W. Lorenz offers another example of this well-intentioned humanistic position in an article serving, in part, as a foreword to a special
issue of *Zeitschrift für Kulturaustausch* (Journal for Cultural Exchange), a
collection of literary and artistic pieces subtitled *Migrationserfahrung und
Deutschlandbild in der türkischen Literatur der Gegenwart* (Experience of

It is obvious that the problematic reception of *Ausländerli-teratur* does not simply indicate a lack of understanding on the part of the Germans. The normative understanding of the other through the binary opposition of superiority-inferiority does not necessarily mean a simple lack of understanding; it can turn destructive when the success of understanding is accompanied by an axiological rejection, what Todorov calls "an un-derstanding-that-kills."[28] In this dangerous mode of approach to cultural differences—one Todorov sees exemplified by Cortés, the conqueror of the old Mexican civilizations—knowledge becomes an instrument of power. Without this in-strument the Spaniards would not have been able to conquer and destroy the highly civilized cultures of the Aztecs and the Mayas in such a short amount of time. The paradox that un-derstanding facilitates destruction and control rather than sym-pathy with the other is explained by the acceptance of the ax-iological system, a system that is at the core of the colonialist

---

Migration and Image of Germany in Contemporary Turkish Literature) 35 (1985): 9–13. Lorenz explicitly advances his polemic against the clichés which he perceives as barriers to understanding between nations, here spe-cifically between Turkey and the FRG. He views Turkey as a land which for decades, but especially since the worker migration of the 1960s and 1970s, has been treated with an appalling lack of understanding and even with hostility and indifference by its great historical "friend," Germany. The consequence, according to Lorenz, is a deep disappointment on the part of the Turks. To combat this state of affairs Lorenz from his idealistic standpoint is always ready to point out the achievements of Turkey, albeit as an abstract, only semihistorical entity (the Turks are the inventors of the coffeehouse), in order to rectify the crudity of his German compatriots and rescue the honor of the Turks. Lorenz's efforts to construct a more ade-quate image of Turkey for the Germans become problematic when one rec-ognizes the premises behind his sentiments. The Turks, he insists, possess enough cultural-historical refinement to rank among the other countries of the West. And it is their undeniable, if peripheral, historical and geograph-ical connection to the West which lends them credibility. The same Euro-centrism which Lorenz consciously seeks to escape enters through the back door of his discourse. He does not argue for the value of Turkish culture in its own right, but for recognizing it as a contributor to an advanced Western European culture.

28. Todorov, *The Conquest,* p. 127.

reception of differences. Edward Said's *Orientalism* convincingly demonstrates that we can trace in a series of literary, journalistic, and scientific texts of the nineteenth century about the Orient the geopolitical awareness of the Westerner, an awareness that shapes the image of the non-Westerner.[29] In light of these critical insights it becomes impossible to accept integration as unproblematic and an easy solution to the cultural conflicts present in the West German milieu. The implications of integration, if pursued within Eurocentric parameters, are either the prejudice of a universally valid concept of equality ("identifying the other purely and simply with one's own 'ego ideal' "[30]), or the exclusion of the other on the basis of one's own self-perception as the superior instance. It is true that German intellectuals often combine their progressive concern with the minorities with a strong self-critique. But only rarely does this reproach mean that the Germans would be ready to give up their position of authority over against the foreigners. The reception of the literary works of the minorities illustrates this unwillingness clearly.

I have already noted that the publication of *Ausländerliteratur* in West Germany frequently occurs in the form of anthologies, neatly ordered according to thematic categories. The authoritative posture of the German mediators is once again manifest in the collective reviews of these literary texts by the German critics, which correspond to the collective publications in the book market. To a certain extent, the foreign authors are also responsible for this global treatment. The publishing houses founded by the foreigners themselves help—unintentionally—reinforce the idea that the literature of minorities only deserves to be treated collectively. These publishers, too, organize the texts as a collective statement; the anthologies are divided into thematic units recalling those published by the Germans. But the marginal treatment of *Ausländerliteratur* by German literary critics cannot be completely explained by the large number of anthologies. Many publications of in-

29. See Edward Said, *Orientalism* (New York: Vintage, 1979).
30. Todorov, *The Conquest*, p. 165.

dividual authors are available to the critics interested in writing monographic or comparative analyses similar to those written for mainstream German literature. Yet such in-depth studies are rarely published.[31] In a programmatic essay, the Syrian author Suleman Taufiq maintains that *Ausländerliteratur* can only be freed from its isolation if the German cultural establishment deals with this literature "normally." But for Taufiq "normal" treatment does not mean that the criteria of German literary criticism be immediately applied to the works of the foreign authors: "For we always write, almost unintentionally, against the prevailing rules and norms of German literature. If one looks for the roots of our texts, one can find them in our own rootlessness."[32] Taufiq's depiction of *Ausländerliteratur* clearly shows that neither the assimilationist treatment of the differences, nor the authoritatively posited value judgments which ascribe the literature of minorities an inferior place altogether, can adequately describe the voice of the other.

The reflections of the minority writers themselves on the reception of their literature reveal, in fact, the most crucial aspects of the problem. In the programmatic anthology *Die Reise hält an* (The Journey Goes on), editor Carmine Chiellino explains the scarce reaction to the literature of minorities in German literary criticism with the false notion that this literature represents some sort of petit-bourgeois appeal: "The foreigners tell us about their discontent in the German society and we should be concerned about them. The literary quality of the poems, stories, satires, fairy-tales, children's stories and novels written by the foreign authors has nowhere been taken into consideration."[33] According to Franco Biondi, another leading

31. The Institute for German as a Foreign Language in Munich has certainly helped to attract greater attention to the literature of the foreigners, although the Institute's manner of mediating the *Ausländerliteratur* through anthologies and competitions is not free of clichés. According to information from Yüksel Pazarkaya, a dissertation has now been written on his work; it is not unlikely that there have been other similar studies initiated in the framework of the Institute in Munich.

32. Suleman Taufiq, "Natürlich: Kritik" (Of Course: Critique), in *Eine nicht nur deutsche Literatur,* p. 77. My translation.

33. *Die Reise hält an,* p. 31. My translation.

figure among the minority authors, Germans have a distorted perception of *Ausländerliteratur* because they have had little experience with literatures of minorities, and none with so-called subcultures, their forms and metaphors: "Actually, they only have experienced a literature which was produced by popes of literature, or by acknowledged personalities."[34] In Biondi's critique, this lack of experience with alterity in German literary criticism often leads the German critic to reductionist clichés, through which the literature of minorities is rendered a harmless phenomenon: "There is a tendency to say it is a literature of the degraded. They think that they have put us into a ghetto, and that our literature can only exist in that we reproduce our immediate experiences as the affected."[35]

With this statement Biondi radically rejects defining the literature of minorities in the Federal Republic by its content. Instead, he proposes that aesthetic experience alone should characterize *Ausländerliteratur*, not the immediacy of the experience. Another minority writer, Rafik Schami, sees in this aesthetic experience a means which could serve to alter the established definitions of literature in the West German intellectual milieu. This is a crucial task in Schami's view, since "Literature smells here like a sanctuary."[36] The task is difficult given the resistance of the established concepts of literature, not only in the minds of an educated public and the literary critic, but also in the institutions representing these concepts. The programmatic discussions of *Ausländerliteratur* by its authors attest to the beginnings of a new poetics depicting the characteristics of this literature. But as Yüksel Pazarkaya observes, the representatives of *Ausländerliteratur* have not yet been given the opportunity to lecture on their aesthetic program in the German universities (I should add that this aesthetic program is by no means a unitary one; it includes a variety of directions); they have not been given the chance to discuss their literature within academic institutions. This ex-

---

34. *Die Reise hält an,* p. 31. My translation.
35. *Die Reise hält an,* p. 32. My translation.
36. Rafik Schami, "Eine Literatur zwischen Minderheit und Mehrheit ("A Literature between Minority and Majority"), in *Eine nicht nur deutsche Literatur,* p. 56. My translation.

clusion becomes more ironic if we consider the fact that Pazarkaya himself earned his doctorate under the supervision of Fritz Martini, one of the prominent voices of contemporary criticism in West Germany.

The questions I have discussed in the context of the reception of *Ausländerliteratur* are related to a specific aspect of the broader problem of how to speak about cultural differences. Again, from a critical perspective it becomes evident how *not* to speak about alterity. My concern is that the problematization of representation may lead any critical study today to a dead-end with respect to an undistorted understanding of cultural manifestations other than one's own. Undermining the privileged authorial position of the Western mind, the prevailing mode of critique in the last decades of the twentieth-century threatens to result in a cultural solipsism, in a kind of claustrophobia. Although the aim of these studies is precisely to break the boundaries of a Eurocentric notion of culture, the perception of multiple voices leaves the Western critic no choice but to become a "participant observer" of these voices.[37] The claustrophobic aspect of this remorseful gesture is that the "participant observation" does not necessarily lead to an adequate understanding of what the participant is listening to. "Participant observation" is rather the self-punishment of the participant, or if the critic is a non-Westerner, a prescriptive punishment given to the Westerner. In any case, the punishment implies the denial of the possibility of rational understanding, which the Western mind has cultivated since the Enlightenment. But this (self) punishing gesture is self-referential; it clearly is a self-confrontation of the Western mode of thinking, for which the problematic other occasions a redefinition of its own categories.

In the special issue of *New German Critique,* Arlene Akiko Teraoka offers an illuminating critique of the stereotypical representation of the Turk by two German authors, Günther Wallraff and Max von der Grün.[38] The critic goes on to explore a

37. See Clifford, *Predicament,* p. 24.

38. Arlene Akiko Teraoka, "Talking 'Turk': On Narrative Strategies and Cultural Stereotypes," *New German Critique: Special Issue* (1989): 104–128.

third mode of representation which she finds free of the clichéed images that dominate Wallraff's and von der Grün's
texts. Teraoka finds this mode in Paul Geiersbach's *Bruder,
muss zusammen Zwiebel und Wasser essen! Eine türkische
Familie in Deutschland* ("Brother, Must Together Eat Onion
and Water! A Turkish Family in Germany"). Geiersbach's text
threatens abiding clichés by emphasizing the "participant observer" position of the West-German narrator who listens
to the stories, told by the remote others of West German society, the Turks. Teraoka welcomes this model since she sees
in it the only possibility for a nonauthoritative depiction of the
culturally different by a hegemonic group: "Not our label for
the Other, but the Other's own voice, speaking to us directly
in its own idiom, which we do not yet understand: the model
is no longer a visual one promising direct access and denying
the possibility of two-way communication, but a *dialogic* one.
They speak, we learn to listen. We are no longer sovereign or
manipulative toward their reality but suddenly unsure and ig-
norant. And it is only when the Self can suspend its own sure
beliefs that it can even begin to listen carefully to what the
Other is saying."[39]

Teraoka's depiction of the nonsovereign, nonmanipulative
model of communication in Geiersbach's text leaves the
question of understanding as a *not yet* achieved goal. She
underscores the position of the German narrator as listener,
his unsureness and ignorance vis-à-vis the voices that he does
not—yet—understand. In spite of the term "dialogic communication," the model proposed by Teraoka is not primarily
concerned with how the "not yet" is eventually to lead to understanding. What is crucial is the symbolic self-execution of
the German narrator in his rejection of his Eurocentric premises. The focus of attention is thus the transformation of the
Western mode of thinking for which the Turkish speakers in
Geiersbach's quasi-documentary text provide the occasion.

The fusion of horizons which one expects to result from the
Westerner's attention to non-Western voices is not self-
understood. Abdul JanMohammed, for example, whose stance

---

39. Teraoka, *New German Critique*, pp. 127–128.

is similar to Teraoka's, sees here an insurmountable hermeneutic difficulty: "Genuine and thorough comprehension of Otherness is possible only if the self can somehow negate or at least severely bracket the values, assumptions and ideology of his culture . . . However, this entails in practice the virtually impossible task of negating one's very being, precisely because one's culture is what formed that being."[40]

JanMohammed's pessimistic outlook concerning the possibility of *dialogic* communication is the consequence of what Todorov calls "excessive relativism." The opposite mode of thinking, namely "excessive universalism," has already gained a bad reputation: "What has been presented as universality has in fact been a fair description of white males in a few Western European countries."[41] But for Todorov the relativistic attitude represented in JanMohammed's stance implies today greater dangers than the Eurocentric one, for to deny the possibility of communication among cultures means to postulate a discontinuity within the human species; the danger of such a conception is that it resembles some kind of apartheid. "We are so busy battling stereotypes in the description of Others that we end up refusing these Others any specificity at all."[42] This critical point illuminates my questions concerning the positive model of cultural encounter that Teraoka traces in Geiersbach's text. Geiersbach's narrator attempts initially to undermine what Todorov calls "excessive universalism," that is, seeking to absorb the other into one's own categories for the sake of a false assumption of universality: he lets the other speak and is learning how to listen. Although this implies that barriers in communication can be surmounted, the model does not provide the theoretical premises of surmountability. The voices of the Turks become for the German narrator more and more confusing. How, then, will the *dialogic* communication

40. Abdul R. JanMohammed, "The Economy of Manichean Allegory: The Function of Racial Difference in Colonialist Literature," in *"Race,"* *Writing, and Difference,* ed. Henry Louis Gates, Jr. (Chicago: University of Chicago Press, 1986), p. 84.

41. Todorov, "'Race,' Writing, and Culture," in *"Race," Writing, and Difference,* p. 374.

42. *"Race," Writing, and Difference,* p. 373–374.

ever come about? Geiersbach seems to postulate an argument
contrary to JanMohammed's. But his model, and Teraoka's
evaluation of it, ultimately fall back on the same "excessive
relativism," since they lack the premises of communication.
Geiersbach's model thus provides an example of what
JanMohammed proposes as "the only genuine and thorough
comprehension of otherness," namely to "negate or at least
severely bracket the values, assumptions, and ideology of
his culture." But the process gets no further than this; the
difficulties inherent in this bracketing as indicated in
JanMohammed's pessimistic commentary remain unresolved.

A possible escape from this dilemma is present in Todorov's
reintroduction of the category of universality, albeit different
from the Eurocentric concept. In response to JanMohammed's
relativistic stance Todorov argues that "we are not only separated by cultural differences; we are also *united* by a common
human identity, and it is this which renders possible communication, dialogue, and in the final analysis, the comprehension
of Otherness—it is possible precisely because Otherness is
never radical."[43]

Following Todorov I will argue that only this uniting human
identity provides minority discourse with the epistemological
foundation for a depiction of cultural difference. Reflection
upon this new concept of universality is the second step in critical studies of alterity, the first and necessary step being the
undermining of excessive universalism. This first step is tran-
sitional, leading to a second stage where theorists of alterity
may explore without inhibitions, and on the basis of a shared
idea of human identity, what the nature of otherness is.
Todorov agrees that "the Orient" is an inaccurate category alluding equally to Middle Eastern and Far Eastern cultures, and
revealing more the ideology of those who created it than the
characteristics of the "Oriental" cultures themselves. "But
does this mean that there is no such thing as a Japanese culture
or Near Eastern traditions—or that this culture and these traditions are impossible to describe?"[44] In line with this rhetori-

---

43. *"Race," Writing, and Difference,* p. 374 (emphasis mine).
44. *"Race," Writing, and Difference,* p. 374.

cal question, it is my contention that the overdetermined critical awareness of present studies of culture implies the danger that they become self-reflexive texts only—critiques of Eurocentrism and attacks on Western epistemological premises. They consequently tend to forget to listen to the voice of the other for whose sake the whole debate was presumably started. The texts proposing a nonauthoritative approach to cultural differences are addressed to Western (literary) critics. They are part of a Western critical discussion of the other. The subject-object split which these critics try to avoid or abolish enters their analyses through the back door.

While I propose Todorov's redefined concept of universality as a productive means to pursue cultural studies, I also find reflection on the critic's own premises an indispensable part of such studies. In the words of Jeffrey Peck, "Any institutional claim to minority studies needs to address the self-reflexive question of the positions of participants—those writing and those who are written about—that constitute the practice of minority studies as such. In this context, two categories, discipline and nationality, figure prominently in defining the position of the contributors to this volume."[45] Not as a new privilege, but perhaps as instigating a different critical awareness do I understand my own—and similar—positions concerning discipline and nationality in the context of the issues at stake. The Czech writer Ota Filip, currently living and publishing in the Federal Republic of Germany, describes the state of displacement in a negative way: "The émigrés or people who have lost their homeland are once and for all losers of the history of our time."[46] Similarly, Todorov describes the exiled person as "a being who has lost his country without thereby acquiring another, who lives in a double exteriority."[47] But unlike Filip, Todorov also sees an emancipatory aspect in the ex-

45. Peck, "Methodological Postscript," p. 204.
46. Ota Filip, in *Eine nicht nur deutsche Literatur,* p. 84.
47. Todorov, *The Conquest,* p. 249. I should add that I understand "exile" here to entail more than just political exile. The so-called private exile (see Aras Ören, in *Die Reise hält an,* p. 165) can also lead to similar experiences. This form of exile, too, can be seen as a situation of loss, but also of gain.

perience of exile: "It is the exiled person who today best in-
carnates, though warping it from its original meaning, the ideal
of Hugh of St. Victor, who formulated it this way in the twelfth
century: 'The man who finds his country sweet is only a raw
beginner; the man for whom each country is as his own is already strong; but only the man for whom the whole world is
as a foreign country is perfect' (I myself, a Bulgarian living in
France, borrow this quotation from Edward Said, a Palestinian
living in the United States, who himself found it in Erich Auer-
bach, a German exiled in Turkey)."[48]

Again taking Todorov's lead, I understand my own situat-
edness in a foreign nation, the United States, where I work in
the field of German studies, (although German is not my native
language either)—a discipline that is itself marginal in this geographical location. Without making this triple exteriority a
privileged starting point, I might use it to look at the critical
discussions on the question of alterity from without, although
I am aware that the category of a "without" does not hold
absolutely valid, and that through my own discussion I may
have entered the realm of "within." Nevertheless, the critic's
own hermeneutic premises, formulated by Peck as discipline
and nationality, should become a constituent part of the critical reflection. I should therefore admit that the aim of my
engagement in minority studies does not completely coincide
with the concerns of those critics who undermine the categories of the Western intellectual tradition from within. It is
perhaps the geographical proximity of my Turkish national origin to the Bulgarian Todorov that leads me to agree with him
that "Otherness is never radical," and that universality can be
regained without giving up diversity. Already in his study of
Renaissance discoveries Todorov defines a new way of experiencing alterity as "an affirmation of the other's exteriority
which goes hand in hand with the recognition of the other as
subject."[49] Recognition of the other as a subject reflects clearly
Todorov's universal postulate of the human being as an auton-

48. Todorov, *The Conquest*, pp. 249–250.
49. Todorov, *The Conquest*, p. 250.

omous subject. Although Todorov understands the experience of exteriority and the acceptance of autonomy as a simultaneous process, I would argue that the latter constitutes the basis for the former. My "interests of knowledge"[50] in this study are most concretely related to Todorov's postulate, since I can identify myself from within with the others as autonomous subjects, who have yet to be seen that way according to the still dominant monocentric Western mode of thought.

The paradigm of exile or displacement proves productive in overcoming traditional boundaries and viewing cultural questions in unconventional ways. Jeffrey Peck, for example, quotes the Germanist Henry Schmidt's advice, which was inspired by a Black feminist, to "marginalize yourself!"[51] Clifford chooses in his critique of cultural representation the works of Conrad and Malinowski, who share a common Polish national origin and were "condemned by historical contingency to a cosmopolitan European identity; both pursued ambitious writing careers in England"—and in other than their native language.[52] In Conrad's *Heart of Darkness* and in Malinowski's *Diary,* both works concerned with cultures other than their authors' homelands and their topos of exile, Clifford sees "an experience of loneliness, but one that is filled with other people and with other accents and that does not permit a feeling of centeredness, coherent dialogue, or authentic communication. In Conrad's Congo his fellow whites are duplicitous and uncontrolled. The jungle is cacaphonous, filled with too many voices—therefore mute, incoherent. Malinowski was not, of course, isolated in the Trobriands, either from natives or from local whites. But the *Diary* is an unstable *confusion* of other voices and worlds."[53]

The lack of centeredness and coherence in Conrad's and Malinowski's writings is closely related to their exile from their

---

50. I am alluding here to Jürgen Habermas's term *Erkenntnisinteresse.* See Habermas, *Erkenntnis und Interesse* (Frankfurt am Main: Suhrkamp Taschenbuch, 1975).

51. Peck, "Methodological Postscript," p. 207.

52. Clifford, *Predicament,* p. 98.

53. Clifford, *Predicament,* pp. 102–103.

native land and tongue. Their emancipatory questioning of the established categories of coherence and meaning, their proximity to what Clifford calls the "postcultural situation," stems from their doubly displaced position. In Clifford's argument, neither writer directly abolishes the notion of subjectivity within culture and language. Rather, they offer "two powerful articulations of this subjectivity." Their heightened awareness of language and culture necessarily leads, as Clifford argues, to a relativizing of culture, parallel to what Nietzsche has accomplished while remaining in his own German culture and native language, in his "On Truth and Lie in an Extra-Moral Sense."[54] As Clifford puts it, "Conrad accomplished the almost impossible feat of becoming a great writer (his model was Flaubert) in English, a third language he began to acquire at twenty years of age. It is not surprising to find throughout his work a sense of the simultaneous artifice and necessity of cultural, linguistic conventions. His life of writing, of constantly becoming an English writer, offers a paradigm for ethnographic subjectivity; it enacts a structure of feeling continuously involved in translation among languages, a consciousness deeply aware of the arbitrariness of conventions, a new secular relativism."[55]

Clifford's interpretation of Conrad clearly demonstrates why exile—in writing—can serve as a most productive paradigm for the awareness of relativity or alterity. This liberating effect, resulting from a writer's exteriority to the language he or she is using, is reiterated in Deleuze and Guattari's reading of Kafka.[56] The critics see Kafka's cultural exteriority as the stimulus for a new mode of writing. In this new mode, which is facilitated by being linguistically and culturally in a foreign domain, Deleuze and Guattari envision the potential for a new, subversive avant-garde. The question they ask themselves and their fellow Western critics and artists is at the same time an

54. Clifford, *Predicament*, p. 95.

55. Clifford, *Predicament*, pp. 95–96.

56. See Gilles Deleuze and Félix Guattari, *Kafka: Toward a Minor Literature*, trans. Dana Polan (Minneapolis: The University of Minnesota Press, 1986).

imperative: "How to become a nomad and an immigrant and a gypsy in relation to one's own language? Kafka answers: steal the baby from its crib, walk the tightrope."[57] What Deleuze and Guattari long for is to create the dream of "becoming-minor" by exploring the "linguistic Third World zones by which a language can escape"; the critics see the example of this escape not only in Kafka, who used Prague German, a "paper language," for his revolutionary narrative strategies, but also in what they call polylingualism, in pop music, pop philosophy, pop writing.[58] Deleuze and Guattari propose a new aesthetic and critical program: the only hope for the monocentric Western mind to gain a new consciousness is by imitation of the experience of alterity through and in the language; by becoming *like* the other; by transforming into one's own the experience of the immigrants and of their children who have to live in a foreign language and who "no longer, or not yet, even know their own and know poorly the major language that they are forced to serve."[59] Deleuze and Guattari's treatment of Kafka as the prime example of a "minor writer" is extensive and highly complex, a breakthrough not only for Kafka scholarship, but also for critical culture studies in general. Contrary to the prevailing metaphorical, allegorical, transcendent, and psychoanalytic readings of Kafka, Deleuze and Guattari find in his work a questioning of the established norms of "great" literature and its canonized forms. It is precisely the emphasis on this questioning that renders Deleuze and Guattari's *Kafka* a productive starting point for exploring *Ausländerliteratur* within the context of contemporary German literature. But there is a danger of becoming too absorbed with the question of creating a subversive form of writing for the Western tradition. This new form, in Deleuze's and Guattari's view, will certainly help to overcome the conventional categories and open up ways of understanding differences. Kafka's narrative strategies become the *organon* leading in this direction. But Deleuze and Guattari are engaged primarily in grasping this

57. Deleuze and Guattari, *Kafka*, p. 19.
58. Deleuze and Guattari, *Kafka*, pp. 26–27.
59. Deleuze and Guattari, *Kafka*, p. 19.

tool to pursue a confrontation with their own tradition. *Kafka* is finally a text written to question Western literary institutions; it is concerned with these institutions and addressed to them. The experience of alterity, explored in Kafka, remains a tool for the critics' final goal.

A more productive point of departure for determining the categories that are characteristic of the diversity of writings subsumed under the label *Ausländerliteratur*, could be obtained by going back directly to the source of Deleuze and Guattari's concept of "minor literature." I mean here the discussions, in Kafka's diaries, of the *kleine Literaturen* ("the literature of small peoples").[60] Kafka's portrayals of contemporary Jewish literature in Warsaw and contemporary Czech literature are provocative. He sees them emerging from a specific form of national consciousness; they are lively and characterized by "less constraint." Kafka understands here "less constraint" as: "1. absence of principles; 2. minor themes; and 3. the easy formation of symbols." When applied to *Ausländerliteratur*, these characteristics reveal the collective program of this literature as a countercurrent against established "major" or "great" literature. These three aspects may also explain why the literature of minorities in West Germany has been treated by literary critics as marginal, a subspecies of "genuine" literature. At this point, we should remember Biondi's statement that Germans are not used to the cultural manifestations of subcultures. We might also recall Taufiq's point that the minority authors write against the established norms of the German literary tradition. A fourth point in Kafka's description involves a "throwing off of the untalented." This point seems at first obscure, since Kafka alludes in the same diary entry to the "literature of small peoples" as "lacking outstanding talents." But while he juxtaposes this type of literature to the conventional definition of "great" literature created by individual talents, he maintains that "a literature not penetrated by a great talent has no gap through which the

60. Franz Kafka, *The Diaries of Franz Kafka: 1910–1923* ed. Max Brod; trans. Joseph Kresh (New York: Schocken Books, 1948), pp. 191–195.

irrelevant might force its way."[61] Thus he arrives at the "throwing off of the untalented." Seen in this light the question of individual talent in West German minority literature points toward new answers.

Kafka's condensed and rather cryptically described category of "the literature of small peoples" warrants further application in critical inquiry into *Ausländerliteratur*. It would be equally important to explore its relevance for the programmatic writings of the minority authors. Many of the programmatic writings already see the task of *Ausländerliteratur* as "showing to the Germans the way to a coexistence with minorities, something that they don't know yet."[62] The literature of minorities attempts to fulfill this task in that it reorganizes the German language, a language of a homogeneous society, toward one including the experience of diversity. Several minority authors agree that this new experience can only be gained through new cultural impulses. Yet Aras Ören maintains that no culture is capable of developing these impulses from within. Thus it becomes necessary "to penetrate into the cosy living rooms of the Germans, with all possible artistic means, sometimes through cunning."[63] Pazarkaya understands the appropriation of the German language and the German literary tradition as a process of "blood-transfusion," and the path that *Ausländerliteratur* has followed as leading "from cultural shock towards a cultural synthesis."[64]

The definition of *Ausländerliteratur* by its own authors reveals the same premise of a redefined universality as proposed

61. *The Diaries of Franz Kafka*, p. 192. Deleuze and Guattari see in this collective aspect of minor literature a political function, an act of solidarity: "Indeed, precisely because talent isn't abundant in a minor literature, there are no possibilities for an individuated enunciation that would belong to this or that 'master' and that could be separated from a collective enunciation. Indeed, scarcity of talent is in fact beneficial and allows the conception of something other than a literature of masters; what each author says individually already constitutes a common action, and what he or she says or does is necessarily political, even if others aren't in agreement." *Kafka*, p. 17.

62. Franco Biondi, in *Die Reise hält an*, p. 35. My translation.

63. *Die Reise hält an*, p. 164.

64. Yüksel Pazarkaya, in *Die Reise hält an*, pp. 104 and 108.

by Todorov. From the most radical to the most traditional, the authors share the belief that diversities are communicable. The mediation of identity for them means the mediation of difference; but it does not mean cultural solipsism, for "Otherness is never radical." The task awaiting the literary critics in German studies is not to reflect upon how to speak about the other only, but also to focus on the writings of ethnic minorities; to treat these texts normally, yet with an awareness of their different status. The programmatic writings by the minority authors should constitute an important part of this focus, for in these writings we can trace a literary history in its genesis. This history of the "literature of small peoples" may not be as specialized as the literary-historical tradition of the "major" German literature, but it is nonetheless critical. About the literary-historical records of the "small peoples" Kafka notes: "there are, to be sure, fewer experts in literary history employed, but literature is less a concern of literary history than of the people."[65]

65. *The Diaries of Franz Kafka,* p. 193.

JON KLANCHER

Transmission Failure

If written words from time are not secur'd,
How can we think have oral sounds endur'd?
Which thus transmitted, if one mouth has fail'd,
Immortal lies on ages are intail'd. . . .
The fly-blown text creates a crawling brood,
And turns to maggots what was meant for food.

   —John Dryden, "Religio Laici"

The following is an account of an episode in the history of criticism. Since literary history is one of the genres of cultural transmission, the present crisis in the authority of literary history has called forth the spectre of a general failure in the process of cultural transmission itself. Such a failure has been imagined since the dawn of modernity; Dryden's "fly-blown text" is an early example of many increasingly dark and apocalyptic forms it has taken, in what might be called the discourse on cultural transmission that runs from the seventeenth to the late twentieth century. Perhaps the most consequential speaker of that discourse was Samuel Coleridge, whose literary lectures provide an occasion to understand how literary transmission is a dialectical process, and one that contradicts the larger ideological discourse that has long tried to govern it.

From 1808 to 1819, Coleridge delivered lectures on Shakespeare, Milton, and literary history to audiences in London's newest cultural arena—the scientific, philosophic, and literary lecturing institutions. There he transmitted Shakespeare to contemporary listeners, but his Romantic criticism was also an influential discourse *about* the corruption of liter-

173

ary language and the survival of classic texts in history. I want to grasp Coleridge's discourse in light of a well-known fact: what he said in those public lectures has never been properly transmitted to us. Unlike Emerson or Hazlitt, Coleridge never published his own lectures, nor did he often use what fragmentary lecture notes he prepared in manuscript. Hence we have no actual text of these ambitious lectures—only the scattered Coleridge notes and an array of second-hand reports by listeners such as John Payne Collier or J. H. Green. For modern editors and scholars this represents the worst of textual scenarios—a transmission failure, a moment when Romantic discourse fell into history, and a history of corrupt reproductions at that.

To see why this transmission failure nonetheless produced an ideological success—the vast influence of Coleridge's discourse on Shakespeare and classic texts in history—I will return briefly to its point of origin in the London lecturing empire, where Coleridge's criticism first entered the reproductive cycles of social and cultural capital. I will then investigate the persistent efforts in literary study to restore the line of authentic communication from Coleridge's lecturing voice to the modern reader's eyes and ears. Many genres of transmission are involved in this reproductive history: the most recent is the textual editing of Coleridge in the ambitious *Collected Coleridge,* a monumentalizing edition that seeks to put Coleridge's discourse at the center of modern Romantic and critical studies. For this claim it does not matter so much that Coleridge's Shakespeare criticism no longer commands the wide assent it once did, nor that his organicist theory of poetry now belongs to history rather than to modern critical practice. What matters most to this edition is Coleridge's Romantic discourse on cultural transmission, which joins hands today with the widely voiced jeremiad on the corruption of classic texts and traditions. Coleridge made his own transmission of Shakespeare the vehicle and proof of an earlier and more complicated form of this jeremiad, which he first sketched out in the London lecturing empire.

I

Witnesses pointed to a startling event in the London lecturing halls: Coleridge transforming himself into a Shakespearean presence. It was a transmission so intense that Coleridge's listeners could measure themselves being sublimely reduced in the act of beholding it. "I felt myself more humble," reported the young John Payne Collier, "than the meanest worm before the Almighty."[1] The *Morning Post* reporter had to apologize to his readers for being unable to "convey to others what he remembers with a consciousness of pleasure, unfortunately as vague as it is intense" (*CC* 5, II:335). Like narrators of a collective Gothic novel, the lecture listeners reported an unreproducible experience testifying to an overwhelming transmission. Modern readers are often told how this intensity verifies Coleridge's unique power, as when Alfred Harbage marvels that, while other critics "present Shakespeare at a remove . . . Coleridge's is the criticism with immediacy, the power to evoke the works criticized; when he speaks, Shakespeare is *there*."[2]

Nineteenth-century intellectuals like Coleridge learned how to produce this "im-mediated" transmission effect in the performative arena of the English scientific lecturing institutions and the American lyceums.[3] Yet Coleridge did not learn it eas-

1. Transcript of 21 November 1811 in *Lectures 1808–1819 On Literature,* ed. Reginald Foakes, vol. 5 of *The Collected Works of Samuel Taylor Coleridge* (Princeton: Princeton University Press, 1987), I:203. All citations from this edition will be hereafter identified in the text as *CC* 5.

2. Introduction to *Coleridge's Writings on Shakespeare,* ed. Terence Hawkes (New York: Putnam's, 1959), pp. 21–22; my italics.

3. The importance of Emerson's lecturing in American lyceums, little noted by Americanist critics, is the subject of Mary Cayton's fascinating essay, "The Making of an American Prophet: Emerson, Audiences, and the Rise of the Culture Industry in Nineteenth-Century America," *American Historical Review* 92 (1987): 597–620. The modern university also produces the transmission effect: Emerson and Arnold brought it from the lecturing world to Harvard and Oxford. From such points onward, the transmission effect has become the key pedagogic device for a now well-established paradigm of teaching. In his recent Norton Lectures at Harvard, Harold Bloom performed it uncannily as he turned himself into Falstaff at the lectern,

ily. As a young radical utopian, he had preached to the audiences of Bristol of 1795, yet he was hardly prepared for the
new London lecturing world that began to flourish in the early
1800s. He was introduced to this world by Humphry Davy, the
charismatic scientist and chief lecturer at the Royal Institution,
which was founded in 1799 by fifty aristocratic landowners
who themselves had set out on a remarkable project: to wed
science to commerce, philosophy to technology, and literary
traditions to the newest conditions of modernity. Outfitted like
a Roman emporium, the Royal Institution developed an audience of well-heeled "fashionables" to behold spectacular dem-
onstrations of the new technological science, shows put on by
dazzling lecturers like Davy, who turned dry technicalities into
star performances. What these audiences witnessed in scientific lecturing was the transmission of God's natural text as
experimentally revealed to man. A famous portrait of Michael
Faraday lecturing at the Royal Institution (figure 1) shows us
a beam of light shining down from the upper left that illuminates both the audience and Faraday himself as his hand guides
the light across the apparatus of science toward the divine text
of nature now displayed by technological means upon the dark-
ened cathedra behind him. This hushed, revelatory scenario of
1856—pictured in the Royal Institution's ideal image of itself—
already belongs to the later, more professionalized phase of
that institution and of British science. In Coleridge's time, it
was not so serene.

Everything implied by the portrait of Michael Faraday is
briskly contradicted in James Gillray's caricature of 1802 (figure 2). Here the scientific lecturer achieves a more startling
effect by turning experimental science against one of its new
aristocratic promoters, the embarrassed Sir John Hippisley.
Gillay adroitly undercuts the Royal Institution's claim to trans-

---

while denouncing those Marxist dialecticians who think you can explain the
effects of transmission rather than acting them out. It was a flawless
Coleridgean reproduction, a true Romantic transmission effect. Bloom's
performance underwrites his own theory of cultural transmission, as it most
recently appears in *Ruin the Sacred Truths: Poetry and Belief from the Bible
to the Present* (Cambridge, Mass.: Harvard University Press, 1989).

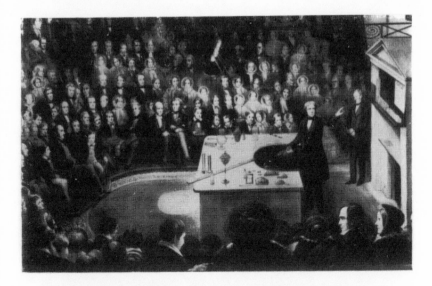

Figure 1. Michael Faraday lecturing at the Royal Institution, 1856. Photograph reprinted from Thomas Martin, *The Royal Institution* (London: Longmans, 1948), by courtesy of the Widener Library of Harvard University.

mit Enlightenment, exposing by satire what was in fact a serious struggle for power waged between the aristocrats who were using scientific technology to raise capital for their own projects, and research scientists, like the Dr. Garnet pictured here, who resented the new lords of the lecturing institutions now sponsoring them. The pivotal figure in this scene is the man looking anxiously bemused just behind the lecturer. That is Humphry Davy, who is not yet a famous lecturer, but whose expression suggests what he is actually waiting for—to see who will take control of the Royal Institution so that he will know which master to serve: scientific truth or aristocratic capital.

Michael Faraday holds his high place in scientific history partly because he was not Humpry Davy, the flashy, prestige-hungry, and, as Coleridge and Southey suspected, corruptible figure of the new Romantic science. The social historians of British science now confirm that Davy did, in effect, sell him-

178   Jon Klancher

Figure 2. "Scientifick Researches!" by James Gillray, 1802. Reprinted from *The Works of James Gillray*, ed. Thomas Wright (London: Chatto & Windus, 1873), by courtesy of the Mugar Library of Boston University.

self out as a serious intellectual by twisting Enlightenment, the project to edify and emancipate all humankind, into an explicit program of class privilege. "The unequal division of property and of labour, the difference of rank and condition amongst mankind," Davy proclaimed at his inaugural lecture, "are the sources of power in civilized life, its moving causes, and even its very soul."[4] He bent himself to the will of the aristocratic wing of capital—in Coleridge's bitter phrase, "prostituting and profaning the name of Philosopher." Meanwhile Coleridge himself was attending these lectures, watching how the scientific lecturer transmitted God's natural text and the moral philosopher transmitted His moral text. What Coleridge began in 1808, when he started lecturing on literature at Davy's desk in the Royal Institution, was a complicated effort to transmit literary culture without becoming a corrupted intellectual himself.

II

These lecturing institutions founded a new kind of social and cultural reproduction in the early nineteenth century, quite distinct from what was disseminating from the publishing industry

4. Quoted in Henry Bence-Jones, *The Royal Institution: Its Founder and Its First Professors* (London, 1871) p. 327. In addition to this classic source, I am indebted to the social historians who have been excavating the ideological origins of modern British science, especially Morris Berman, *Social Change and Scientific Organization: The Royal Institution 1799–1844* (Ithaca: Cornell University Press, 1978) and "Hegemony and the Amateur Tradition in British Science," *Journal of Social History* 8 (1975): 30–50; Ian Inkster and Jack Morrell, eds., *Metropolis and Province: Science in British Culture 1780–1850* (Philadelphia: University of Pennsylvania Press, 1983); Sanborn Brown, *Benjamin Thompson, Count Rumford* (Cambridge, Mass.: MIT Press, 1979); J. N. Hays "The London Lecturing Empire 1800–1850," in *Metropolis and Province*, pp. 91–119, and "Science in the City: The London Institution 1819–40," *British Journal for the History of Science* 7 (1974):146–162; Jack Morrell and Arnold Thackray, *Gentlemen of Science: Early Years of the British Association for the Advancement of Science* (Oxford: Clarendon Press, 1981); K. D. C. Vernon, "The Foundation and Early Years of the Royal Institution," *Proceedings of the Royal Institution* 39 (1963); D. S. L. Cardwell, *The Organization of Science in England* (London: Heinemann, 1972).

and the periodical press. In Gillray's caricature, the grotesques in the front row are mostly aristocratic members of the Royal Institution, but among and behind them are bankers and colonialists. They would shortly break away from these aristocrats to found the London Institution in 1805, soon to be known as a more prestigious and lavishly financed institute than its precursor. Once the institutional lecturing scene was divided between these two fractions of capital, it was a short matter of time before what Charles Lamb called the "ten thousand institutions" of current cultural exchange were functioning within this field of discursive force.[5] The Cork, Surrey, Russell, and Philomathic Institutions were built and run on the model of the Royal; even the London Philosophical Society, organized in 1794, remade itself to fit the new lecturing world. This was not the dilettantish gentleman's science of the old Royal Society, nor the Baconian science associated with radical dissent in the provinces, from which both Coleridge and Davy had emerged. Rather, it was, for some thirty years, a world of science and philosophy governed by landowners, bankers, colonialists, industrialists, wealthy lawyers and doctors—all the fractions of capitalist ambition.

The audience originally meant for the new scientific institutions never materialized. In 1799 the Royal Institution had originally planned and half-constructed what would have been the first mechanics' institute in England—long before the Mechanics' Institutes of 1825. Had this plan been carried out, we can only imagine how different the social history of Romantic England might have been from the one we now know— either far more radically challenged by its artisans and mechanics, or far less. But the prospect of teaching science and technology to the readers of Thomas Paine's *The Rights of Man* began to alarm both the industrialists and the aristocrats. Halfway through its construction, the Royal Institution reversed its gears and chose to become instead a high-profile lecturing institute for the wealthy. This upper-class audience, un-

5. Charles Lamb, Letter to Thomas Manning (26 February 1808) in *The Letters of Charles Lamb,* ed. E. V. Lucas (London: J. M. Dent, 1935), p. 51.

able to take learning tours of the Continent in the age of Napoleonic war, now took a learning tour of the new industrial phase of the bourgeois revolution by going to the lecturing institutions instead.[6]

Among this audience, the lecturers discovered listeners they could hardly anticipate in the masculine world of technical science. Women filled the lecture halls. Even Robert Southey, who took no interest in what the scientific lecturers had to say, came to observe the men taking snuff or falling asleep while the women of rank were "all upon the watch . . . with their tablets and pencils, busily noting down what they heard, as topics for the next conversation party."[7] Others perceived a more political effect of the scientific institution on the female audience: it would help "make the real blue-stockings a little more disagreeable than ever and sensible women a little more sensible. . . . Your chemists are metaphysicians in petticoats are altogether out of nature—that is, when they make a trade or distinction of such pursuits—but when they take a little general learning as an accomplishment, they keep it in very tolerable order."[8] But it took the imaginative Humphry Davy to grasp the full reproductive opportunity here. Motherhood, he told these note-taking women, transmits instruction "by an object beloved and venerated" to the child and the family.[9] Incre-

6. G. Caroe, *The Royal Institution: An Informal History* (London: John Murray, 1985), p. 32; see also Bence-Jones, *The Royal Institution*, pp. 114–209; Berman, *Social Change*, pp. 1–31.

7. Robert Southey, *Letters from England* (1807), ed. Jack Simmons (London: Cresset, 1951), p. 453.

8. Francis Horner to Sydney Smith, quoted in Bence-Jones, *The Royal Institution*, p. 264.

9. For the full lecture to and about the women in the audience, see Davy's 1810 lecture quoted in Bence-Jones, *The Royal Institution*, pp. 297–298. Both the English and American lecturing worlds came to be recognized as substitute universities for women, yet their learning was ritually devalued by observers from Southey to Coleridge, Dickens, and other nineteenth-century intellectuals who associated feminine education with a cheapened intellectual sphere. I thank Anne Mellor for pointing out to me a parallel process in the nineteenth-century publishing industry, where the novel tended to be devalued as long as women novelists dominated the field; see also Gaye Tuchman, *Edging Women Out: Victorian Novelists, Publishers, and Social Change* (New Haven: Yale University Press, 1989).

dibly, the women of rank who appeared at the institution to learn the new "useful knowledge" heard themselves being hailed as mothers of the Industrial Revolution: not bluestocking authors, not feminist cultural producers in their own right, but full-blooded reproducers charged with transmitting the new knowledge through the domestic cycles of the sexual system. Humphry Davy had been absorbing Romantic paradigms of feminized learning from Coleridge and Wordsworth for many years. But here he went far beyond his precursors by adapting those Romantic *topoi* to the harshest of disciplines—the capitalist project to dominate nature in *all* of its forms.

We can begin to see why the scientific lecturing institution was becoming—in its capacity to channel the knowledge explosion according to class and gender—an extraordinary device of social reproduction. Unlike the publishing house or the periodical quarterly, the lecturing institutions offered the owners of capital a direct, hands-on control of the new cultural technology: the place, the time, the audience, the lecturer, and the program. Former research scientists became charismatic popularizers; former preachers became literary lecturers. As one social historian of science remarks, it was as though the University of London had been welded to the Crystal Palace.[10] These institutions were driven by the accelerated powers of bourgeois revolutionizing to which Marx would pay ample respects in 1848; the responsibility of the scientific and moral lecturers was to percolate their discourse throughout the social world. But the Romantic critic was perhaps its most complicated product.

Coleridge, himself once a Unitarian preacher, understood from the start that these new lecturing institutions were promoting the perverse religion of "Theomammonism." What they perverted was the Protestant model of transmission, which Coleridge describes in an important passage of the 1816 *Lay Sermon* as a way of transmitting God's meanings through the speaker's "Look and Hand."[11] Now the great works of the mind Coleridge signified by the generic term "Philosophy"—

10. J. N. Hays, "Science in the City," p. 147.

11. With the Reformation, Coleridge argues in 1816, there was "no need to visit the conventicles of fanaticism" in order to "See God's ambassador

the natural, moral, and aesthetic philosophies that were all modes of reading God's text to man—were being drastically reduced to mean what Andrew Ure, himself a product of the Royal Institution, would eventually codify as *The Philosophy of Manufacture* (1835). The temple of Theomammonism—as Coleridge's neologism implies—was in fact an insidious new mechanism for turning divine Transmission into capitalist Reproduction. Coleridge thought he could make his way in this world by resisting that reduction, trying not to be Davy, the corrupted functionary of the new cultural order. Yet he pleaded for its support, signed its owners and managers up to read his periodical *The Friend,* and even told readers of the *Biographia Literaria* in 1817 that it was not in his publications, but in the "numerous and respectable audiences" who "honored my lecture-rooms with their attendance" that his ultimate moral and cultural worth was being proved.[12]

III

It was not mere money that compelled the nineteenth-century intellectual to stoop to lecture. It was the prospect of raising impressive volumes of cultural and social capital which the successful act of transmission promised to reward. These forms of capital were to be raised among the unmistakable signs of moneyed wealth, where the lecturer dissimulated that wealth by transmitting the priceless cultural treasure.[13]

---

in the pulpit stand, / Where they could take notes from his Look and Hand; / And from his speaking ACTION bear away / More sermon than our preachers used to SAY." These are the figural gestures of the seventeenth-century mode of transmission that now seem to be profanely literalized by the capitalist machinery of the lecturing institutions—the speaking action, the note-taking audience, the charismatic "Look and Hand." Coleridge, *A Lay Sermon,* in *CC* 6:198–199.

12. On Coleridge's struggle to save the "divine poetic voice" of Wordsworth from the commodification of the publishing industry, see Robert Maniquis, "Poems and Barrell-Organs: The Text in the Book of the *Biographia Literaria,*" in *On Coleridge's "Biographia Literaria,"* ed. Frederick Burwick (Columbus: Ohio State University Press, 1990).

13. On these forms of capital see Pierre Bourdieu, "The Forms of Capital," in *Handbook of Theory and Research for the Sociology of Education,* ed. John G. Richardson (New York: Greenwood Press, 1986), pp.

To his lecturing audiences Coleridge transmitted a "respect-able Shakespeare," a "philosophical aristocrat delighting in . . . hereditary institutions" (*CC* 5, II:272). Such a Shakespeare resisted absorption by the "fashionables" crowd-ing the lecturing halls; he brought the spirit of the old heredi-tary institutions into the soulless frames of the new capitalist institutions. Unlike the anxious bourgeois social climber or the middle-class reformer, Coleridge's Shakespeare does not gen-eralize or theorize: everything is tacit, embodied, "philosoph-ical" only by the implication of his language, the gestures of his characters, the vast design of his organically constructed plays. A. W. Schlegel's German Shakespeare lectures armed Coleridge with this body of aesthetic device, and with it Coleridge tried to carve out the "respectable" audience to which he could transmit a Shakespeare whose "judgment was equal to his genius"—that tacit, knowing judgment of the phil-osophical aristocrat and the correspondingly responsive lis-tener. For Coleridge, the "respectable" did not yet signify the philistine, as it would for the Victorian critics, but the self-conscious: listeners to whom one could really transmit be-cause they had somehow shaped themselves self-consciously from within, as though they were the human equivalents of an aesthetic "imitation" that, as Coleridge often pleaded, forms itself deep from within—as opposed to the vulgar, fashionable, mass-produced "copy" whose shape and ethos can only be stamped upon it cynically from without.[14]

Coleridge also gendered these distinctions in the lecture hall—more than once he urged male friends to seat their wo-

241–258; and for a precise formulation of the relation between economic and cultural capital, see especially Bourdieu, "The Field of Cultural Produc-tion, or: The Economic World Reversed," *Poetics* 12 (1983): 311–356.

14. Teaching the "fashionables," as the mordant modern calculator of cultural capital, Pierre Bourdieu, suggests, would mean having to teach the "transmission code" in order to transmit the text, as Humphry Davy did. To transmit an implicitly philosophical Shakespeare to the "respectables" meant Coleridge could "dispense with the code" and transmit "to a public prepared by insensible familiarization to understand [his] tacit meanings." See Pierre Bourdieu, *Reproduction in Education, Society, and Culture*, trans. Richard Nice (Beverly Hills: Sage, 1977), p. 164.

men in the lower gallery while the men should sit in the upper
rows "with the most *respectable* part of my audience." In the
publishing world, as recent feminist critics argue, Coleridge
designated high culture as masculine, the emerging mass culture as feminine.[15] But in the lecture halls, Coleridge went
further—he began to think, as he told Hugh Rose in 1818, that
"in one form only would Lecturing meet my own judgement
and inclination, namely, with from 20 to 30 young men of in-
genuous birth and education," aged 18–26, with whom Coleridge could finally "*go thro'* a steady course on Philosophy."
No women, no fashionables, no capitalists. Philosophical
Shakespeare, it seems, was a crucial step on the way toward
this little Platonic academy, to be conducted far from the noise
of the London lecturing empire.

For Coleridge could never be sure if and how his lecture-
transmission was taking effect. Women and men, fashionables
and respectables, promiscuously intermingled in these London
audiences. Hence we may understand why Coleridge so fran-
tically searched for the visual symbols of transmission, as
when he first sought out, then rejected the Coachmaker's Hall
for his 1811 Shakespeare lectures, a place where the fashionables were taught how to dance. At the last minute Coleridge
switched to Scot's Corporation Hall in Fetter Lane: "a spa-
cious handsome room with an academical Stair-case & the
Lecture room itself fitted up in a very grave authentic poetico-
philosophic Style with the Busts of Newton, Milton,
Shakespeare, Pope & Locke behind the Lecturer's Cathedra."[16] Here Coleridge stood heralded by the icons of transmission as he transmitted the greatest Englishman of all among

15. See Julie Ellison, "Rousseau in the Text of Coleridge: The Ghost-
Dance of History," *Studies in Romanticism* 28 (1989): 417–436; and Karen
Swann, "Literary Gentlemen and Lovely Ladies: The Debate on the
Character of *Christabel*," *ELH* 52 (1985): 397–426.

16. Quoted in Foakes, *CC* 5, I:156–157. See letter to Crabb Robinson, in
Collected Letters of Samuel Taylor Coleridge, ed. Earl Leslie Griggs
(Oxford: Clarendon Press, 1959) 3:342. The Foakes edition gives us more of
this kind of literary context for Coleridge's lectures than any previous edition or work of scholarship, while it more or less rigorously excludes the
decisive historical and ideological framework I have been drawing from the
social history of science.

the array he called the "Peerage of undying Intellect." Unfortunately the surrounding neighborhood of Fetter Lane reeked of sausage and cabbage. There was plenty of cultural display inside the hall of the London Philosophical Society, but a meaner struggle for daily existence taking place outside it. Half of the landed "respectables" for whom Coleridge prepared his 1811 performances stayed prudently at home.

We know the men of letters did come: Crabb Robinson, John Payne Collier, Hazlitt once or twice, even Byron, ominously silent. Among them were listeners experienced at taking shorthand notes—and these are the surviving forms of what Coleridge said at the lectures. This textual record, to which I now turn, was left by the "respectables" rather than the "fashionables." Here, what happened in one part of the culture industry—the lecturing institutions—was translated into another, the newspaper press and the publishing houses. For what is so often opaque in the history of cultural transmission—the moment when the individual utterance becomes a collective, institutional project carried out in the individual's now mystifying name—is unexpectedly made visible in this case. It is here that one can locate more precisely the moment of transmission failure, and then the claim of miraculous recovery which extends down to the most recent claims for Romantic critical authority in modern critical editions like the *Collected Coleridge*.

Coleridge's words were taken down by experienced shorthand reporters who were a regular feature in the lecturing world. But the shorthand notetakers at Coleridge's lectures made serious mistakes they could hardly avoid, thanks to the peculiar shape of Coleridge's sentences. The experienced shorthand notetaker had no trouble with the usual lecturer at the institutions, for as Coleridge's nephew explains, "He could almost always by long experience in his art, guess the form of the latter part, or *apodosis* of the sentence by the form of the beginning: but the conclusion of every one of Coleridge's sentences was a *surprize* upon him. He was obliged to listen to the last word."[17] Readers of *The Friend*, which Coleridge was

17. H. N. Coleridge, quoted in Foakes, *CC* 5, I:lxxxiii; cf. *Coleridge the Talker*, ed. Richard Armour and Raymond Howes (Ithaca: Cornell University Press, 1940).

composing about the time of his 1808 and 1818 lecture series, can estimate what kind of sentence style frustrated the shorthand reporters. It was not the linear style of a normal institutional lecturer, but a looping style distinctive for its connectives, its "hooks and eyes of intellectual memory" that Coleridge self-consciously adapted from the prose posture of the seventeenth-century divines. And this could hardly be taken down in the mechanical transcription of any English shorthand method. What disseminated from Coleridge's lectures were phrases, key-words, or memorable formulae, but not the syntactic patterns that alone gave distinctive form to his sentences. Even the key-words and phrases were fouled up when the shorthand reporter found himself gaping in awe at Coleridge's intensely performed Shakespeare transmission while the reporter's hand fumbled to take a note.

One set of surviving shorthand notes reveals the amplification it required to get these notes back into readable shape. They belong to the same John Payne Collier who sat sublimely senseless in Coleridge's 1811 lectures on Shakespeare, and who rediscovered these shorthand notes in 1854. What he published in 1856, *Seven Lectures on Shakespeare and Milton by S. T. Coleridge,* has been until recently a key part of the Coleridge canon, appearing in all versions of the Shakespeare criticism. Romantic critics have been quoting from it for 130 years. Collier based his 1856 version on both his shorthand notes and a longhand transcript he made days after the lecture in 1811. To Victorian readers he promised a faithful rendering of Coleridge's text; he pledged not to change or add a word. To authenticate his account of Coleridge's lecture, he made Coleridge speak in the first person. It looked and sounded like a true transmission; it is and was a remarkable fabrication.

Below I quote three versions, beginning with the shorthand notes John Payne Collier took at the ninth lecture in 1811; then a transcription he made days after the lecture, and finally the published version offered Victorian readers in 1856. Here Coleridge is trying to show why two lines from *The Tempest,* Act 1, scene 2, are natural to the speaker Prospero rather than, as Pope believed, an unnatural moment revealing either Shakespeare's erratic control of the play or a corrupt interpolation by someone else.

(1811 SHORTHAND) But he would try this by the introduction how does Pros introduce it. He has told Ma a story which affects her most deeply and has lulled her into sleep and the actress ought to have represented it with her eyelids sunk down and living in her dreams

(1811 TRANSCRIPT) But *Coleridge was content to* try this passage by its introduction: How does Prospero introduce it? He has just told Miranda a story which deeply affects her and *afterwards for his own purposes* lulled her to sleep, & *Shakespeare [makes her] wholly inattentive to the present when she awakes & dwelling only on the past.* The Actress *who truly understands the character should have* her eyelids sunk down & [be] living *as it were* in her dreams.

(1856 PUBLISHED) But *I am* content to try *the lines I have just quoted* by the introduction *to them, and then, I think, you will admit, that nothing could be more fit and appropriate than such language.* How does Prospero introduce them? He has just told Miranda a *wonderful* story, which deeply affected her, *and filled her with surprise and astonishment,* and for his own purposes he afterward lulls her to sleep. *When she awakes,* Shakespeare has made her wholly inattentive to the present, *but wrapped up in* the past. An actress, who understands the character of Miranda, would *have her eyes cast down, and her eyelids almost covering them,* while she was, as it were, living in her dream.[18]

Coleridge here assumes what eighteenth-century editors since Dryden assumed: that Miranda could not have had the mind or will to make the famous speech to Caliban—"Abhorred slave . . . I took pains to make thee speak"—which precedes the two lines in question here. When he reproduces Coleridge, John Collier further reduces Miranda to a dreaming idiot, "wholly inattentive to the present . . . & dwelling only on the past." He makes Shakespeare emerge to verify this reading. Each revision makes Coleridge himself sound more and more

18. I quote these passages from the Foakes edition: (1811 shorthand) Appendix B, II:451; (1811 transcript) I:366; (1856 published text) II:527. The 1811 texts were first published by Foakes in *Coleridge on Shakespeare* (Charlottesville: University Press of Virginia, 1971). When he relegates the 1856 text to Appendix C in the *Collected Coleridge,* Foakes underlines passages he believes Collier added long after 1811. I have extended this practice, by way of italics, to the 1811 transcript, which Foakes now considers the "best text."

confident, while the reader of 1856 is reduced to passively admitting the overpowering logic of this Shakespearean design. That coercive phrase—"you will admit that nothing could be more fit and appropriate than such language"—also dissimulates Collier's own Victorian man-of-letterese as the authenticated, first-person "vivid and peculiar phraseology" of the Romantic critic himself. What Victorians and nearly all modern readers have read as "Coleridge" here is a transmission effect, simulated and swelled up into a grand program of Romantic interpretive performance and authority.

We may now think of Collier's gooey Victorian doxa as quaintly belletristic, as though modern critical methods somehow free us from its bad ideological aftertaste. But Collier's idiom belongs to a more pervasive discourse, what Bakhtin quite rigorously clarifies as the discourse of "general literariness," with "the socially sealed-off quality of a privileged community ('the language of respectable society')." This is a language that accommodates a particular utterance, like Coleridge's in 1811, so that it can, as Bakhtin puts it, be "easily dealt with against that background without its being dialogized, without calling forth any sharp dialogic cacophany between context and what is said." This is, in short, the "smoothing and ironing-out of style."[19] It is a way of contextualizing a historical utterance so that it seamlessly meshes with—that is, *reproduces*—the discourse of the "socially sealed-off" group of transmitters. To raise your own cultural capital by transmitting a cultural treasure, you do not accentuate the "sharp dialogic cacophany" that puts your own discourse of transmission into a dissonant critical light. What you do is "iron out" the style—here, Coleridge's "vivid and peculiar phraseology"— into a hybrid discourse that blends your language with the authorizing language of the cultural treasure being transmitted. The result is a monologic transmission—to borrow Bakhtin's well-known adjective—that conceals the dialectical movements of its constitution.

19. Mikhail Bakhtin, "Discourse in the Novel," in *The Dialogic Imagination,* ed. Michael Holquist (Austin: University of Texas Press, 1983), p. 381, my emphasis.

This transmission effect can be performed in many ways. Coleridge cleansed his Shakespeare of all historical dross in order to philosophize Shakespearean language as a natural language of poetic design. Shakespeare's imputed philosophic intention appears to mesh with the abstract critical discourse that Coleridge used to reveal it. But Collier reversed that method when he transmitted Coleridge. He relentlessly saturated a philosophically abstract Coleridgean discourse in the socially specific language of the transmitter and his local world of cultural capital. This happens all through the 1856 text: Coleridge's "mighty nation" becomes Collier's "mighty empire," the phrase "giant nations" becomes Collier's "great nations," a "story" becomes a "wonderful story," "affects her most deeply" becomes "filled with her surprise and astonishment." Even music history undergoes the same change, as Coleridge's "cadenza" becomes Collier's "piece of music"— a particularly suggestive translation that shows Collier himself performing a soloist cadenza on his own earlier shorthand notes. When John Collier improvises Coleridge in order to accredit himself as a valuable transmitter, he inducts Coleridge into a later, more intensely commodified world of cultural capital—where "cadenzas" become "pieces of music"—by translating him "word for word."

We know too that this is partly how Coleridge performed his own Shakespeare lectures, which he sometimes translated closely from the German text of A. W. Schlegel to unsuspecting English listeners. Coleridge's plagiarism is indeed not fundamentally different from the fabrication I have shown Collier performing here. Both were surreptitious methods of cultural transmission—stealthy reproductions. The invisible German hand in Coleridge's spoken lecture, and the invisible Victorian hand in the 1856 printed lectures, were both silent means of accumulating the profits of cultural capital that come to the literary transmitter who denies his hidden mediators. To John Payne Collier the model for this mode of cultural transmission, if not exactly the method, was Coleridge himself.

Yet is was not only a practice of literary transmission we see being handed down here: it was also the discourse *about* cultural transmission and textual corruption. Collier was very sensitive to that discourse, as we see in these passages, for which the shorthand notes have not survived:

(1811 TRANSCRIPTION) How grateful he exclaimed should we be that the works of Euclid & Plato still remained to us, & that we were yet possessed of those of Newton of Milton & of Shakespeare, the great living dead men of our island & that they would not now be in danger of a second eruption of the Goths & Vandals. They will never cease to be admired till man shall cease to exist and at the present moment the greatest name our isle can boast had but received the first fruits of his glory which glory must for ever increase wherever our language is spoken.

(1856 PUBLISHED) How grateful *ought mankind* to be, that *so many of the great literary productions of antiquity have come down to us*—that the works of *Homer,* Euclid, and Plato, have been preserved—while we possess those of *Bacon,* Newton, Milton, Shakespeare, and of *so many other* living-dead men of our own island. These, *fortunately, may be considered indestructible: they shall* remain to us till the end of time itself . . . A second eruption of the Goths and Vandals could not now endanger their existence, *secured as they are by the wonders of modern invention and by the affectionate admiration of myriads of human beings. It is as nearly two centuries as possible since Shakespeare ceased to write, but when shall he cease to be read? . . . English has given immortality to him, and he has given immortality to English.*   (*CC* 5, I:208 and II:472.)

This is only half of what Collier amplified in 1856. It isn't just that Homer has now joined the ancient canon, and Bacon the modern, nor that "mankind" rather than "we" English are grateful for what is now a vastly larger cohort of the "living dead." Nor is it even that Coleridge now appears to embrace all those technical "wonders of modern invention" promoted by the scientific lecturing institutions where he began, very apprehensively, lecturing on Shakespeare. It is also that Coleridge's historical act of transmission in 1811 now becomes what he seems to memorialize in his own voice. Collier presents Victorian readers with a time warp: Coleridge appreciating the historical outcome of his influential transmission of Shakespeare at the very moment he seems to be making it in

1811. This is the recursive cycle by which the Romantic discourse on cultural transmission begins to explain and validate itself. As its hidden mediator, John Collier updates this Romantic discourse by amplifying Coleridge in order to raise his own cultural worth as a transmitter of the "living dead."

IV

Today the *Collected Coleridge* exposes the 1856 Collier text as a brazen corruption, a faked transmission. Editor Reginald Foakes substitutes for this embarrassing text the 1811 longhand transcript from which I've quoted the initial passage above. He then reprints the 1856 text as an appendix to volume II of *Lectures 1808–1819 On Literature,* replete with heavy black underlines to show where Collier fabricated passages of his own. Foakes does not do the same with the 1811 transcript, which he now considers the "best text," though I've shown how this transcript amplifies the shorthand at least as much as 1856 amplifies the transcript. The modern editor knows how unstable all of these texts are, but he prefers a "sense" of transmission to Collier's embarrassing simulation. Now, rather than make Coleridge speak the language of "general literariness," the editor speaks it himself, in some 300 pages of introductions and footnotes. Readers of the *Collected Coleridge* generally know the sound of this discourse: it appears most insistently when the editor rushes to discredit an unfriendly witness or critic of Coleridge—so we get a "sneering" William Hazlitt, a "hostile" John Thelwall, a "malicious" Edward Jerningham, or among modern critics, a menacing, "crude" Norman Fruman.[20] But it also echoes throughout these volumes as the reading instructions for hearing Coleridge's voice, compelling us to read all these different texts as though they said the same monologic thing.

To hear only that voice in these lecture volumes means hav-

20. Since the publication of *Coleridge: The Damaged Archangel* in 1971, Norman Fruman's critique of Coleridge's plagiarism has made him the chief nemesis of the editors of the *Collected Coleridge,* an edition that has, ironically, institutionalized Fruman's attack by using the editorial apparatus of the Bollingen-Princeton volumes to refute it.

ing to ignore the diversely social responses of the many lecture listeners whose reports made Coleridge's lecturing transmissible at all. This is why Reginald Foakes regularly diminishes their importance in favor of the fragmentary Coleridge notes, reorganizing all these materials so that now—unlike the previous Thomas Raysor editions—the modern reader will give preference to the Coleridge manuscripts, even though we know that Coleridge almost never spoke from them.[21] As we now read, for each lecture, first the Coleridge notes and then the relevant report, we constantly bridge the gap for ourselves—we are supposed to get a sense of transmission since we cannot have the real thing. The new edition cannot truly be a transmission—it cannot produce the actual text of Coleridge's lectures. But as a modern, expert work of cultural technology, it can and does labor very hard to simulate a transmission by producing a fine-tuned transmission effect.

Unfolding since the 1960s, the *Collected Coleridge* has been an unusually polemical scholarly project, designing a wide range of transmission effects that appear variously in the new editions of the *Marginalia, The Friend, Biographia Literaria, Lectures on Literature,* and other volumes. Such effects depend on what particular mode of communication Coleridge adopted, what apparatus of the nineteenth-century culture industry shaped his discourse, and how the editors devise a means for reproducing Coleridge's mode of communication to us.[22] Such editorial devices have been guided by the more gen-

21. In his 1930 and 1960 editions of *Coleridge's Shakespearean Criticism,* Raysor separated Coleridge's private notes in volume 1 from the lecture reports, Collier's chief among them, in volume 2. Volume 1 of Raysor's edition, however, presents another kind of transmission effect: arranged in the order of Shakespeare's plays, genre by genre, the Romantic critic's notes give the impression of being the spontaneous critical self-consciousness latent in the Elizabethan plays themselves.

22. This is a local way of putting the more general case, made with clarity by Jerome McGann, that a truly "critical edition is a kind of text which does not seek to reproduce a particular past text, but rather to reconstitute for the reader, in a single text, the entire history of the work as it has emerged into the present"; see *A Critique of Modern Textual Criticism* (Chicago: University of Chicago Press, 1983) p. 93. For specific critiques of the Coleridge edition's insistent partisanship as it has affected particular

eral principle, announced by the chief editor, that Coleridge's writings would be transmitted according to the "forms of communication" he used in texts that obeyed none of the usual boundaries between genres or subject areas. But it is just these forms of communication—the means of cultural transmission—that cannot be reproduced without bending them to the will of the broader *discourse* on cultural transmission that makes itself heard throughout the *Collected Coleridge*.

The transmission effect can be described theoretically as the relation *between* the ideological discourse on cultural transmission and the practices of communication that try to carry it out. Critical editions and literary history use different methods to achieve it; literary lectures bodily perform it. As John Payne Collier performed it in his remarkable text of 1856, it results in an internal commodification of Romantic critical language. In our time, the discourse on cultural transmission has become a best-selling jeremiad that produces the anxious readers of Allan Bloom and the dictionaries of "cultural literacy"— a commodity on the market of symbolic goods. At the same time, it is politically useful Romantic abstraction. It defends the same general narrative that emerged after World War II as perhaps the most important genre of modern literary history, namely "the history of criticism." Such a history displaced the older, principally nationalist literary histories by giving an account of *Western* transmission—the unfolding of ethical and aesthetic consciousness from Athens and Rome to Jena, London, and then New York, Ithaca, New Haven, and Cambridge. The authors of that vastly influential critical history—M. H. Abrams, W. J. Bate, René Wellek, among others—made Romantic criticism, with its indelible links to the

---

volumes, see Elinor Schaffer's review of the "textus" in the new *Marginalia, Studies in Romanticism* 21 (1982): 531–540; Dierdre Coleman's rereading of *Coleridge's The Friend 1809–1810* (Oxford: Clarendon Press, 1989); and Norman Fruman's critique of the *Biographia Literaria* volumes edited by W. J. Bate and James Engell, in *Studies in Romanticism* 24 (1985): 141–173.

French Revolution, the pivotal turn in Western transmission.[23] The Coleridge project was founded upon this larger enterprise and shows us, like no other work of modern scholarship, the impact of ideological commitments upon cultural technologies that link us to the past.

Today the Western narrative of transmission is surely in crisis; the critique of Romantic ideologies—among them, the ideology of cultural transmission embedded in projects like the *Collected Coleridge*—has helped delegitimate some of its key intellectual devices. Yet it would be an illusion to think, as Jonathan Culler seems to think, that humanists in the contemporary university can simply turn away from the older effort to "transmit a heritage" to the more enlightened and genuinely modern quest to "produce knowledges."[24] The logics and narratives of transmission do not merely disappear, no matter how severely they may be challenged or discredited. The postwar "Western" rationale of transmission was itself fashioned out of the fragmented materials of the older theological and nationalist narratives, and it may well furnish, in the decades to come, the materials for an emerging, equally powerful model of transmission that will be based on a North/South disposition of power and capital rather than the West/East geopolitical frame of the past fifty years. One response to this historical turn—symbolized now by the political transformations of 1989—is to show that cultural transmission is a dialectical movement of persons and institutions, agents and structures, economic and cultural capital. Its rhetoric produces powerful and consequential effects, even when the process itself appears to fail. What we have to produce is the knowledge of how that process works in what Marx called the "ceaseless revolutionizing" of capitalist modernity as a whole.

23. I have analyzed the history of English Romantic criticism as it inflects modern politics in "Romantic Criticism and the Meanings of the French Revolution," *Studies in Romanticism* 28 (1989): 463–491.

24. Jonathan Culler, *Framing the Sign* (Norman, University of Oklahoma Press, 1989), p. 19.

JEROME MCGANN

History, Herstory,
Theirstory, Ourstory

Because "history" takes place as a matter of pluralities, it
should always—like Herodotus' exemplary work—be written
in the plural. But of course it is not, of course people tend to
write Theirstories in the singular, tend to write *a* history of
something or other, and tend to suggest thereby that history is
integral, uniform, and continuous. We are all familiar with
Thesestories—for example, with the commonplace view that
there are basically three theories of history, the degenerative,
the progressivist, and the cyclical (with due allowance made
for the spiral variant, usually imagined as moving in an upward
rather than a downward direction).

Thistory, thus imagined, creates problems for people who
work as historians, a fact which people who work as anthro-
pologists have been pointing out to them for some time now.
But history thus imagined is worse still for people who write
and study literature; indeed, the linear imagination of history
was probably the single most important factor in separating
literary work from historical studies in the twentieth century.

In literary criticism, for example, the classic argument
against a historical method in criticism has been that facts in
poetry are not like facts in history: a fact is a fact in history
(whether we mean by the term "history" the historical event

196

or the historical text), but in poetry facts transcend any one-to-one correspondence relation. In poetry facts are taken to be multivalent, or as we sometimes like to say, symbolic. They are open to many readings and meanings, and any effort to explicate them by a historical method, it is believed, threatens to trivialize the poetic event into a unitary condition. Furthermore, to the degree that a poem solicits a historical condition, to the degree that it seeks to define itself locally and topically, to that extent, it is argued, does the poem abandon its poetic resources. Byron's "Fare Thee Well!" became one of the most notorious pretenses to poetry in the language, so far as the academy was concerned, precisely because the academy *knew* that it was a poem written to his wife on the occasion of their marital separation, and because the academy therefore knew—or thought it knew—what the poem meant. Its meaning *is* simple because its meaning *was* simple, worse still, that meaning is and was sentimental and mawkish.

I will return to the example of "Fare Thee Well!" at the end of this brief essay. For the moment I want merely to emphasize that the historicity of the poem is no more linear or unitary than is the historicity of any other human event. The problem of understanding the historicity of poems is grounded in a misunderstanding of what is entailed in facts and events, whether poetical or otherwise. Every so-called fact or event in history is imbedded in an indeterminate set of multiple and overlapping networks. The typical procedure in works of history is to choose one or more points in those networks from which to construct an explanatory order for the materials. Furthermore, works of history commonly cast that explanatory order in a linear form, a sequential order of causes and consequences. These procedures are of course perfectly legitimate heuristic methodologies for studying human events, but they foster the illusion that eventual relations are and must be continuous, and that facts and events are determinate and determinable in their structure.

But in *fact* history is a field of indeterminacies, with movements to be seen running along lateral and recursive lines as well as linearly, and by strange diagonals and various curves, tangents, and even within random patterns. Such variations are a consequence not merely of the multiplicity of players in the field (persons, groups, institutions, nonhuman forces, chance events, and so forth), but of the indeterminate variations in scale and speed which operate in dynamic sets of events. Herodotus wrote his *Histories* out of his understanding of the play of such variations, and Tolstoy constructed *War and Peace* from a similar imagination. In our day Marshall Sahlins's *Islands of History*[1] used Captain Cook's voyage to Hawaii as a dramatic instance for showing how a set of events may be seen to have different and antithetical meanings because the same set of events is incommensurate with itself— because the same set of events is, appearances notwithstanding, *not* the same set of events, is not equal to itself but is multiple.

In telling Thatstory Sahlins wrote History (a history, or perhaps A-history). That is to say, he sought to define, for certain critical and heuristic purposes, a structure of particular events. He produced a new order of explanation which restored commensurability to the order of events whose problematic character he had initially exposed. (The new order involves the introduction of anthropological categories into a historical field.)

These matters are important for anyone interested in the relation of history and literary work because facts and events *in history* are likewise not integral or stable or commensurable with themselves. They are multiple, and normative historical texts seek to regularize them only because such texts are committed to using their materials to develop explanations and to moralize events. These regularizing procedures are essential to the tasks, for example, of history and philosophy; and while they operate as well in poetry (for example, in a poem's expository and ideological materials), even the most rationally grounded poetical work—Lucretius, say, or Pope—resists and scatters its regularizing orders.

This is why so many commentators have observed that poetry operates as a kind of second nature (or, more exactly, an imitation of the human world). As in the world it refigures, a

1. Marshall Sahlins, *Islands of History* (Chicago: University of Chicago Press, 1985).

poem (as it were) strives to become the locus of a complex agenting structure. Facts in poetry therefore appear as *facta*, and the Latin form of the word reminds us, as the English form does not, that facts are *made* things. The poem itself, the artifice of its madeness (*poiesis*), is thrust forward as the sign under which all its materials stand.

Brecht's crucial reflections on epic theatre have helped to remind us that the ultimate subject of *poiesis* is the global event of the work: not simply the tragic story of Romeo and Juliet, but *The Most Excellent and Lamentable Tragedy of Romeo and Juliet*. The *Tragedy* is the globe (in several pertinent senses) that contains the tragic history, and when the *Tragedy* is seen as such it appears, in its turn, as a complex event (or, more strictly, set of events) carried out in a larger world.

In a poetical field we are asked to observe a play of complex interactions between the various agents who are responsible for the *poiesis*. Even lyric poems are "theatrical" in Brecht's sense. *Poiesis* is the display of active agents carrying out deeds which later agents (call them critics and historians) remake through their subsequent acts of reflection. So, if it is a fact that Byron wrote "Fare Thee Well," that fact was (and still is) an event involving multiple agents and authorities. The *writing of* "Fare Thee Well!" is only one act (or fact) in the much more complex fact which (for example) literary critics are interested in when they study the work that goes by the name "Fare Thee Well!" If we look even cursorily at the *printing history* of the poem we discover very soon that "Fare Thee Well!" is a work which will be only partly (and very narrowly) defined by the horizon of its composition and its composer.

Elsewhere I have explicated some of the factive network of acts and events which are comprised under the title of the lyric "Fare Thee Well."[2] The poem was written by Byron, initially,

2. In "Byron and 'The Truth in Masquerade'," forthcoming in the collection of papers given at the Hofstra Bicentennial Conference on Byron, edited by Alice Levine. See also David V. Erdman, "'Fare Thee Well!'— Byron's Last Days in England," in *Shelley and His Circle: 1773–1832,* ed. Kenneth Neill Cameron (Cambridge, Mass.: Harvard University Press, 1970) IV, 638–665; and W. Paul Elledge, "Talented Equivocation: Byron's 'Fare Thee Well!'," *Keats-Shelley Journal* 35 (1986):42–61.

but even that act summoned a larger context that he had already partially imagined when he wrote the poem. But Byron had not been able to summon in his own consciousness the entire context of his work, or the ways in which other agents in the field of Byron's particular activities would make their own special contributions to the *fact* we (think we) know as the poem "Fare Thee Well." That larger context, which includes various particular people and institutions, is written into—is assumed in the structure of—the work we know as "Fare Thee Well," though not all of what the *work* assumes was assumed by Lord Byron, the titular workman who made the poem. What all this means is that the poem is initially made in a certain way, and that we can glimpse the complexity of its initial facticity by (for example) looking at the different ways the poem was read by its various early readers: by Byron, Lady Byron, Thomas Moore, John Cam Hobhouse, Wordsworth, Mme. De Stael, and many, many others. These different readings overlap and converge at some points, but they veer away and differ at others. The diversity is an index of the work's factive heteronomy, and when we remember that many different agents read and refashion the work over time and across spatial and political boundaries, we begin to glimpse the abyss of human agencies which underly everything we call a fact. No one person or group of persons can control this enormous field of human activities, all the agents are swept up by inertias in which they have played their parts.

Normative historical texts try to regularize these complex eventual networks. The facts that come to us through these explanatory and moralizing agencies become those so-called empirical facts which most people think of when they think about facts. When Coleridge said that "objects *as* objects are fixed and dead," he was referring to this kind of empirical facticity.[3] Coleridge was wise to distinguish the empirical from the phenomenological order of things, as he did when he made that remark, but he was less shrewd when he suggested that the empirical order comprises "fixed and dead" objects. The fac-

---

3. See *Biographia Literaria,* ed. James Engell and W. Jackson Bate (Princeton: Princeton University Press, 1983) I, p. 279.

tive object of the empirical imagination is itself a *factum*, a thing made to be (seen) in this way by certain agenting processes. The "object as object" is not dead, even though the life it leads is far removed from the life we solicit through poetry.

Among the Romantics, it was Blake who saw most clearly into the peculiar reality of the fact. His understanding is nicely exposed in the following passage: "The reasoning historian, turner and twister of causes and consequences, such as Hume, Gibbon and Voltaire, cannot with all their artifice, turn or twist one fact or disarrange self evident action and reality. Reasons and opinions concerning acts, are not history. Acts themselves alone are history . . . Tell me the Acts, O historian, and leave me to reason upon them as I please."[4] Blake's distinction between facts and reasonings underscores his view of the fact as a kind of deed or event which opens a field—which itself *constitutes* the opening of a field. By contrast, reasoning upon the facts entails for Blake the emergence of what Coleridge called the fixed and dead object. Blake's reasoning is a structure of thought which limits and organizes the active agencies of the factive realm. The latter, for Blake, comprises the *order* of imagination—with order in this sense principally signifying a performative rather than a structural phenomenon.

These poetical orders increase one's sense of the incommensurability of facts, events, and the networks of such things.[5] Poetry, in this view of the matter, does not work to extend one's explanatory control over complex human materials (an operation which, as we know, purchases its control by delim-

4. *The Complete Poetry and Prose of William Blake*, rev. ed. by David V. Erdman, with commentary by Harold Bloom (Berkeley: University of California Press, 1982), pp. 543–544.

5. Of course some poems solicit an incommensurable reading more actively and thoroughly than others; moreover, certain texts which are not formally poetical—Plato's dialogues, for example, Gibbon's *Decline and Fall*, the essays of Montaigne, Herodotus' *Histories*, and so forth—are highly "poetical" in the sense of the term that I am using here (where, if metaphor remains the central sign of a poetical text, it is taken to be the figure which holds "opposite and discordant qualities" together in an antithetical and unresolved state). Poetry's central function, in this view, is to expose the differentials which play within the apparitions of wholeness and order.

iting the field of view); rather, poetry's function is to "open the doors of perception," and thereby to reestablish incommensurability as the framework of everything we do and know. In this sense poetry is a criticism of our standard forms of criticism—which is, I take it, approximately what Aristotle meant when he said that poetry is more philosophical than history and more concretely engaged than philosophy. Its philosophical (critical) task could not be executed, however, if poetry took its direction from the orders of reason rather than from the orders of facticities and minute particulars.

If poetry operated solely within physical and biological horizons, we would perhaps say that it represents a kind of Second Nature, with the matter of its universes disposed according to a human rather than a divine consciousness. But the horizon within which poetry operates is sociological (or, more strictly, sociohistorical). It represents not the natural but the human world, an eventual field with two important features that distinguish it from a natural world: first, it functions within the complex networks of various conscious agencies, and second (but contradictorily), those networks undergo constant and arbitrary change. This means, among other things, that whereas such a world is always both reflexive (like God) and integral (like Nature), its consciousness and integrity are both indistinguishable and incommensurable.

The antithesis of poetry displays that world for us through its special modes of acting within such a world. The clearest way I can think of to explain this is to contrast what I would call "poetry in action" from what Bruno Latour has called *Science in Action*.[6] The latter involves consciousness in immensely complex sets of goal-directed operations: literary criticism, including this essay and the book in which it is included, are perfect instances of "science in action." The object of these activities is knowledge. Latour uses the analogy of a road map to define the complex networks of scientific activities, because the road map is for him the sign of the human preoccupation with destinations and the desire to be master of destinations.

6. See Bruno Latour, *Science in Action* (Cambridge, Mass.: Harvard University Press, 1987), esp. pp. 215–223.

When science is in action, the best road map is the one that most clearly defines the relative importance of different places on the map and the relative mobility which comes with the various roads. Old maps and new maps, good maps and bad maps, none of these are *prima facie* without importance or interest to science in action. Everything depends upon the object in view, the goal, the destination. An old map might be more useful, might function with more useful information, than a new one—depending on your goals and purposes.

When poetry is in action, the situation appears quite different. The poetical object in view is precisely not to set limits on the objects in view. Of course, poems will always have very specific goals and objects set for themselves—by the original authors, by various readers, early and late. Poems do not achieve their vaunted universality from the fact that their authors set out for themselves transcendental goals: were this the case, we would have no mute inglorious Miltons (Milton Friedman, Milton Eisenhower, Milton Berle? or perhaps Alexander Ha*milton*). Nor is it that they affirm nothing and deny nothing—explicitly didactic poetry is merely the index of the ideological dimension which is a necessary component of any use of language, including poetical language.

The poetical use of language is special insofar as it preserves materials which—according to any of the work's possible sociologics—may be experienced, through a poetical deployment, as heterodox, irrelevant, contradictory, enigmatic. Poetry operates with the same kind of sociologics which Latour observes in *Science in Action,* but it veers away from the pragmatistic horizon of scientific knowledge. It is consequently the framework within which a critique of scientific knowledge is alone possible, for this reason: only a poetical deployment of language can make one aware how every ordering of knowledge is at the same time, and *by the very fact of its orderliness,* a calling to order of what must be experienced simultaneously as noncongruent and irrational.

Near the outset of this essay I mentioned Byron's "Fare Thee Well!" as a kind of epitome of the factive poem—a work fairly defined by what Blake called "minute particulars." Some have taken those particularities as a sign of the poem's poverty of its merely local habitations. Others have read those particulars with a different negative twist: the poem is bad not because it is full of particularities, but because it is absurdly sentimental. But though Ronald Reagan has imagined, and said, that "facts are stupid things," they are by no means stupid—nor are they fixed and dead, as Coleridge thought. Byron understood, as all poets more or less consciously understand, that facts are what Blake would call the "vehicular forms" of social events. They are neither dead nor stupid, and "Fare Thee Well!" illustrates *that* fact very well.

Many—myself included—have missed the factive life of Byron's excellent poem because we have imagined its facts were, perhaps like the poem's author, "stupid things," and hence have imagined the poem to be as stupid and sentimental as this way of reading the poem. In *fact,* the poem is as much a work of revenge, hatred, and hypocrisy as it is a work of suffering, love, and cant-free talk. Its minute particulars tell a set of contradictory stories, and finally make up one story whose central subject is contradiction itself—a contradiction we know as the torments of love and jealousy which were realized and played out through the break-up of the Byron marriage. This poetical work is at once a part of and a reflection upon that immensely complex set of connected and contradicted events.

"Fare Thee Well!" tells HIStory, then—let us call it Byron's story, pretending that even his-story is unitary and unconflicted. But in venturing Thatstory the work also calls out HERstory—let us call it Lady Byron's story, on a similar heuristic pretense. Because neither of Thesestories are simple or commensurable (and least of all pretty or sentimental), in thosestories the work develops Theirstory as well. Theirstory, however, never belonged entirely to HIM and HER; from the outset it comprised numerous otherstories which wove themselves into the fantastic network of Thesestories. As the locus of Thistory, "Fare Thee Well!" makes possible a number of other stories, which we would probably not be entirely wrong to call ourstory. All Thesestories began among the first transmitters of the poem, and they continue to work their ways down to and beyond ourselves.

But that is what poetry is supposed to do. What we forget sometimes is the *fact* that it will do so only as it works with minute particulars—with those hard facts (linguistic, biblio-graphical, sociological) which can never be made commensu-rate with the meanings we lay over them. It is in this context that we should say, therefore, after Lyn Hejinian's excellent prose sequence, that "Writing is an aid to memory."[7] Norma-tive histories and memorial forms tend to use writing in order to disable the contradictions and differentials which constitute the field of memory. But writing in Hejinian's poetical imagi-nation functions to multiply those differentials, and thereby to increase our potential access to ranges and ways of remember-ing we might otherwise have hardly known.

7. See Lyn Hejinian, *Writing Is an Aid to Memory* (Great Barrington, Mass.: The Figures, 1978).

MICHAEL VALDEZ MOSES

Caliban and His Precursors: The Politics of Literary History and the Third World

Remember
First to possess his books; for without them
He's but a sot, as I am; nor hath not
One spirit to command: they all do hate him
As rootedly as I. Burn but his books.

The Tempest, III.ii.91–95

It has become a commonplace of contemporary critical thought that scholarship can never be perfectly objective or disinterested. As the heirs of Hegel, Marx, Nietzsche, and Heidegger, professors in the humanities acknowledge the historicist basis of their thinking. This is nowhere more apparent than in contemporary efforts to reconstruct literary history.[1] Generally the first move of any revisionist critic is to question the motives, interests, and prejudices which informed the work of prior generations of literary historians. The normative claims of prior scholars, most especially any pretense to objectivity, are met with the utmost skepticism. In short, literary

1. Sacvan Bercovitch provides an eloquent statement of this position in a recent essay: "I would like to declare the principles of my own ideological dependence. I hold these truths to be self-evident: that there is no escape from ideology; that so long as human beings remain political animals they will always be bounded in some degree by consensus; and that so long as they are symbol-making animals they will always seek in some way to persuade themselves (and others) that *their* symbology is the last, best hope of mankind." See "The Problem of Ideology in American Literary History," *Critical Inquiry* 12 (1986): 636.

history is viewed as a political rather than an objectively scientific enterprise.

But if the recognition of the essentially political character of literary history has liberated us from the shackles of scientific objectivity, it has by no means settled any of the fundamental disputes among literary historians and critics; it has merely transposed those disputes to a different battleground. The charge of false objectivity which may justly be leveled against the norms that often governed prior literary evaluation does not in itself constitute a refutation of those norms, nor can it serve to validate new ones. Acknowledging the political component of literary historical activity does no more (or less) than transform what appeared to be purely theoretical disputes into essentially political ones. The particular problem of Third World literary history and its problematic relation to the literary history of the First World may serve as an example of the political issues at stake for contemporary literary historians.[2]

It may at first seem odd to attempt to illuminate the controversies of contemporary American or European literary history by reference to the sorts of disputes one finds among artists, intellectuals, and scholars in Latin America or Africa. Literary controversies in such countries as Nigeria, South Africa, or Kenya would seem to provide us with only special cases, of marginal interest to Western literary historians. But I will argue that the politically charged atmosphere of Third World cultural disputes has the advantage of bringing out into the open ideological conflicts that have a direct bearing on the construction, preservation, and transmission of literary history in regimes of the First as well as the Third World. In pursuit of this goal, I consider three works of literary scholarship and cultural criticism which bear directly on the problem of literary history: *Toward the Decolonization of African Litera-*

2. I am aware that the terms Third World and Third World literature are controversial. In fact, I have many reservations concerning the ways in which these terms tend to obscure or even eliminate political and literary distinctions which are of considerable importance. For the sake of convenience I have nevertheless used these terms as a kind of shorthand, with the understanding that many of the writers from the so-called Third World use these terms themselves.

ture by Chinweizu, Onwucheckwa Jemie, and Ihechukwu Madubuike, *White Writing* by J. M. Coetzee, and *Decolonising the Mind* by Ngugi wa Thiong'o.[3]

II

From the start, it ought to be noted that none of these three works of criticism may be regarded as example of academic literary history on the model, say, of *English Literature in the Earlier Seventeenth Century* by Douglas Bush. While all re-flect upon the problem of literary history, they are not, strictly speaking, attempts to lay out the comprehensive and detailed literary history of a people, race, nation, continent, or even a given movement or genre. Moreover, though all the authors have held academic positions, they are not confined to strictly academic roles. Chinweizu and Jemie are prominent Nigerian poets, Ngugi a Kenyan novelist and political dissident, Coet-zee a (white) South African novelist, and Madubuike was the Minister of Education of Nigeria at the time *Toward the Decolonization of African Literature* appeared. It is of course not unheard of that writers of the First World engage in schol-arly or political activity; one thinks for example of Nabokov and Barth, Sartre and Grass. Nevertheless it is much more fre-quently the case within the Third World that literary and schol-arly figures are also political ones. (Mario Vargas Llosa, the Peruvian novelist, has long been prominent in his country's politics). In any case, the lack of any strict division among the spheres of art, academics, and politics within much of the Third World leads us to question whether the designation of literary history as a purely *academic* problem is universally valid, rather than historically contingent upon and politically delimited by the norms of Western liberal democratic regimes.

3. The editions to which I refer are as follows: Chinweizu, Onwucheckwa Jemie, and Ihechukwu Madubuike, *Toward the Decolonization of African Literature: African Fiction and Poetry and Their Critics*, vol. I (Washing-ton, D.C.: Howard University Press, 1983); J. M. Coetzee, *White Writing: On the Culture of Letters in South Africa* (New Haven: Yale University Press, 1988); Ngugi wa Thiong'o, *Decolonising the Mind: The Politics of Language in African Literature* (Portsmouth, N.H.: Heinemann, 1986).

In fact, if one does not insist on disciplinary boundaries between the practices of literary history and literary art, one begins to discover that many poems, plays, and novels from the Third World are actively engaged in the construction of literary history. In his most recent novel, *Foe,* Coetzee self-consciously rewrites the story of Robinson Crusoe.[4] Coetzee's revisionary version differs from that of Defoe (or Daniel Foe as he was sometimes known) in several fundamental respects, the most important being that Crusoe himself no longer plays a central role in the narrative. Two other figures—Susan Barton, a shipwrecked woman washed ashore on Crusoe's island, and Friday—come to occupy the gravitational centers of Coetzee's narrative. Coetzee's Kafkaesque novel pits Barton and Friday against the enigmatic Daniel Foe; Barton struggles against Foe in an attempt to communicate her own and Friday's versions of life on the island, versions at odds with the one Foe is busy composing. *Foe* is thus a self-conscious intervention into the politics of literary history. Though it is not a scholarly or academic work, its aim is nonetheless to reconstruct literary history as it has come to be received in the Western tradition in general, and the South African tradition in particular. In the place of the literary and cultural history which legitimizes the goals and aspirations of the European white male bourgeois imperialist, Coetzee substitutes the literary and cultural history of those whose voices have not typically been heard or recorded, in particular the voices of women and the nonwhite peoples of the Third World.

A similarly revisionary objective characterizes Chinua Achebe's *Things Fall Apart.* This novel, which dramatizes the tragic life of Okonkwo, a leading man among the Igbo people during the advent of British colonialism in Nigeria, ends with a sudden and dramatic shift in perspective. Although the whole of the action has been presented from the perspective of the Igbo people, at its close *Things Fall Apart* suddenly presents us with the way these events are viewed by the British District Commissioner: "The story of this man who had killed a mes-

4. J. M. Coetzee, *Foe* (New York: Viking, 1987).

senger and hanged himself would make interesting reading. One could almost write a whole chapter on him. Perhaps not a whole chapter but a reasonable paragraph, at any rate. There was so much else to include, and one must be firm in cutting out details. He had already chosen the title of the book, after much thought: *The Pacification of the Primitive Tribes of the Lower Niger.*"[5] Achebe has in mind the kind of book which British colonial administrators did in fact write about Nigeria, such as *In the Shadow of the Bush* (1912) by C. Amaury Talbot.[6] Moreover, Achebe's concluding sentences are a veiled reference to another famous report, that of Kurtz to The International Society for the Suppression of Savage Customs. With his startling reversal in narrative perspective, Achebe implicitly challenges the way in which the political and literary history of the Igbo people has become little more than a footnote within the political and literary histories of the West. The whole of Achebe's novel may be seen as his self-conscious attempt to rewrite literary history so that it begins to reflect the cultural and political narrative of Africa from the perspective of the Africans.[7]

Revisionism is only one goal of much contemporary Third World fiction. A significant number of works engage in the literary historical task of consolidating and promoting an indigenous or non-European literary tradition. For instance, in Achebe's most recent novel, *Anthills of the Savannah,* a central chapter begins with David Diop's poem "Africa."[8] Part of the novelist's aim is to lend greater stature and importance to the work of the Senegalese poet, to claim an African work as the literary heritage of Achebe himself as well as his Nigerian characters.[9]

5. Chinua Achebe, *Things Fall Apart* (London: Heinemann, 1958), pp. 147–148.

6. See Robert M. Wren, *Achebe's World* (Washington, D.C.: Three Continents Press, 1980), p. 17.

7. For a general statement of his purpose, see Chinua Achebe's "An Image of Africa: Racism in Conrad's *Heart of Darkness*," in *Heart of Darkness,* ed. Robert Kimbrough (New York: Norton, 1988), pp. 251–261.

8. See Chinua Achebe, *Anthills of the Savannah* (New York: Doubleday, 1988) p. 123.

9. In this regard one might also consider Ngugi's epigrammatic use of

These various examples suggest that a fundamental questioning of what contemporary American or European scholars mean by the term "literary history" is in order. In many ways, our unreflective use of the term to indicate a strictly academic history of literature assumes that writers themselves do not have a sense of literary history or work to construct one. In this view, the historical sense is provided by the academic critic, rather than by the writer or writers under investigation. To be sure, some studies of literary influence take into consideration the psychological burden of literary belatedness; Harold Bloom offers an exhaustive account of the immanent historical development of poetry that occurs through the intergenerational struggle of strong poets. But what one sees explicitly at work in contemporary Third World writing is something more than just literary influence or poetic *agon*. The relationship between these contemporary writers and their precursors is not merely that between the great tradition and the passive (and unselfconscious) receivers of that tradition, nor is it the purely psychological (Oedipal) struggle between ephebes and their strong predecessors. Coetzee and Achebe consciously acknowledge Defoe and Conrad; the link is charged with a cultural and political significance which lies outside the boundaries of Bloom's theory. These authors do not simply strive for their own personal voices, for their individual places within a cultural and historical continuum. In fact they attempt to speak for an entire culture or nation and at least in part to reconstitute the entire cultural context in which their work will appear. For Coetzee and Achebe to rewrite Defoe and Conrad, or for Achebe to signal an indebtedness to Diop, is fundamentally to alter the cultural coordinates of their readers and their cultures, to define them against a purely Western literary historical tradition.

---

biblical quotations throughout *A Grain of Wheat*. Ngugi's aim is the appropriation, or "transgressive reinscription" (the term is Jonathan Dollimore's), of a work central to the Western tradition. By means of a deliberate recontextualizing of passages from the Old and New Testament, Ngugi transforms a text which was used ideologically to subdue the Gikuyu people, into one which serves as a vehicle for their liberation from British imperial rule.

In short, the strict division between literature and literary history, which contemporary academics in the West tend at least implicitly to acknowledge, depends upon something more than the formalistic differences that are usually noted between the two disciplines. It also depends upon a residual belief in the separate and autonomous realms of art and scholarship, and also upon the assumption that it is the literary historian (as opposed to the artist) who is in some final sense responsible for the transformation of an artistic fact into a culturally determinative influence. That assumption may itself be traced back to the peculiar legacy of modernist aesthetics which, in turn, was partly a reaction to the more isolated position the modern artist came to occupy in an increasingly more democratic and commercial culture.[10] If instead, one starts from the assumption of many Third World writers that artistic practice is not separable from larger cultural and political activity, then one is inclined to understand the works of these writers as seeking to effect cultural tasks which in the contemporary United States are felt to be the preserve of educators and academicians or politicians and civil servants. The novel, poem, essay, biography, or drama becomes the inert object of literary historical interest only when it is understood to have lost its historical agency, to have become a mere museum piece. Academic literary history would then appear as a peculiarly modern phenomenon, cut off from the active engagement with political history as an ongoing challenge and danger.

III

The critical works of Chinweizu, Jemie, Madubuike, Ngugi, and Coetzee thus suggest that the problems of Third World

10. The increasing allusiveness and obscurity of modernist novels and poetry, the deliberate cultivation of difficulty, may be understood as both a response and objection to the commercialization of art in democratic capitalist regimes. With no hope of aristocratic patronage as a source of critical and financial support, the modernist artist such as Eliot or Joyce turns to the academy. Making less and less pretense of speaking to a mass audience or of influencing society as a whole, the artist gradually accedes to a dependency upon the academic establishment which will interpret and transmit the work of the modernist to a larger audience. To be sure the artist can

critics have unsuspected consequences for their counterparts in the First World as they begin to challenge the validity of Western political and cultural norms. In each of these three works the author strives to delineate a cultural and literary heritage that may be claimed as the unique possession of a people, regime, or continent which lies at the periphery of Western culture. But in every case this new or emerging culture is necessarily defined against the backdrop of the modern Western world. While vast differences in approach and subject matter separate the three works, collectively they share a common objective: they aim to discriminate between elements within the Western cultural tradition (part of the legacy of European imperialism) that can be fruitfully incorporated into an indigenous cultural history and those that cannot.

For example, Chinweizu, Jemie, and Madubuike, often referred to as the *bolekaja* (meaning "come down and fight") critics, argue that the standards used by both European and African literary critics to evaluate contemporary African literature are on the whole Eurocentric, and hence inappropriate. In particular they charge that the norms of the Victorian or realist novel are imposed on contemporary African fiction, and those of Euromodernist poetry on contemporary African poetry, in each case to the great disadvantage of African literature. While arguing for a decolonization of African literary standards and for the substitution of standards drawn from a renewed historical appreciation of earlier African literature and "orature,"[11] the *bolekaja* critics simultaneously argue that in some respects the usual Western standards employed by literary historians for judging contemporary African literature ought to be reversed. The African novel is better appreciated if one evaluates it on the model of the Euromodernist novel, while contemporary African poetry is better understood in relation to pre- or nonmodernist European poetry. I shall return

---

come to resent and even resist this hieratic structure, disdaining those upon whom he depends—the professors of literature.

11. *Orature* is a term derived from Ngugi, coined on the model of *literature*, and is used to refer to all forms of oral discourse in African culture, including poetry and rhetoric.

later to the obvious contradiction in evoking European standards of aesthetic judgment (even in revised form) while calling for the total repudiation of Eurocentric norms. For the moment, however, I wish to dwell on the fact that *Toward the Decolonization of African Literature* offers a thoroughgoing critique of the deficiencies and weaknesses of Euromodernist poetry, concentrating on its obscurantist, elitist, and apolitical tendencies, while demonstrating an appreciation for the narrative innovations of Euromodernist novelists who have dispensed with the cumbersome description, plot, and detailed characterization of nineteenth-century realist fiction. The authors view the obscurantist poetic influence of Hopkins, Eliot, and Pound on contemporary African poets like Wole Soyinka as corrupting insofar as it severs the poet from his audience, thereby precluding any active and responsible engagement on his part in shaping the culture of an emerging nation.[12] By contrast, the innovative fiction of Joyce, Kafka, Proust, Faulkner, and Dos Passos has something to offer to the Third World writer, making possible the fuller and more accurate representation of non-Western cultures which have yet to become fully secularized. In particular, Euromodernist subjectivity allows for the fuller representation of the "magical" or "divine" elements still present within the consciousness of many African peoples, used in abundance in the works of a writer such as Amos Tutuola.[13]

In his *Decolonising the Mind,* Ngugi takes an approach similar to that of the *bolekaja* critics (not surprising, since they are influenced by Ngugi's writings). While Ngugi argues for the purging of neocolonialist elements from African literature and culture, including the repudiation of European languages as the vehicle for composition, he nonetheless credits writers like Conrad with having discovered narrative techniques which are particularly well-suited for conveying an African story. Ngugi

12. *Toward the Decolonization of African Literature,* pp. 208–238.
13. *Toward the Decolonization of African Literature,* pp. 18–23 and 132–133. In this regard, the influence of Faulkner and Conrad on the practitioners of "magical realism" within Latin American literature such as García Márquez takes on a new significance.

suggests that many of Conrad's preferred narrative devices—
the shifting points of view of time and space, the multiplicity
of narrative voices, the narrative-within-a-narrative—better reflect the "conversational norms" of the African peasantry than do the devices of the nineteenth-century realist
novel.[14]

Coetzee's *White Writing,* unlike *Toward the Decolonization
of African Literature* and *Decolonising the Mind,* does not explicitly aim at the repudiation of all European cultural standards and the complete Africanization of African culture.
Nevertheless, Coetzee posits as the central problem of white
writers throughout South African literary history the grave difficulty and sometimes the impossibility of adapting European
literary conventions to a non-European environment. Whether
the issue is how best to represent the quite foreign terrain of
the South African landscape or how to embody the speech and
consciousness of the non-European native, Coetzee insists
upon the cultural relativity and politically interested character
of all such adaptations.[15] One of the necessary by-products of
Coetzee's study is a reassessment of a number of central Western texts, including the King James Bible, Rousseau's *Social
Contract* and the *Discourses,* and Wordsworth's poetry, to
name only a few. Coetzee views Rousseau's *Discourses,* for
example, as having revolutionary implications within the context of the imperial conquest of South Africa. Rousseau's representation of "natural man" and the implicit defense of "idle-
ness" as a happier state than that of civilized man are seen as
a challenge to the Protestant work ethic, which helped to legitimate the rule of the Afrikaners over the native tribes,
the Khoi and the San, and later the rule of the British
over the Afrikaners.[16] In Coetzee's view, the notable absence
of the Rousseauian view of natural man from "white writing"
is no accident; its inclusion could help to forward "the demise
of White Christian civilization at the tip of Africa."[17]

14. *Decolonising the Mind,* p. 76.
15. *White Writing,* pp. 36–62, 115–135, 167–177.
16. *White Writing,* pp. 12–35.
17. *White Writing,* p. 35.

In all of these above instances an interesting phenomenon is
at work; the very act of describing or reconstituting the literary
and cultural history of a non-European or non-Western regime
(South Africa being an equivocal case) makes possible, indeed
necessitates, a reconsideration and reevaluation of Western literary and cultural history. In the very act of severing ties or
discriminating differences, the Third World critic begins to alter the view we have of our own (Western) literary tradition.
In a short essay, Borges aptly characterizes this phenomenon:

Once I planned to make a survey of Kafka's precursors. At first I
thought he was as singular as the fabulous Phoenix; when I knew him
better I thought I recognized his voice, or his habits, in the texts of
various literatures and various ages . . . If I am not mistaken [these]
heterogeneous selections . . . resemble Kafka's work: if I am not mistaken, not all of them resemble each other, and this fact is the significant one. Kafka's idiosyncrasy, in greater or lesser degree, is present
in each of these writings, but if Kafka had not written we would not
perceive it; that is to say it would not exist . . . The word "precursor"
is indispensable in the vocabulary of criticism, but one should try to
purify it from every connotation of polemic or rivalry. The fact is that
each writer *creates* his precursors. His work modifies our conception
of the past, as it will modify the future.[18]

I disagree with Borges's insistence that we purify the word
"precursor" from "every connotation of polemic or rivalry."
In fact, I would suggest that the precursor is created out of a
felt rivalry which is more than personal, psychological, or
merely literary; it is a rivalry which is profoundly political in
the most comprehensive sense of that term. While the specific
consequences of the rivalry between Third World writers and
First World literary history I have noted are particular and limited, they make possible a reconsideration of Western literary
and cultural history which is far more sweeping.

For example, looking at Western literary history from a
Third World perspective forces us to reassess what it is that
we consider of greatest importance, of "world historical" sig-

18. Jorge Luis Borges, "Kafka and His Precursors," in *Other Inquisi-
tions,* trans. Ruth L. C. Simms (New York: Simon and Schuster, 1964),
pp. 106, 108.

nificance (to borrow Hegel's phrase), within our tradition. To take only one example, our sense of which modern authors or movements are most influential and worthy of critical attention may change. Some of the high modernists—Woolf, Pound, Eliot, James—may appear of lesser importance than those writers with whom Third World writers have carried on a more active and fruitful crosscultural conversation—Conrad, Kipling, and Dinesen, for example. It is the latter writers, as opposed to the former, who most directly and powerfully deal with the phenomenon of imperialism, colonialism, and the emergence of the Third World. Specific works, which, while respected, have hardly held a prominent place in the modern canon—*Under Western Eyes* or *Kim,* for example—suddenly appear as seminal works of global importance when they are transformed within the emerging literature of the Third World such as Ngugi's *A Grain of Wheat* or Salman Rushdie's *Midnight's Children.*

Moreover, from the perspective of non-Western cultures, what constitutes the decisive contribution of any given author or thinker in the Western tradition can change dramatically. Whereas Joyce has customarily appeared to his English and American academic defenders and promoters as the embodiment of high modernist aesthetics and *l'art pour l'art,* he is seen elsewhere as a politically engaged Third World writer. From this perspective many of the technical innovations of *Portrait of the Artist* or *Ulysses* suddenly seem less directed toward purely formal or stylistic revolutions in literary technique than toward the representation of the consciousness of an intellectual elite within the Third World which is still under the dominion of an imperial power, a consciousness disoriented and alienated by that experience; one that endeavors to find a new voice for an emerging culture—in Stephen Daedalus's words, "to forge in the smithy of my soul the uncreated conscience of my race." Even a writer apparently so utterly apolitical as Beckett can appear different when viewed from this new angle. In his case, it is possible to view the rigorously postmodern aesthetics of his post-Joycean work as the result of a complete dissolution of a nationalistic perspective into the cosmopolitanism of contemporary Europe. A writer who abandons the (colonial) language of his native country, who seeks to forge a language outside political boundaries, one whose work refuses to represent the political and social realities of any given regime—is it so surprising that his career begins with a deliberate rejection of a postcolonial Irish identity?

In short, the whole of Western literary history changes its features when seen in relation to the emerging literatures of the Third World. Of late, the most notable realliances have occurred as a result of the perceived and often openly acknowledged affinities between the writers of sub-Saharan Africa, those of the Caribbean, and those of African American descent, as well as the links between Latin American and Chicano writers.[19] This realliance has been welcomed by those who set themselves up as critics of a white patriarchical hegemony within the Western literary and cultural tradition. But paradoxically, a non-Western perspective on Western literary history challenges the previously accepted notion of hegemonic uniformity, if Joyce, Yeats, Synge, and other Irish writers are seen as representatives of the Third World. Nor can the example of these Irish writers be dismissed as exceptional. Within the American literary tradition, a whole set of canonical writers from Irving and Brockden Brown to Cooper, Hawthorne, and Melville may appear as writers of an immediately postcolonial environment. To take just one more example, that of Walter Scott, writers who are perceived to be at the very center of a British tradition can suddenly seem culturally marginal and paradoxically deserving of greater attention. For Scott's historical novels rehearse many of the same problems that Achebe's or Ngugi's do a century and a half later: how to represent a culture that has undergone an experience of imperial domination by a foreign power, how to preserve the distinctive linguistic experience of the colonized consciousness in the language of the colonizing country, how to keep what is best from a precolonial form of life, a tribal life, given the increasingly modern economic and political conditions that come with integration into a national economy and

19. For a recent example of this realignment, see José David Saldívar, *The Dialectics of Our America,* forthcoming from Duke University Press.

culture. In the very act of distinguishing the Western literary tradition from its other, one discovers unsuspected fissures and highly stratified levels of cultural sedimentation at its foundation.

IV

At virtually every level of analysis appropriate to literary history the consideration of the peripheral case begins to alter our perception of the metropolitan one. Our conception of the rank order of authors, of the significance of their particular contribution to world literature, of their categorization according to historical period or literary movement, of the preeminence and importance of given generic or formal innovations, all become subject to revaluation. More than the content of literary history and the significance of that content is challenged; in addition, a set of methodological practices, themselves grounded in a set of philosophical assumptions, are drawn into question.

The attack on formalism within literary studies has been under way for some time, most recently in the name of a historicist and relativistic approach which is radical and motivated by a generational revolt against the political and cultural norms of what was once quaintly termed "the establishment." Our attention to the specific problem posed for Western literary studies by the Third World would seem to be in line with just such an approach. But it is possible that an attack on formal literary history in the name of politics might lead instead to a more fundamental reexamination of all political agendas. Let me offer some examples of how the consequences of my previous analysis suggest an approach to literary historical studies (and to cultural studies in general) that may call into question the specific goals of the current generation of revisionist literary historians.

To begin with, the transcultural approach to literary history suggests that it is a mistake to evaluate literary forms without reference to their political context. As we have seen, modernist narrative techniques—those of Joyce or Conrad, for example—take on new meanings within Third World writing insofar as they become the vehicles of political aims which may have been entirely alien to their originator's intent; for Ngugi they can, for instance, better represent the conversational norms of the African peasantry whose political objectives he shares, and which he understands to be opposed to those of Western capitalism. While the historicist approach therefore subverts the particular or local conception of the purpose of a given formal device, it cannot do so without reference to some alternate political aim if that initial subversion is to be effected. In other words, if the historicist position depends upon the invocation of cultural relativism to undermine the teleological biases of a Western tradition, it must be prepared to put forward alternate goals and defend their validity.

Put another way, our analysis has attempted to demonstrate that any history of literary or cultural forms depends upon an implicit or explicit set of political norms to make sense of those forms. Any literary or cultural history, insofar as it attempts to avoid Eurocentrism or the premature belief in the essential rightness of a given set of cultural practices, will of necessity have to embrace the rightness or superiority of an alternative, if only implicitly. The content and significance of literary and cultural history become comprehensible only in regard to a particular regime and its conception of what is best for its citizens. Any construction and evaluation of literary or cultural history will ultimately depend upon some concept of the political good, even those revisionary histories which initially appeal to cultural or historical relativism.

I mentioned earlier that Chinweizu, Jemie, and Madubuike fault Eurocentric critics for applying the wrong (Western) standards of aesthetic and political judgment to African literature. But they nevertheless enlist those standards, in a revisionary way, to justify a higher estimation of African fiction and poetry. The contradiction between a thoroughgoing, uncompromising Africanization of African literary history and the appropriation of Western standards suggests to me that the real issue for these critics is not the so-called relativity of Western cultural standards, but instead, how best to constitute a new culture out of both African and Western traditions. This goal is finally articulated by them in their defense of syncretism:

Our basic assumption in this essay is that contemporary African culture is under foreign domination. Therefore, on the one hand, our culture has to destroy all encrustations of colonial mentality, and on the other hand, has to map out new foundations for an African modernity. This cultural task demands a deliberate and calculated process of syncretism: one which, above all, emphasizes valuable continuities with our pre-colonial culture, welcomes vitalizing contributions from other cultures, and exercises inventive genius in making a healthy and distinguished synthesis from them all.[20]

The ultimate standard for judging the appropriateness of cultural syncretism is their conception of what would constitute the best possible regime for contemporary Nigeria. Behind their objection to Western cultural or literary standards being imposed on non-Western cultures is a much more basic objection to the inappropriateness of those regimes as comprehensive models for contemporary African states. The singular virtue of Ngugi's writing is his more or less explicit insistence upon this judgment.

The weapon of cultural relativity, wielded so forcefully by revisionary critics, does nothing to defend them from the charge that such revisionism must finally acknowledge its own political ends, ends which must be made concrete in one kind of regime or another. This necessary consequence becomes evident just as soon as a critic attempts to delineate the scope and scale of any literary historical project. For the *bolekaja* critics, the use of the term "African" is a case in point. In speaking of African literature, these critics use the term in at least four different senses: to distinguish a given tribal lan-

20. *Toward the Decolonization of African Literature,* p. 239. Such syncretism implicitly acknowledges that some Western standards are potentially beneficial to a new African culture. It is no surprise to discover that many of the so-called indigenous African cultural standards are fully compatible with the aesthetic principles of many Western critics. Consider, for example, the recommendation of the three authors with regard to structure and logistics: "Efficient structure and logistics is valued in orature, for it takes one through to the climax without tedious or unnecessary diversions. Contemporary poetics should make the same demand upon writers." *Toward the Decolonization of African Literature,* p. 247. Aristotle would have been pleased.

guage or identity (Yoruba or Igbo), to identify a given nation, the boundaries of which have been more or less determined by the legacy of European imperialism (Kenya, Nigeria), to delimit an entire region made up of several different nations that once constituted a political entity during colonialism (French West Africa, British East Africa), and finally to indicate the whole continent from its earliest history to the present (including Pharaonic Egypt, South Africa, the black African states). To speak of African literature or of European is nearly as problematic as to speak of Western or Third World literature.

Now of course each of these designations has a useful descriptive function. The question remains, however, which one is to be determinative when it comes time to evaluate, criticize, or construct a literary history, much less a culture. To choose among them is fundamentally a political decision that addresses at some basic level the question of what constitutes the best regime. And in the case of Ngugi as of the *bolekaja* group, the effective result is a recognition of the primacy of the nation-state—Kenya or Nigeria—as the necessary foundation for the construction of a new culture. To be sure, a case can be made for applying the cultural norms of one Third World or African country to another, but the concrete suggestions of these critics finally are directed toward rewriting and reshaping the culture of an already existing political regime. In short, pan-African culture can only come about as a result of the collective actions of particular African regimes. Moreover, the particular standards according to which such an African literature and culture will be constructed, recorded, and evaluated are linked with a definite notion of what sort of regime is to be singled out as a model. In Ngugi's case, the decolonization of cultural life is part of a political program calling for the establishment of democratic socialism within Kenya.[21] While the objectives of the *bolekaja* critics are less easily identified with a specifically Marxist agenda, they are directed toward the

21. We note in passing the obvious contradiction between an "authentic" return to African cultural and political norms and the call for socialism along Marxist principles, principles which are, of course, specifically Western in origin.

promotion of African nationalist identities which would overcome tribal divisions without sacrificing the contributions of
distinctive tribal traditions.

Current American critics of E. D. Hirsch are not likely to
appreciate the irony of this position, insofar as the practical
steps called for by these African critics are ultimately far more
restrictive, exclusionary, and centripetal than those recommended in *Cultural Literacy*. The *bolekaja* critics, for example, call for the organization of three departments within the
reconstructed African university. In strict order of their importance and centrality they are to be: (1) the department of
African Languages, Literatures, and Oratures; (2) the department of Comparative Literatures (which will emphasize
European, South American, Chinese, Indian, North American, Russian, and South Asian literatures, presumably in
translation); (3) the department of Colonial Languages. This
last department is ultimately to be abolished.

When the departments of African languages, literatures and oratures
have done their work and Africa has evolved a continental official
language to replace the colonial ones, then the department of colonial
languages would have to be abolished. It is important to emphasize
that the department of colonial languages should not be permitted to
teach the national literatures of England, France, Portugal, etc. . . .
Whatever exposure to English language literature one needs in order
to learn the English language should be acquired by studying African
literature in English, Afro-Caribbean literature in English, and Afro-
American literature.[22]

I will not presume here to evaluate the prudence or practi-
cality of such schemes. Rather, I wish only to point out that
African critics who speak of the cultural relativity of Western
culture and literary tradition openly advocate a specific and
exclusionary cultural program which is ultimately legitimated
by a political vision of what constitutes a well-ordered African
state. Cultural relativism is thus immediately (and perhaps
wisely) abandoned when it comes in conflict with political aims
which are deemed to be of greater urgency and importance. If

22. *Toward the Decolonization of African Literature*, p. 299.

American or European counterparts insist upon cultural diversity as opposed to cultural hegemony, such calls make sense only within liberal regimes which have come to identify diversity with the twin democratic virtues of tolerance and individual freedom. In short, literary history, even as it presently constitutes itself in a revisionary mode, is premised upon the acceptance of cultural norms underlying the contemporary political context. At the very least, revisionary critics must make clear to themselves and to others what political consequences are implicit in their reconstruction of a cultural tradition and what sort of regime it is that might conceivably embody that tradition.

V

If literary and cultural history always implies a conception of what constitutes the best regime, does this mean that the historian can only reflect the given political and historical prejudices of the time? Is there any choice in the literary history we choose to write? For some of the most influential and seminal historicist thinkers, Hegel and Marx, this question was to be answered in the negative. For both conceived of themselves as writing at a uniquely privileged moment, an absolute moment at which the only legitimate kind of regime had become the only kind which possessed an historical future. That is, both Hegel and Marx conceived of themselves as coming at or near the end of history, a history which could finally be objectively understood, and which had disclosed the inevitability of a certain form of government. For Hegel it was the modern German state founded upon the idea of freedom articulated in the "Rights of Man"; for Marx it was the inevitable socialist or communist community. There is, in short, perfect agreement between their historicist conception of History, including literary and cultural history, and the necessary and inevitable historical triumph of a particular, optimal kind of regime.

Modern historicist scholars are understandably uncomfortable with the specific conclusions of Hegel and Marx. Following Nietzsche, they have tended to opt for a historicism which does not insist upon the end of history, is not in some final sense objective. All cultural epochs and literary traditions are relativized and historically limited. Practitioners of this Nietzschean form of historicism are quite willing to consider that their own historical insights, including the historicist insight itself, possess only relative value. The tactical advantage of such a strategy is that it appears to make human and political choice possible, while preserving the historicist insight. *Toward the Decolonization of African Literature* might serve as a representative example of this particular gambit. But the Nietzschean historicist premise argues against any single or particular political choice—if cultural standards are truly relative, then why prefer Afrocentric to Eurocentric culture? The apparent appropriateness of different standards to different peoples, ages, or regimes (an appeal to organicism, another early form of historicism) merely begs the question. For the issue then becomes why one cultural tradition or one conception of literary history is more appropriate than another.

The rhetorical appeal to one's *own* literary history, to one's *own* culture is a powerful one, but it is based on little more than prejudice and provinciality. Moreover, it merely transforms the question of what is objectively best for one's own culture into the question of what actually is or should be the character of one's culture. The *bolekaja* critics, to say nothing of Ngugi, must raise this question in relation to the precolonial tradition of African "orature." Colonialism has deprived African peoples of what was once theirs, namely a great tradition of oral poetry. This tradition is essentially African and therefore it belongs essentially to Africans as their particular cultural heritage. (Were it not *essentially* African, then it would have been imposed by non-Africans, and hence would not be the specific inheritance of African peoples.) This however raises the question of how the essence of a culture can ever be lost. The *bolekaja* critics are well aware of this possibility both in the past and in the future. That is why they insist that contemporary African writers need "more than a haphazard and unconscious exposure to the African tradition . . . They need *conscious, determined, meticulous,* and *thorough study*. They need extended *immersion* in the traditional mode and *apprenticeship* in its methods."[23] This means that a given tradition is not in any sense historically inevitable, nor is it in any sense guaranteed. Only human intervention in history makes possible the construction and preservation of a particular culture. History, it would appear, is in constant need of human agency to come to its rescue.[24]

If History has no identifiable *telos,* and therefore cannot determine history or culture in the political sense, what becomes of historicism? What ought to direct political and cultural ends? How is it possible to choose among cultural traditions, or in the case of Chinweizu, Jemie, and Madubuike, to combine cultural traditions in a "healthy" syncretistic fashion? I can offer only a modest suggestion as to how such a fundamental question might be approached. The virtue of a work like *Toward the Decolonization of African Literature* rests in large measure not in its invocation of cultural relativism or even in its practical suggestions for contemporary African literature and culture, but in its attempts to base its conclusions on what might be regarded as transcultural, even transhistorical comparisons. To be alert simultaneously to both the Western and African literary traditions, to rely upon the knowledge of both to make fruitful comparisons and judgments strikes me as eminently reasonable and just. More broadly speaking, it suggests that any conception or construction of literary or cultural history benefits from a transcultural comparative approach. And more fundamentally, it suggests that any truly comparative approach to literary historical studies would benefit from a truly comparative understanding of different political regimes. It is an old paradox that by becoming a stranger to one's own culture, one is in a better position to judge it— dare we say—objectively.

23. *Toward the Decolonization of African Literature,* p. 234.
24. Consider in this regard Walter Benjamin's critique of Hegelian historicism in his "Theses on the Philosophy of History," particularly theses VI and VII. The essay is to be found in *Illuminations,* trans. Harry Zohn (New York: Schocken, 1968), pp. 253–264.

MARK PARKER

Measure and Countermeasure: The Lovejoy-Wellek Debate and Romantic Periodization

The concept of a literary period has a curious status in critical writings: there is wide agreement about what periods do, general discontent at these activities, and no consensus about alternatives to them. Thomas Vogler could speak for many when he describes periods in a recent article: "Like all literary phenomena, literary periods are not factual givens, but continuously changing historical constructions. Once the general outline of a period is more or less in place . . . it can be modified and redesigned almost endlessly."[1] Yet words like paralysis, scandal, embarrassment, crisis, confusion, and detour are regularly employed in critical discussions of periodization. This range of terms suggests a kind of hysteria. Treatments of period and periodization have grown more indirect, entwining discussions of this concept with questions of Romanticism, critical pluralism, deconstruction, sociologies of literature, canons, the position of the critic, and literary history generally.

Recently Romanticism has come to designate not only a period but the place where genetic concepts of history took hold.[2]

1. Thomas Vogler, "Romanticism and Literary Periods," *New German Critique* 38 (1986): 155.
2. Vogler, "Romanticism," pp. 132–133. See also Paul de Man, "Genesis and Genealogy," in *Allegories of Reading* (New Haven: Yale University Press, 1979), pp. 79–102.

If this is the case, then we might expect discussions of Romanticism to take up, implicitly or explicitly, the question of periods and periodization. In fact, even a cursory glance at these discussions reveals a rich history of critical preoccupation. Further, it reveals that the implications of the exchange on the nature of Romanticism between Lovejoy and Wellek are still crucial to a discussion of periodization. Care must be taken, however, to avoid reading this exchange "romantically"—that is, in terms of an originary moment. What is necessary is a genealogical history in the sense that Foucault has used the term—a history that maps descent, not development. By unraveling this exchange as it winds through the work of other Romantic critics, we can begin to produce the "effective" history discussed by Foucault, a history whose events are "the reversal of a relationship of forces, the usurpation of power, the appropriation of a vocabulary turned against those who had once used it, a feeble domination that poisons itself as it grows lax, the entry of a masked 'other.'"[3] And by this process we can begin to effect a cure.

To recall briefly, Lovejoy, in his 1924 "On the Discriminations of Romanticisms," states that "the word 'romantic' has come to mean so many things that, by itself, it means nothing."[4] He offers de Musset's humorous account of the "twelve years of suffering" spent by the unfortunate Messrs. Dupuis and Cotonet in defining Romanticism, their eventual exhaustion, and their withdrawal from the pursuit. The choice is simple, according to Lovejoy: abandon the term "romantic" altogether or use it in the plural to weaken the illusion of unity and coherence that the singular implies. Perhaps more illuminating is Lovejoy's terse consideration of Romanticism in 1941: "new ideas of the period were in large part heterogeneous, logically independent and sometimes essentially antithetic to one another in their implications."[5]

3. Michel Foucault, "Nietzsche, Genealogy, History," in *Language, Countermemory, Practice*, trans. Donald Bouchard (Ithaca: Cornell University Press, 1977), p. 154.

4. Arthur Lovejoy, "On the Discrimination of Romanticisms," *PMLA* 39 (1924):232.

5. Arthur Lovejoy, "The Meaning of Romanticism for the Historian of Ideas," *Journal of the History of Ideas* 2 (1941):261.

Wellek provides a sharp rejoinder. Lovejoy's ironic account of period definition, which seems to consider the difficulty essentially a procedural matter, is met by a different kind of rhetoric, one with a strong ethical component. The nominalist position is that Romanticism is "nothing discoverable in reality, but merely a linguistic label for any section of time which we want to consider in isolation for the practical purpose of analysis and description."[6] This statement is more notable for its affect than its literal claims; take away the reductive implications of "merely" and "in isolation," the lack of specificity suggested by "any," and the faint irony in "practical," and the statement is little more than a repetition of Lovejoy's recommendation. The ideological commitment that informs this opposition is not concealed, however: Wellek fears that nominalism, which "leaves us with a chaos of concrete events on the one hand and purely subjective labels on the other," might lead to skepticism. Further, the nominalist point of view assumes that "reality is a continuous, directionless flux."[7]

Wellek's response to Lovejoy in this and in later articles lays the ground for much of the subsequent discussion of period and periodization. Certain recurring features emerge: that the nominalist position is "tantamount to giving up the central task of literary history";[8] that since periods must be conceived of in terms of a series, a period concept entails a theory of literature;[9] that history must be conceived of as continuous; and finally that a period is a "dynamic regulative concept and is not either a metaphysical essence or a purely verbal label."[10] But it would be a mistake to conceive of Wellek's contribution as simply positive—that is, as defining and characterizing the problem. Wellek establishes a rhetorical atmospherics that has had far more effect on later discussions of periodization. Each of his articles has an embattled tone, but perhaps none exploits

6. René Wellek, "Periods and Movements in Literary History," in *English Institute Annual 1940* (New York: Columbia University Press, 1941), p. 74.

7. Wellek, "Periods and Movements," p. 74.

8. Wellek and Warren, *Theory of Literature* (New York: Harcourt Brace and Jovanovich, 1977), p. 261.

9. Wellek, "Periods and Movements," p. 74.

10. Wellek, "Periods and Movements," p. 92.

this crisis rhetoric so successfully as the discussion of periodization in his influential *Theory of Literature*. Significantly, in
the book's culminating chapter, "Literary History," Wellek is
preoccupied with the difficulties of periodization.

It is likely that a critic like Wellek would be the first to scoff
at poststructuralist bromides about what has been called the
"delusive" difference between literature and criticism.[11] But
few articles are so worthy of being read with this strategy in
mind as Wellek's chapter on literary history in *Theory*. Wellek
proposes two views of "period": the metaphysical, "an entity
whose nature has to be intuited," and the nominalistic, "an
arbitrary superimposition on a material which in reality is a
continuous directionless flux."[12] Although Wellek modifies the
position he took in earlier articles on Romantic periodization,
he expresses strong reservation about Lovejoy's notion of a
plurality of romanticisms, arguing that this approach would
make all schemes of literary history impossible. Wellek then
begins the negative dialectic which marks his discussion: in
what follows, he dwells more on the problems attending on
periodization than on a working definition of the term. He expresses impatience at the frequency with which periods take
their names from political events; he chafes at the "motley"
array of labels they assume.[13] The waters of discontent part
momentarily for a rather general definition: "A period is thus
a time section dominated by a system of literary norms, standards, and conventions, whose introduction, spread, diversi-
fication, intergration, and disappearance can be traced."[14] He
refines this claim by reference to Romanticism: "a historical
category or, if one prefers the Kantian term, a 'regulative idea'
(or, rather, a whole system of ideas) with the help of which we
interpret the historical process."[15]

But a rift is visible between these two formulations. In the
move from general to specific Wellek's prose adopts an array

11. Paul de Man, *Allegories of Reading* (New Haven: Yale University
Press, 1979), p. 19.
12. Wellek, *Theory*, p. 262.
13. Wellek, *Theory*, p. 263.
14. Wellek, *Theory*, p. 265.
15. Wellek, *Theory*, p. 265.

of qualifying devices. And as the discussion shifts from definition to the problem of change, Wellek's discontent with periods increases. He recounts several theories of change—Formalist, Marxist, generational—but they are dismissed as incomplete, impractical, or obviously wrong. Wellek concludes by further hedging his bets: "Obviously we should not expect too much from mere period labels: one word cannot carry a dozen connotations. But the sceptical conclusion which would abandon the problem is equally mistaken, as the concept of a period is certainly one of the main instruments of historical knowledge."[16] Thus Wellek concludes with an impasse, an aporia without the self-promoting drama of deconstruction. Periods are unacceptable yet constitutive of historical knowledge. The term itself is inherently unstable, always already the site of competing meanings and subject to a conflict of interpretations. *Theory of Literature,* in many ways a benchmark for modern Anglo-American criticism (and a kind of strawman for most later accounts), offers a discussion of "period" in a surprisingly tentative way. Wellek, while assuming the centrality of the term to literary history, has charted its resistance to definition.

Consider the parallels between the rhetoric here and that of recent, self-consciously deconstructive articles. Wellek sketches the impasse more bluffly, but the basic moves in each argument are very similar. In each treatment, the term at stake is unacceptable yet constitutive of critical practice. Each discussion contains a performative element, an enactment of the difficulties posed by definition. Perhaps the difference lies in the attitude toward the impasse: Wellek is frankly discontented, but deconstructive critics revel in the ironies attendant on the aporia or head off any emotive reaction with cool praise of the lucidity provided by their readings.

Perhaps the best measure of Wellek's success is the number of times his performance has been repeated with variation. Ulrich Weisstein's 1973 discussion of period is a typical testimonial to the force of Wellek's argument. He adopts the same conflicted rhetoric, paralleling even Wellek's modest lament over

16. Wellek, *Theory,* pp. 267–268.

criticism's "clumsy" methods by remarking "how much work remains to be done in this domain."[17] Weisstein places greater emphasis, however, on the instrumental function of periods; they can bring "order into the seeming chaos of ceaselessly unfolding and constantly flowing events, the 'directionless flux,' as Wellek calls it."[18] In a more expansive but still fundamentally reassertive way, Claudio Guillén's "Second Thoughts on Literary Periods" refuses to "surrender" to nominalism.[19] But his campaign is defensive: like Wellek, he is besieged by problems and discontents. His final recommendation, that we solve the difficulties of periods by recognizing that authors and works live in many different periods or durations at once, is almost a capitulation. In spite of Guillén's optimism, his proposed defense against nominalism threatens a dispersal so complete that the term "period" would become useless.

What these later discussions omit, significantly, is Wellek's relentless undoing of the period concept itself. By emphasizing the instrumental function of periods, they shore up the tenuous quality of Wellek's presentation. A genealogical account of these discussions finds (as Foucault, following Nietzsche, predicts) that if we take Wellek as an "origin" of period discussion, we find "something altogether different" from what we expect, a "disparity."[20] Rather than make positive claims about periods, Wellek submits them to a nervous deconstructive examination. In other words, his insistence on periods and on continuous reality marks out the site of their loss. His attempt to secure them signals their unavailability. Wellek's mediation on period concepts is permeated with an odd kind of nostalgia, one which argues for the existence of a past it desires.

Similar discontinuities, slippages, and falsifications can be traced in the less direct treatments of periods and periodization

17. Ulrich Weisstein, *Comparative Literature and Literary Theory,* trans. William Riggan (Bloomington: Indiana University Press, 1973), p. 92.

18. Weisstein, *Comparative Literature,* p. 67.

19. Claudio Guillén, *Literature as System* (Princeton: Princeton University Press, 1971), p. 464.

20. Foucault, "Nietzsche," p. 152.

that follow. It is not surprising that some of the most telling of these indirect discussions are found in the work of M. H. Abrams and, predictably, in the reviews of and response to *Natural Supernaturalism.* It is evident in this survey that the concept of the period has begun acting covertly, informing criticism but rarely becoming its object. It often performs its silent work in a critical arena that claims to have done away with the category altogether. Far from being thrown away as instrumental critical ladders, such outmoded and exploded terms display a durability and persistence.

We can begin tracing the reflex of the Wellek/Lovejoy exchange in Abrams's familiar 1963 article, "English Romanticism: The Spirit of the Age." Clearly consonant with the conception of Romanticism expressed later in *Natural Supernaturalism,* the argument seeks to clarify the relation of "revolutionary upheaval" to Romantic poetry. After nearly collapsing the two, Abrams qualifies his thesis:

Romanticism is no one thing. It is many very individual poets, who wrote poems manifesting a greater diversity of qualities . . . than those of any preceding age. But some prominent qualities a number of these poems share, and certain of these shared qualities form a distinctive complex which may, with a high degree of probability, be related to the events and ideas of the cataclysmic coming-into-being of the world to which we are by now becoming fairly accustomed.[21]

The passage verges on contradiction. There are two claims here: of "diversity," seemingly allied to Lovejoy's embrace of a heterogeneous plurality of romanticisms, and of "a distinctive complex," a position closer to Wellek's desire for an idealist conception of Romanticism. Yet it is hard to take exception with Abrams's careful formulation, largely because the contradiction is so firmly embedded within the critical tradition. The passage, although it makes no mention of period or periodization, enacts the dialectic between nominalist and realist. The tension between unity and heterogeneity informs the passage and its cautious, hedging, accretive rhetoric. The im-

21. M. H. Abrams, "English Romanticism: The Spirit of the Age," in *The Correspondent Breeze,* ed. Jack Stillinger (New York: Norton, 1984), pp. 46–47.

agery used in making the second claim, in which "prominent qualities" are first shared, then "form a distinctive complex," and finally have a "coming-into-being," suggests a process of recognition. It is a wonderfully effective bit of writing, but it dodges the issue.

Abrams's approach in *Natural Supernaturalism* is more straightforward, but the reflex of the Wellek/Lovejoy exchange can still be easily detected. In the preface, he writes that the claims of Shelley and Hazlitt that there is a "spirit of the age" are justified, and he adopts their position. But he does so with a difference. Abrams will not use their phrase: "for economy of discussion" he will employ "the conventional though ambiguous term 'Romantic,'"[22] The opening pages of the book examine one poem as deeply indicative of the age's spirit, and suggest that Abrams has moved closer to Wellek's early definition of period: a time when a system of norms, discoverable from literature itself, is "dominant," and in which "every individual work of art can be understood as an approximation to one of these systems."[23] Abrams abstracts this dominant system from Wordsworth's Prospectus to "The Excursion," and then moves to a series of analyses of other poems and authors. *Natural Supernaturalism* follows the structure of what Abrams in another article calls "the greater Romantic lyric":[24] the conclusion to the book returns to the Prospectus. Seemingly, the period concept of Wellek has won out.

Abrams never mentions Wellek in *Natural Supernaturalism*, and his references to Lovejoy are few. (The only remark directed toward their discussion of periods is embedded in his monumental footnotes, where he remarks that a passage "incidentally, indicates how mistaken it is to reduce Lovejoy's position on 'Romanticism' to simple 'nominalism' which denies validity to any application of the term to a period of human thought and culture."[25] Here he seems to second Wellek's

22. M. H. Abrams, *Natural Supernaturalism* (New York: Norton, 1971), p. 16.

23. Wellek, "Periods and Movements," p. 92.

24. Abrams, "Structure and Style in the Greater Romantic Lyric," *The Correspondent Breeze*, pp. 76–108.

25. Abrams, *Natural Supernaturalism*, p. 506.

fears of the skeptical direction of nominalistic uses of "period" while rescuing Wellek's chosen antagonist from the enemy camp.) Reviewers of *Natural Supernaturalism,* however, rarely fail to engage Abrams on the subject of periods and periodization. The quickness with which they apply the familiar moves in the Wellek/Lovejoy exchange shows how pervasive the exchange has become.

E. D. Hirsch concludes his review of Abrams's book in *The Wordsworth Circle* with this thumping Q.E.D.: "by the thoroughness of its documentation, it sweeps away, like the lightest chaff, earlier controversies about the essential unity of the Romantic movement. Lovejoy's plurality of romanticisms does not stand up to this weight of evidence, and must acquire whatever truth it has at a lower level of insight and discrimination."[26] Other reviewers were less willing to take up the "homogeneous" line of Romanticism. Herbert Lindenberger, while shy of the nominalism anathematized by Wellek, sketches a jostling plurality of romanticisms which undermines Abrams's synthesizing turn. But when his dissatisfaction leads to a more general discussion of periods and periodization, his remarks, like those of Wellek, return to the difficulties of conceiving periods at present. When the ideas of a given period are, in their turn, historicized, the "autonomy" and "individuality" of the period dissolve, and the historian of ideas becomes a "mediator" performing an impossible activity. Worse, each period is built on a "distinct bias."[27] For Lindenberger, as for Wellek, the present embarrassments connected with trying to apply the concept of Romanticism and of periodization are consuming, and he concludes with a wistful meditation on Abrams's apparent freedom from darker, less affirmative views of each. Lindenberger's nostalgia for some simpler scheme of periodization, although it seems born of discontent specific to the present, essentially repeats Wellek's simultaneous loss of and insistence on periods. But, as with all repe-

26. E. D. Hirsch, review of *Natural Supernaturalism, Wordsworth Circle* 3 (1972):20.
27. Herbert Lindenberger, review of *Natural Supernaturalism, English Language Notes* 10 (1972):153.

titions, there is a residue of difference. Wellek's antinominalist account has been transformed from tenuous defense to a more stable description of periods. The "Wellek" who underwrites Lindenberger's remarks is not the Wellek who charted the term's resistance to definition.

Other reviews seek relief from the confines of the Lovejoy/Wellek debate. J. Hillis Miller, in a review article in *Diacritics,* attempts to redefine the historical sequence traced by Abrams in terms of a different set of metaphysical suppositions. In place of Abrams's traditional pattern of original unity, fall, and redemptive reconstruction, Miller posits original dispersal, de-centering, and displacement. In place of Abrams's synec-dochic construct, in which certain poems like the Prospectus reproduce the spirit of the age or a period's dominant ideas, Miller would employ the "concept of a centerless repetition in which no element in the series is the commanding exemplar of which the others are copies."[28] The effect of such a point of departure on the concept of a period is clear. Neither Wellek's unitary view nor Lovejoy's plurality would do; the period must mark out the space of a dispersion.

But Miller's deconstructive account of language has implications for the relations between the very periods he has made unthinkable. He argues that Abrams's strategy of interpretation in *Natural Supernaturalism,* which assumes that "a text has a single meaning which is more or less independent of the play of relations, repetitions, and differentiation within the work itself," must be replaced by readings that regard poems and philosophical works as "the crossroads of multiple ambiguous passages."[29] Such dialogism, in addition to making a text's adherence to a given set of period concepts problematic, makes the relation of texts from different periods—concepts of source and influence—equally vexed. Miller draws out the implications of this deconstructive view of literary history in a review of Joseph Riddel's *The Inverted Bell:*

If every text is "dialogical," no text will fit any univocal period definition. The idea of homogeneous literary periods must be discarded. Each period is itself equivocal. Periods differ from one another be-

---

28. J. Hillis Miller, "Tradition and Difference," *Diacritics* 2 (1972):13.
29. Miller, "Tradition," pp. 11, 12.

cause there are different forms of heterogeneity, not because each
period held a single coherent "view of the world." There is literary
history because texts are "undecidable," rather than the other way
around, since one side of the aporia of deconstruction is always referential statements, that is statements which point to time and history.[30]

A referential reading of a group of texts might produce a period, but the subsequent deconstruction of this referentiality,
culminating in the familiar impasse or aporia, would make it
unavailable. One interpretive direction offers a literary history
with homogeneous periods; the deconstructive turn makes
them impossible. By aligning the desire for periods and periodization with the Western metaphysics of presence, Miller implies that such constructions are always already vulnerable
and problematic. Yet he calls for a heterogeneity that, paradoxically, would be somehow normative—or at least regulative—for a given period. While implicitly undermining the idea
of a period, he seems to envision a new conception of it that
would still allow the critic to situate a given poem or work in
one of the "different forms of heterogeneity" that his revisionist account would generate. It is a notion that still relies on
period distinctions, while self-consciously replacing Abrams's
reliance on similarity and consonance with a deconstructive
practice based on difference and Deleuze's "enigmatic" repetition. What keeps Miller's account from making literary history an "impossibility" (as Abrams later charges it does) is the
resilience of the critical desire for some version of a period
concept.[31] The desire for periods animates Miller's account of
literary history, as it does Wellek's traditionalist view.

Other responses seek a productive loosening of period
claims or a wholesale redrawing of periods. Characteristic of
this shift are Jerome McGann's remarks in a 1972 review article
that devotes much attention to *Natural Supernaturalism*.
McGann, like other critics, begins by noting the exclusivity of
Abrams's account of Romanticism and tracing its deficiencies.

30. J. Hillis Miller, "Deconstructing the Deconstructors," *Diacritics* 5
(1975):31.
31. M. H. Abrams, "Rationality and Imagination in Cultural History: A
Reply to Wayne Booth," *Critical Inquiry* 2 (1976):458.

But setting the historical record straight is not the goal here. What emerges in McGann's conclusion is a radical reconstruction of periods in either of two ways. The first, which makes all literature in the nineteenth and twentieth century Romantic, asks scholars to identify and describe "different sorts of Romantic traditions."[32] The second, a prescient description of much future "new historical" scholarship, proposes a difficult task of imposing a "flexible set of interacting limits—formal, substantive, geographical, and historical" on Romantic literature.[33] The first possibility continues the search for a regulative or normative set of period concerns (albeit on an impossibly large and diverse body of material), and the second, by looking to the contingencies and particularities of microhistory, tends to defer, by the constant differentiation of "interacting limits," the formation of period concepts on the scale pursued by Wellek, Abrams, or even Lovejoy.

Such a loosening of period claims has been pursued in the work of many critics. But such projects often reveal the inexpungeable presence of the critical framework set out by the Wellek/Lovejoy debate. Marilyn Butler's remarks in *Romantics, Rebels and Reactionaries* on the coherence and homogeneity that mark Abrams's and Wellek's accounts of Romanticism are characteristic of the uneasy confluence of the debate's original terms. Reflecting on how the book has "tended to highlight differences" between writers, she concludes that "Romanticism is inchoate because it is not a single intellectual movement but a complex of responses to certain conditions which Western society has experienced and continues to experience since the middle of the eighteenth century."[34] This passage, which strikes an uneasy balance between the "inchoate" and the structure (or at least structuring process) implicit in "a complex," at once succinctly embodies the formative pressures that the debate has placed on subse-

32. Jerome J. McGann, "Romanticism and the Embarrassments of the Critical Tradition," *Modern Philology* 70 (1972):256.

33. McGann, "Romanticism," p. 257.

34. Marilyn Butler, *Romantics, Rebels, and Reactionaries* (New York: Oxford University Press, 1982), p. 184.

quent scholarship. The echoes of Abrams's "distinctive complex" and his 200-year view of Romanticism, albeit probably unintentional, serve as reminders of the entanglements that this framework seems to generate.

Although McGann and Butler have been reliable guides to the route taken by subsequent researchers into the era traditionally called Romantic, it would be a mistake to see the Lovejoy/Wellek confrontation as solved or rendered irrelevant. The caution with which they invoke Lovejoy's position indicates the lingering force of Wellek's concept of a period. Significantly, when McGann returns to this debate in *The Romantic Ideology*, he speaks of Lovejoy as "the most useful scholarly method that one could adopt *at this juncture*."[35] A plurality of romanticisms is offered as a cure for the widespread critical practice of reifying recent homogeneous period histories and employing them as standards against which to judge individual works. Butler tacks throughout *Romantics, Rebels, and Reactionaries*, noting that nothing in her book "directly challenges Professor Wellek's formulation" of a "closely coherent" Romanticism.[36] Such moves have been enormously productive, perhaps in part because they cause a deferral of questions of period and periodization, but the old difficulties still persist.

Oddly enough, nowhere can the tension between Wellek and Lovejoy be better observed in all its contradictory splendor than in Abrams's own responses to his reviewers. In several articles, most notably "A Note on Wittgenstein and Literary Theory," Abrams emphasized the performative and narrative dimensions of his historical practice. What Wittgenstein proposed as a justification for certain uses of language was adopted by Abrams to underwrite critical procedures:

The view that the justification for a linguistic procedure is not what forms of expression it uses, but whether it is really "doing work," is neither inhibitive nor prohibitive, but liberative. And such a view may be taken to confirm—not in details, but overall—the very diverse

---

35. Jerome J. McGann, *The Romantic Ideology* (Chicago: University of Chicago Press, 1983), p. 20.

36. Butler, *Romantics,* pp. 183–184.

ways that our best literary critics have in fact used language in order
to achieve their profitable discoveries and conclusions, as against
what some recent analysts claim that the critics have done, or should
instead have done.[37]

This entails, most surprisingly in the case of Abrams himself,
a move from representation to production as a measure of critical success. In addition to affecting the kind of claims one can
make about the world, the "fluidity and variability in our ways
of speaking," put at a premium in this instrumentalist conception of language, have ramifications for the kinds of stories one
can tell about a given literary period.[38]

This is seen most clearly—even startlingly—in Abrams's cor-
rection of suggestions by many reviewers that he is in the Wellek or essentialist camp. Not only does he assert that he is a
nominalist like Lovejoy, he goes on to say that his work has
been misread. His use of the term "Romanticism" is an "expository convenience": "I don't believe that there exists an
abstract entity, named 'Romanticism,' whose essential features are definable."[39] But such a claim is not unambiguous;
Abrams is reorganizing the essential issues in the debate.
Rather than framing the issue as a choice between Lovejoy and
Wellek, he opposes R. S. Crane's term "Platonist" (ferried
into the discussion by Wayne Booth in the article which pre-
ceeds Abrams's reply) to nominalist. Given the difficulties
posed in finding a "Platonist historian," this looks suspiciously
like an empty category, or at least an irrelevant one. However,
having invested himself in the nominalist cloak, Abrams, in
suggesting what questions a reader should address to *Natural
Supernaturalism,* proceeds to sound like Wellek: "Did the distinctive complex of literary and cultural phenomena I chose to
discuss really take place in the period conventionally called
Romantic?"[40]

These strains culminate in a later discussion of alternative
Romantic histories. Abrams, again in a surprising move,

37. M. H. Abrams, "A Note on Wittgenstein and Literary Theory," *English Literary History* 41 (1974):544.
38. Abrams, "A Note," p. 544.
39. Abrams, "Rationality," p. 450.
40. Abrams, "Rationality," p. 451.

sketches out an "imaginary history" based on the principles of Romantic irony. Although he wishes us, through the experience of *Natural Supernaturalism,* to assent to the "distinctive complex" he traces, he can "imagine" alternative accounts, can "almost imagine writing" one, and would "ungrudgingly accept" such a book as "valid."[41] This would seem a position in keeping with his embrace of Lovejoy's nominalistic plurality of romanticisms. Yet, in a passage that recalls Wellek's fears of the skepticism implicit in Lovejoy's nominalism, Abrams carefully distances himself from the relativism apparent in this move. Does the acceptance of alternative histories make for critical relativity?

Not, I think, in any dismaying sense of that word, for it does not obviate the claim that both books tell a story which is true. Their judgments about Wordsworth seem "contradictory," but they are not so in the logical sense of that word, which assumes that the clashing assertions meet on the same plane of discourse. The disparate judgments about the representative quality and greatness of Wordsworth's poetry, however, follow from different controlling categories which effect a different selection and ordering of the historical facts and implicate a different set of criteria by which to assess what is representative and great. The insights and assessments of each book, in other words, are relative to the vantage point chosen by its author, and each tries to make us see selected goings-on in the Romantic era in a certain way; but these diverse goings-on are there to be seen in that way. Each, that is, tells only a *part* of the truth, but it is a part of the *truth.*[42]

This passage is best evaluated in terms of Abrams's earlier remarks about method, in which he has had a great deal to say about the use of metaphors in critical investigation. Following Wittgenstein in *Philosophical Investigations,* he has called for tolerance of some indistinct and blurred concepts, and he has suggested that the critic employ a variety of similes to prevent the confusion and misdirection that are the inevitable detritus of the use of a single figure.[43] This makes his reliance on one particular metaphor in the passage quoted above significant. Abrams's optical metaphor (later referred to as "almost inevi-

---

41. Abrams, "Rationality," p. 459.
42. Abrams, "Rationality," pp. 459–460; emphasis Abrams's.
43. Abrams, "A Note," pp. 542–544.

table") suggests that the plurality of histories possible for a
given period stems from different critical perspectives, not
from a genuine heterogeneity inherent to the period. Instead of
providing Lovejoy's welter of "logically independent, heterogeneous" ideas that suggest a plurality of "truths," a period
for Abrams has some essential, yet paradoxically unavailable
truth. History is not some "directionless flux," things and
events are there and stable. But the experience of history is
somehow anamorphic. "Different controlling categories"—the
"eyes" in this metaphor—allow access to different aspects of
the same terrain. But it is always the same terrain: theories
don't create facts; they simply allow us to uncover different
facts. There is a deep empiricity to this metaphor, and consequently to the notion of period implicit in it. Heterogeneity is
apparent—a predictable function of critical method—but only
through this plurality of Romanticism (as opposed to Lovejoy's
romanticisms) can we approximate the evasive, unapproach-
able reality of the period. It is hard to miss the consonance
between Abrams's concept of a period and the history of the
period he presents: a redemptive pattern of unity, fall, and a
difficult reconstruction. His attempt to fuse Wellek and Lovejoy is of a piece with the desire for synthesis so evident in
Natural Supernaturalism.

Looked at in terms of a traditional history, Abrams's argument about periods and Romanticism seems to confuse and
distort the terms of the Wellek/Lovejoy debate. But a history
less given to seeking out an origin would offer a different evaluation. Abrams has reinterpreted the debate, changing the
rules set down by Lovejoy and Wellek. Shorn of their agonistic
intensity, Foucault's remarks on historical change are applicable here:

Rules are empty in themselves, violent and unfinalized; they are impersonal and can be bent to any purpose. The successes of history
belong to those who are capable of seizing the rules, to replace those
who had used them, to disguise themselves so as to pervert them,
invert their meaning, and redirect them against those who had initially
imposed them; controlling this complex mechanism, they will make
it function so as to overcome the rulers through their own rules.[44]

44. Foucault, "Nietzsche," p. 151.

Abrams's mastery of what Foucault would call the impositions of Wellek and Lovejoy is evident throughout his work on Romanticism.

The next move in this Romanticist debate on the concept of a period was played out at another level of abstraction: in the confrontation between Miller and Abrams over the possibility of literary history. If one takes, according to Abrams, Miller's ideas on the ongoing constitution and reconstitution of literary fact in his review of *Natural Supernaturalism* seriously, then "any history which relies on written texts becomes an impossibility."[45] Without a determinate and determinable "core of meanings," literary histories simply turn out to be "a history . . . of the historian's will to power." The rhetoric here, both absolutist and apocalyptic, recalls Wellek's dismay at the skepticism he detected in Lovejoy's view. Miller's reply to this threat to the humanist enterprise is blunt: "So be it. That is not much of an argument. A certain notion of history or of literary history, like a certain notion of determinable reading, might indeed be an impossibility, and if so, it might be better to know that, and not to fool oneself or be fooled."[47] In Miller's work, as in that of other deconstructionists, there is a curious, though not contradictory, lucidity to the way he wields the concepts of undecidability and unthinkability. He reminds his reader that the "impossibility" of history does not prevent its being done.[48]

45. Abrams, "Rationality," p. 458.

46. Abrams, "Rationality," p. 459.

47. J. Hillis Miller, "The Critic as Host," *Critical Inquiry* 3 (1977):439–440.

48. By questioning Abrams's account in this way, Miller recalls the constructivist line of thought about periodization and literary history generally. Siegfried Schmidt's "On Writing Histories of Literature: Some Remarks from a Constructivist Point of View," *Poetics* 14 (1985) is typical of this critical approach. Schmidt argues, somewhat like Miller, that since there are no objective literary facts—only the interpretations generated by a given theory or cognitive context—there can be as many literary histories as critics to write them. Hence the criteria for a given production are dictated by use. Implicit in Schmidt's formulation are quasi-Enlightenment ideals of self-awareness and understanding. Consequently, Schmidt's proposals differ radically from those of Miller, who is less sanguine about the possibility of a consciously directed program. While both schemes expect, and even

More recent discussions of the nature of Romanticism have located the question of literary periods in Romanticism itself. Thomas Vogler has recently attempted to historicize the question of periods by reminding us that the writers conventionally dubbed Romantic are often credited with the invention of a sense of history that unfolds in a directed, productive way. The act of periodization, an implicit subscription to "fundamental difference and diachronic variability," makes the historian, in some sense, a Romantic.[49] Yet this investment in change has, paradoxically, led to some spectacularly ahistorical readings of Romanticism and of subsequent periods. Noting the tendency of critics to project binary oppositions—often psychological or literary categories—as "periods," Vogler maintains that historical thinking has evaded us. Synchronic thinking has held us captive: "even if we regret the fact and want a diachronic view, it can be difficult to find one."[50] Considerations of literary history and of periods have shuttled between two exclusive positions: an idealist concept which sees literature as an autonomous, self-regulating domain (a view which ultimately questions the existence of some historical "real"), and a sociologically oriented materialist conception.[51] Vogler traces the way Jauss attempts to step beyond these two alternatives, but he shrewdly questions whether such approaches represent anything more than a "history of the history of literature."[52] Jauss' historical program, while laudable as an attempt to escape the "binary set of alternatives that paralyzes and polemicizes our thought and discourse," may be yet another "Romantic discourse of desire which tries to inscribe a genuine difference in

---

embrace, multiple histories, Schmidt's optimism about the social ends of the making of history could hardly be accepted by Miller's deconstructionist program. For Schmidt, periods are a function of present social needs; for Miller, they are the marks of historians' elusive desires or the results of their awkward entanglements with past critical accounts. Ultimately, Miller enacts such an entanglement when he calls for the recognition of "heterogeneous" periods.

49. Vogler, "Romanticism," p. 133.
50. Vogler, "Romanticism," p. 147.
51. Vogler, "Romanticism," p. 131.
52. Vogler, "Romanticism," p. 154.

the discourse—with the possibility that desire, and its attempts, are the only change there is."[53] Yet however conscious and lucid Vogler's exposition of the Romantic basis of the desire for periods, his rhetoric of vexation and difficulty seems familiar, and his concluding sentence suggests even more strongly the persistence of Wellek's crisis rhetoric in Anglo-American discussions of periodization: "Without a definitive map, a new road may always turn out to be a detour."[54]

In a less direct treatment of the problem, Paul de Man, with characteristic finality, has sought to evade the constraints of the genetic position by inverting and denying it:

Can the genetic pattern be said to be "truly" characteristic of Romanticism? Does this system, with all the conceptual categories that it implies (subject, intent, negation, totalization, supported by the underlying metaphysical categories of identity and presence) remain as unchallenged in writers of the late eighteenth century as it remains unchallenged in most of their later interpreters? It could be that the so-called Romantics came closer than we do to undermining the absolute authority of this system. If this were the case, one may well wonder what kind of historiography could do justice to the phenomenon of Romanticism, since Romanticism (itself a period concept) would then be the movement that challenges the genetic principle which necessarily underlies all historical narrative. The ultimate test or "proof" of the fact that Romanticism puts the genetic pattern of history in question would then be the impossibility of writing a history of Romanticism. The abundant bibliography that exists on the subject tends to confirm this, for a curious blindness seems to compel historians and interpreters of Romanticism to circumvent the central insights that put their own practice, as historians, into question.[55]

The way out hinted at by de Man, a searching deconstruction of the genetic claims apparent in Nietzsche's *Birth of Tragedy,* has all the oblique force of his "exemplary" readings. If it promises more than it delivers, it unsettles more than one might expect. De Man's characteristic deferral of affirmation or positive knowing at the end of the article leaves in place the

53. Vogler, "Romanticism," p. 160.
54. Vogler, "Romanticism," p. 160.
55. De Man, *Allegories,* pp. 81–82.

hypothesis about the genetic bias of Romanticism: "it is in-structive to see a genetic narrative function as a step leading to insights that destroy the claims on which the genetic conti-nuity was founded, but that could not have been formulated if the fallacy had not been allowed to unfold."[56] Yet in rendering that place suspect, consequently making the problems for pe-riodicity posed by the genetic model less pressing than that of the status of the genetic claims, de Man's article is longer on "instruction" than on practice.

Periods run deep in our historicizing. Even when we assume the real to be contingent, periods have an endurance that looks—to all but absolutist or apocalyptic gazes, and in almost all critical practices—eternal. Perhaps this is the Romantic leg-acy: to sense the lack of foundations to the past, the ubiquity of interpretation in recalling it, and its unavoidable made-up quality, yet remain entangled with it. Since the apparent prob-lem of periodization stems from certain critical practices, what is needed is an array of counterpractices—less a solution, an enlightenment, or a synthesis, than a cure. What critical and historical tradition appears to give us is the unfolding drama of an unruly historical sense born of a certain moment. De Man's attempt to undo that moment by reading a counterhistory in Nietzschean genealogy needs to be supplemented (I use the word advisedly) by other practical cures. In the face of the embarrassment, scandal, and crisis of periodization, the appli-cation of the subversive historical sense discussed by Foucault in "Nietzsche, Genealogy, History" offers a countermeasure.

Foucault's three "anti-Platonic" uses of genealogy—the par-odic, the dissociative, and the sacrificial—could go far toward a recovery. By parodic history, which is "directed against real-ity, and opposes the theme of history as reminiscence or rec-ognition," Foucault proposes that the historian produce an exaggerated, self-conscious variety of historical returns, a "concerted carnival" which will undermine the lingering sense of stable reality. Dissociative history would attack the concept of identity, opposing "history given as continuity or represen-tative of a tradition."[57] Through it the heterogenity of a given

56. De Man, *Allegories,* pp. 101–102.
57. Foucault, "Nietzsche," p. 160.

field would become prominent, and the practices that conceal this heterogeneity would be scrutinized. Finally, sacrificial histories would relentlessly question the apparent neutrality of the historical account and the desire of the historian. Knowledge, without its mask of objectivity, would become the will to knowledge.

We can recognize de Man's attentive raveling of the antigenetic strain in a traditionally genealogical text as a dissociative move. Janusz Slawinski has cunningly sketched another such dissociative account. In tracing the reorientation of literary history by reception theory, he reminds us how explosive commonly held concepts of the reader are. If we accept the "reader" as a construct organizing the semantic features of a work, if we also consider the real readers constituted by other textual encounters, and if we assume that meaning is attached to a given work over time by the encounter between these two constructions, we arrive at an entirely different conception of a literary period. Traditional text-centered views of periods, which record discontinuity, revolution, and innovation, must be supplemented by more continuous periods based on "public readership and styles of reception."[58] Although the methodological problems of producing the social history of the "public" reader are formidable, perhaps even insurmountable, taking the measure of Slawinsky's dissociative move, as well as that of de Man, indicates how different such counterhistories would look from most present accounts. Perhaps we have come to a place where an ironic counterhistory of Romanticism, one less intent on closure, one more alive to the accidents and contingencies of descent, is at once possible and necessary. For even as critical journals and conferences bruit the notion of a foundationless and contingent history, we have never really let go of the handrail provided by periods. Fear of "detours" should not deter us, for if the counterhistories of genealogy offer anything, it will be a clearer sense of the detours we have persisted in taking. And without a deeper suspicion of the inexpungeable work of periods and periodization, we will not be able to imagine anything different or better.

58. Janusz Slawinski, "Reading and Reader in the Literary Historical Process," *New Literary History* 19 (1988):526.

DAVID PERKINS

Literary Classifications:
How Have They Been Made?

Classification is fundamental to the discipline of literary history. A literary history cannot have only one text for its subject, and it cannot describe a great many texts individually. The multiplicity of objects must be converted into fewer, more manageable units, which can then be characterized, compared, interrelated, and ordered. The single most necessary assumption of literary history is that one can speak meaningfully of supraindividual entities—periods, genres, traditions, schools, movements, horizons of expectation, discourses, or communicative systems. Such "logical subjects," as Dilthey called them, are the usual protagonists of literary histories, the "heroes" whose rise and decline we narrate.

Classifications map the cultural world. Literature by blacks in the United States can be a separate taxonomic unit, or it can be "integrated" with literature by whites. Langston Hughes can be grouped with Amiri Baraka or with Carl Sandburg. The tendency in German literary histories to demarcate a literary period by the Third Reich has, Alexander von Bormann says, a "perceptibly disburdening function." The period falls "out of our cultural tradition as an exotic," ceases to be " 'present past.' " This changes at once if one proceeds from the thesis of continuity, and pays attention to the many lines of connection."[1] Thus classifications shape our sense of national and personal identity.

The importance of literary taxonomy to the profession cannot be overstated. Classifications are organizing principles of courses ("The Lyric"), library shelves ("Fiction: American— 19th Century"), societies (the divisions of the Modern Language Association), journals (*Studies in Romanticism*), anthologies, collections of essays, conferences, and tenure searches. They are used and contested in struggles for institutional power.

Despite the importance of the topic, not much critical reflection has focused recently in the United States on literary classification and its problems.[2] Furthermore, except in considerations of genre, discussion has been limited to only one

1. Alexander von Bormann, "Zum Umgang mit dem Epochenbegriff," in *Literatur und Sprache im historischen Prozess*. Vorträge des Deutschen Germanistentages Aachen 1982, ed. Thomas Cramer. Vol. I, *Literatur* (Tübingen: Max Niemayer Verlag, 1983), p. 191.

2. For genres see Paul Hernaudi, *Beyond Genre: New Directions in Literary Classification* (Ithaca, N.Y.: Cornell University Press, 1972); Rosalie L. Colie, *The Resources of Kind: Genre-Theory in the Renaissance,* ed. Barbara K. Lewalski (Berkeley: California University Press, 1973); J. P. Strelka, ed., *Theories of Literary Genre* (University Park, Pa.: Pennsylvania State University Press, 1978); *Renaissance Genres: Essays on Theory, History, and Interpretation,* ed. Barbara K. Lewalski (Cambridge, Mass.: Harvard University Press, 1986); Ralph Cohen, "History and Genre," *New Literary History* 17/2 (Winter, 1986), and Cohen's article in this volume; Clifford Siskin, *The Historicity of Romantic Discourse* (New York: Oxford University Press, 1988); and works on particular genres. For problems of taxonomy in general see the very elegant discussion of eighteenth-century taxonomy in the natural sciences in Michel Foucault, *The Order of Things* (New York: Pantheon Books, 1970). For taxonomy and especially periodization in literary history see R. S. Crane, *Critical and Historical Principles of Literary History* (Chicago: University of Chicago Press, 1971); Claudio Guillén, *Literature as System* (Princeton: Princeton University Press, 1971); Ulrich Weisstein, *Comparative Literature and Literary Theory: Survey and Introduction,* trans. William Riggan (Bloomington: Indiana University Press, 1973); Fredric Jameson, *The Political Unconscious: Narrative as a Socially Symbolic Act* (Ithaca, N.Y.: Cornell University Press, 1981); John Frow, *Marxism and Literary History* (Cambridge, Mass.: Harvard University Press, 1986). Among recent discussions in Germany of periodization mention may be made of Uwe Japp, *Beziehungssinn: Ein Konzept*

question, namely, whether literary taxonomies can correspond to historical realities. The terms of this argument are not exactly the same with respect to periods, genres, traditions, movements, and other categories, but they are similar, and our thinking about periodization illustrates the state of the question with respect to literary classifications in general.

In *Theory of Literature* (1949) Wellek rejected both the notion that periods are metaphysical entities and the opposite opinion of Croce that periods are merely conventional. Adapting ideas of the Russian Formalists, Wellek argued that a period is created by a dominant "system of literary norms, standards, and conventions." Thus Wellek secured the objectivity and "relative" unity of periods, while also allowing for a degree of heterogeneity and struggle within them.[3] Wellek's views were accepted, though not without criticism, by Guillén, Weisstein, Japp, and most others who wrote about the theory of literary history. This consensus lasted, though gradually weakening, until the beginning of the 1970s.

At present, we tend to regard periods as necessary fictions. They are necessary because one cannot write history or literary history without periodizing. Moreover, we require the concept of a unified period in order to deny it, and thus make apparent the particularity, local difference, heterogeneity, fluctuation, discontinuity, and strife that are now our preferred categories for understanding any moment of the past.

---

der Literaturgeschichte (Frankfurt am Main: Europäische Verlagsanstalt, 1980); the essays by various hands collected in *Epochenschwellen und Epochenstrukturen im Diskurs der Literatur- und Sprachhistorie,* ed. H. U. Gumbrecht und Ursula Link-Heer (Frankfurt am Main: Suhrkamp Verlag, 1985); Siegfried J. Schmidt, "On Writing Histories of Literature: Some Remarks from a Constructivist Point of View," *Poetics* 14 (August, 1985), pp. 279–301; and Artur Bethke, "Periodisierung als methodologisches Problem der Literaturgeschichtsschreibung," in *Die nordischen Literaturen als Gegenstand der Literaturgeschichtsschreibung.* Beiträge zur 13. Studienkonferenz für Skandinavische Studien (IASS) 10.-16. August 1980 und der Ernst-Moritz-Arndt-Universität Greifswald (Rostock: VEB Hinstorff Verlag, 1982).

3. René Wellek and Austin Warren, *Theory of Literature* (New York: Harcourt, Brace, 1949), pp. 277–278.

Our postmodernist questioning of the unity and objectivity of periods bases itself on the historiography of the *Annales* school and Lévi-Strauss' Appendix to *The Savage Mind,* both stressing the overlap of long- and short-term events (these ideas already modified Guillén's view of literary periodization); the structuralist sense of systematic oppositions or differences within any field we discriminate; the "genealogy" of Foucault and its polemic against totalizations; the orientation to the history of reception, which yields periods quite different from those in the traditional literary history of the genesis of works;[4] the argument of hermeneutics that periods of the past are constructed from a present perspective and change as the present moves on; and *Ideologiekritik,* emphasizing that classifications serve ideological interests.

Also, more traditional objections still have force. According to Croce, a work of art embodies an individual intuition, and hence every work of art differs from all others. The literary field—any assemblage of texts that we wish to divide into groups—is always perfectly heterogeneous. When we classify texts, we put the continuously differing objects into a few pigeonholes. Moreover, Croce agrees with the Russian Formalists and with the modern avant-garde in general that the individual quality or difference of a work of art is the special locus of its value. Since taxonomies are based on features texts share, they foreground what is less valuable in them.

We owe especially to Dilthey the concept that periods are spiritually or ideologically unified tracts of time, but even Dilthey worried that such representations are integral and stable, while "life" is endlessly diverse and changing. Periods are "fixed representations of something in progress, giving fixity in thought to that which in itself is process or movement in a direction."[5] When we speak of the Romantic period, we isolate a duration within a longer duration and suggest, without wish-

4. Janusz Slawinski, "Reading and Reader in the Literary Historical Process," *New Literary History,* 19/3 (Spring, 1988): 526.

5. Wilhelm Dilthey, *Der Aufbau der geschichtlichen Welt in der Geisteswissenschaften, Gesammelte Werke,* 2nd ed., unchanged (Stuttgart: Teubner, 1958), VII, p. 157.

ing to do so, that the process of change ceases within the "period." This point has frequently been noted by theorists of literary history,[6] and the same objection applies to concepts of schools and movements. The phrase "Imagist movement" suppresses not only the differences among the texts it synthesizes but also the development of this style over time, for a typical Imagist poem in the 1930s was unlike one in the 1910s. The previous sentence itself commits the error it criticizes and thus illustrates the problem, which is rooted in the nature of conceptual thinking and language.

Theorists have proposed new taxonomic categories—horizon of expectations, discourse, communicative system, *épistème*—that will, it is hoped, escape the objections to the traditional ones. But emphasis on particularity, difference, and discontinuity undermines confidence in all classifications. At the same time, of course, we must classify, since otherwise we sink into a mass of unrelated details and lose all possibility of understanding them. A typical idea at present is, then, that we must impose taxonomies, but must not believe that they correspond to historical realities. Philippe Forget says that in writing a literary history one must "accept a definite division" of the material, but "in the course or at the end of the investigation" must also make the division appear "unsuitable" and give it up or restructure it.[7] The interrelations of texts and authors in a literary history are not "embedded in the historical process" for the historian to discover, as Wellek maintained,[8] but are constructed by the literary historian. "We must admit," says Siegfried Schmidt, "that we have to apply criteria other than truth, objectivity, or reliability to literary histories,

6. Wellek and Warren, *Theory*, p. 278; Guillén, *Literature*, p. 445; Crane, *Critical and Historical Principles*, p. 28.

7. Philippe Forget, "Literatur—Literaturegeschichte—Literaturgeschichtsschreibung: Ein rückblickender Thesenentwurf," in *Kontroversen, alte und neue*. Akten des VII. Internationalen Germanisten-Kongresses Göttingen 1985. Vol. 11, *Historische und aktuelle Konzepte der Literaturgeschichtsschreibung. Zwei Königskinder? Zum Verhältnis von Literatur und Literaturwissenschaft*, ed. Albrecht Schöne (Tübingen: Max Niemayer Verlag, 1986), p. 44.

8. Wellek and Warren, *Theory*, p. 278.

and that we have to formulate social functions for literary histories other than that of providing a true report on 'what has been the case.' "[9]

But this argument, replacing the consensus created by Wellek, still focuses on the same question: can literary taxonomy be true to the past. On this occasion I bracket this question in order to raise others we have not asked, or are only now beginning to ask, about literary classifications. These questions pertain to their provenance (who made them? how? with what interests or motives?), to their reception (who or what determines their acceptance? why and how do they change?), and to their functions in determining what we read, in modifying our responses to texts and our interpretations of them, in organizing the past, in careers and institutional life, and in society at large. These questions may be asked both about particular classifications and about the process of literary classification in general.

A brief essay can explore only part of this program. I shall attempt to say how, in general, classifications have been made by literary historians. I aim only to describe what have been and still are the common methods, and do not here attempt to suggest what ought to be done if we are to overcome our clearly unsatisfactory practices. The investigation is empirical, in the sense that it concentrates on particular instances of literary historians classifying. The examples are chosen almost at random, and my generalizations are based on studying many more instances than space allows to be analyzed. Another set of examples would not lead to different conclusions.

Obviously, the processes of literary taxonomizing have been contingent and the results irrational. They are not at all like the efforts of Linnaeus and other eighteenth-century naturalists described by Foucault in *The Order of Things,* for the naturalists, though myopic in the criteria on which they based their classifications, were otherwise logical and systematic. Literature has no taxonomic system, but only a confused aggregate of overlapping classifications from different points of

9. Schmidt, "On Writing Histories of Literature," p. 285.

view. To see how literary classifications have actually been made tells us why.

Literary classifications have been determined mainly by six factors: tradition, ideological interests, the aesthetic requirements of writing a literary history, the assertions of authors and their contemporaries about their affinities and antipathies, the similarities that the literary historian observes among authors and/or texts, and the needs of professional careers and the politics of power in institutions. This essay does not analyze examples of the latter, for either the political and career-istic motives are glaringly obvious or they are veiled by more acceptable, apparently objective ones. Contrary to what might naively be supposed, observation of texts is the most unusual method of classification, and it is also the least effective if effectiveness is measured by acceptance. Henceforth I attempt to give these generalizations concreteness and detail by studying particular cases. To me the most surprising thing such cases reveal is the overwhelming role of tradition in the process of taxonomizing.

We may begin by asking why the latest *Cambridge History of Classical Literature* (1985) classifies Greek lyric poetry from the seventh to fifth centuries B.C. into the following categories: elegy and iambus, archaic choral lyric, monody (lyric for solo voice), and choral lyric in the fifth century. Whoever has to classify this poetry is not to be envied, since all that has survived are texts or significant fragments from approximately eighteen poets, widely scattered in time and place, about whom we have little, mostly unreliable information. But no one starting now from scratch to classify this verse would decide that the historical and other interrelations between these poets are best disclosed by a system based mainly on versification and on choral or solo mode of performance. Yet this is the organizing principle adopted in the *Cambridge History,* though the system also takes account of chronology. It does not reflect the different dialects in which the poems were written, their social uses, their provenance, or their subject matters, though we must admit that if we used these criteria, we would find it no less difficult to group the poems in historically meaningful ways.

The system in the *Cambridge History* is essentially the same
as the first classification of these poets, which was made by
Alexandrian grammarians in the third century B.C. They divided the poets of two to four centuries earlier into those who
wrote in elegiac meter, those in iambic meter, and "lyric"
poets (a term they invented) who wrote in stanzas. The "Alexandrian canon" was widely known in the ancient world and
descended through the Middle Ages and the Renaissance.[10]
When the first works that we would recognize as literary histories were composed in the eighteenth century, they naturally
adopted the Alexandrian scheme of classification. An example
is the course of lectures given at Halle in the 1780s by F. A.
Wolf, the famous scholar and teacher whose *Prolegomena ad
Homerum* (1795) first raised the "Homer question." In his lectures Wolf discussed the melic (lyric), iambic, and elegiac
poets separately, and within each classification he followed
chronological order. He frankly admitted that "it cannot and
should not be avoided that a later author is mentioned before
an earlier one in a different genre."[11]

Interesting early attempts to break away from the Alexandrian scheme of classification were made by Herder in his essay on "Alcaeus und Sappho" (1795) and by Friedrich Schlegel in "Von der Schulen der Griechen und Römer" (1798).
They strove to create a taxonomy based on periods and
schools. Herder distinguished a first period of Greek poetry
characterized by epic and elegy and a second period of poetry
of the type associated with Lesbos, the poetry of Alcaeus and
Sappho. Schlegel attempted to make the different Greek tribes
the basis of a taxonomy and described an Ionian school, a Do-
rian school, and so forth. In *Geschichte der Hellenischen
Dichtkunst* (1838–39), G. H. Bode attempted to carry out
Schlegel's idea in detail, making racial stock (*Volk*) the leading
theme of his taxonomy. But this and similar attempts shattered

10. Weisstein, *Comparative Literature*, pp. 111, 120, summarizes the history of this taxonomy in the ancient world, though his information differs
slightly from mine.

11. Friedrich August Wolf, *Vorlesungen über die Altertumswissenschaft*,
ed. J. D. Gurtler and S. F. W. Hoffman. Vol. II: *Vorlesungen über die Geschichte der griechischen Literatur*, ed. J. D. Gurtler (Leipzig, 1839), p. 111.

on their own historical inaccuracy and internal inconsistency,
and the hundreds of literary histories of Greece in the nineteenth century generally reverted to the Alexandrian classification, deploying four categories in two pairs: elegiac and iambic verse, choral and solo lyric.

Of course, classical literary historians argued that versification was regularly associated with other significant features,
thus making their taxonomies seem less arbitrary. K. O.
Müller, for example, maintained that "the Greek poets always
chose their verse with the nicest attention to the feelings to be
conveyed by the poem."[12] But his further exposition showed
that Greek elegiac verses might express a great range of feelings—warlike, erotic, political, convivial, or lamenting. Müller
was thus compelled to seek for other "essential" features
shared by poems in elegiac meter. These were, he said, strong
emotion, "honest and straightforward expression," and a social use: elegies were sung at banquets.[13] In his *Grundriss der
Griechischen Litteratur* (Halle: 1836–45) Gottfried Bernhardy,
who regarded Müller as superficial, sought to correlate verses
in elegiac meter with the racial characteristics of the Ionian
Volk that created the meter and with the historical emergence
of individual self-consciousness. We need not follow these arguments in detail in order to see that the ancient classification
by meter is causing embarrassments. Yet as late as 1929 the
authoritative Schmid-Stählin asserted that "the division according to *literary genres* . . . corresponds for the most part
with the division according to racial stocks and dialects,"[14] a
point that is denied by the 1985 *Cambridge History*.[15]

Thus a dubious scheme of classification has lasted for more
than two thousand years. We might argue that classical schol-

12. K. O. Müller and John William Donaldson, *A History of the Literature of Ancient Greece* (London, 1858), I, pp. 142, 147.

13. Müller and Donaldson, *A History*, I, p. 147.

14. Wilhelm Schmid and Otto Stählin, *Geschichte der Griechischen Lit-
eratur, Erster Teil: Die Klassische periode der griechischen Literatur*. Vol.
I: *Die griechische Literatur vor der attischen Hegemonie* (München: C. H.
Beck'sche Verlagsbuchhandlung, 1929), VII, i., i., 9.

15. *The Cambridge History of Classical Literature*. Vol. 1, *Greek Literature*, ed. P. E. Easterling and B. M. W. Knox (Cambridge: Cambridge University Press, 1985), p. 158.

arship is a special case. Not many people can be involved. The issues are remote from the interests of the present. Yet the grip of tradition is powerful in all cases.

As we write literary histories, a scheme of classification is usually in existence already, as was true for F. A. Wolf and all his successors. If literary historians think about existing classifications, they have already thought with them. The classification is prior, in a sense, to the literature it classifies, for it organizes perceptions of the literature. The validity of the classification confirms itself every time the texts are read, for the classification signals what to look for and therefore predetermines, in some degree, what will be observed.

Imprinted taxonomies are also resistant to change for the simple reason that the number of ideas one has time and occasion to consider and correct is small in comparison to the total number of ideas one harbors. The content of anyone's mind consists mostly of received ideas, including the traditional taxonomies. It takes, to repeat, so much more energy, so much more knowledge and reflection, to disturb the received system than to accept and apply it, that anyone can revise it at only a few points. Hence in any comprehensive literary history the main source of taxonomies will be cultural transmission. To these considerations we may add the conservative influence of the audience. To the extent that readers already know the traditional taxonomies, they expect them in literary histories. A literary historian who proposes different taxonomies must make an argument.

Finally, so far as it is a logical process, taxonomizing involves reasoning in a hermeneutic circle. A literary taxonomy includes a name (for example, modernism), a concept, and a canon of works subsumed under the concept. Reasoning goes from the concept to the canon, from the canon to the concept. Both may be modified, but before the process can start, they must be given. In most cases they are given by tradition, that is, by a previous, already existing classification of these texts. Very large modifications may take place over time, but the process can never completely transcend its beginnings.

In one respect, however, the *Cambridge History of Classical Literature* differs from all previous classifications of ancient Greek lyric. It includes a category of Women Poets. That the reasons are political and ideological is the more obvious because the category has little ground otherwise, few verses by women poets having survived. (The women poets do not include Sappho, who is discussed under a different category, but Corinna, Myrtis, Telesilla, and Praxilla.) This illustrates how quickly and sharply even the most traditional taxonomies are revised if present interests are involved. The history of literary taxonomies might be written, *à la* Foucault, in terms of repression and of protest against it, of the struggle for power in the competition of discourses and literary historians.

I come now to taxonomies formed on the basis of what we may call "external facts"—facts external to the texts themselves. Unlike taxonomies derived from tradition, these presuppose and require positivistic literary scholarship. We may discover, for example, that authors felt affinities with certain of their contemporaries, or even viewed and presented themselves as members of a group in manifestoes, journals, joint publications, anthologies, and the like. To classify them together reflects their own self-understanding and, usually, the perceptions of their contemporaries. It was natural for contemporaries to associate Wordsworth and Coleridge, since they published a joint volume of poems (the *Lyrical Ballads*), and introduced it with a Preface stating their shared views on poetry—at least, they were interpreted as shared views at the time. Moreover, Wordsworth and Coleridge were known to be friends, and Coleridge frequently praised Wordsworth's poetry. It was also reasonable to group Robert Southey with them, since Coleridge and Southey were brothers-in-law and shared the same house. Since all three poets lived within twenty miles of each other in the Lake District of England, they were known as the Lake School. These facts and many others, plus the mere effect of grouping them together, caused a presumption that their poems were similar in style, theme, and Weltanschauung, and similarities were found. The Lake School has interestingly lapsed as a taxonomic term, but Wordsworth and Coleridge are still closely associated in the mind of every reader.

Somewhat similar observations could be made about the Bloomsbury group, the Pre-Raphaelites, the Georgian poets, the Imagists, the association of Eliot with Pound, of Addison with Steele, and many others. Groups of writers may also feel themselves to be united by the influence of the same predecessor or contemporary. The poets of the Auden Group in the 1930s are an example, and so are the poets of the Black Mountain School in relation to Pound and the Sons of Ben in relation to Jonson. In all these cases the taxonomy has become a part of cultural tradition, but it was, to repeat, grounded at first in affinities that the authors and their contemporaries asserted. Generally we do not know about these contemporary perceptions from reading literary texts, but, instead, from ancillary documents, such as letters, manifestoes, and critical essays.

When in 1960 Donald Allen brought out his anthology of *The New American Poetry,* the poets he wished to include were little known. As he said in his Preface, the field was "almost completely uncharted."[16] Yet in presenting his poets, he wished to divide them into groups. Like every thoughtful taxonomer, he knew that his divisions were "somewhat arbitrary," but he thought that classifications were necessary "to give the reader some sense of milieu and to make the anthology more a readable book and less still another collection of 'anthology pieces.'"[17] In order to classify, he relied mainly on "external facts." He made one group out of persons who had published in the same journals, namely, *Origin* and *Black Mountain Review;* several of them had also taught or studied at Black Mountain College. Geography partly determined other groups: the San Francisco Renaissance, the New York Poets. Many of the poets in each group were personally acquainted with others in the group. For example, "John Ashbery, Kenneth Koch, and Frank O'Hara, of the fourth group, the New York poets, first met at Harvard where they were associated with the Poets' Theatre. They migrated to New York in the early fifties where they met Edward Field, Barbara Guest, and James Schuyler, and worked with the Living Theatre and the Artists Theatre."[18]

16. Donald M. Allen, ed., *The New American Poetry* (New York: Grove Press, 1960), p. xiv.

17. Allen, *The New American Poetry,* pp. xii–xiii.

18. Allen, *The New American Poetry,* p. xiii.

Another anthologist, selecting a different set of "external facts," would possibly have produced a different system of taxonomy. Yet Allen's classifications lasted. We talked for many years of Black Mountain Poets, San Francisco Poets, and New York Poets. To some extent we still do. The fact may testify to some virtue of Allen's classification, but it certainly illustrates the inertia of cultural transmission. Once Allen had made his classifications, they organized contemporary poetry for other readers and critics. This taxonomy was now a part of cultural tradition, and any retaxonomizing of the same poets would be done on the basis Allen had provided.

To classify by observing similarities and differences between texts is, as I said, very uncommon in literary histories. More exactly, such observation is frequent enough, but it is used to confirm classifications that have been obtained initially in some other way. Observation and comparison of texts are almost never the *sole* basis of a taxonomy. One sees why if one considers how vulnerable such procedures are to criticisms of the Crocean type. Since texts have innumerable aspects, they can be linked to innumerable other texts with which they share one or a few aspects, though otherwise the texts thus linked may be quite unlike. If, in other words, we chose only a few aspects as the basis of our classification, addressed only one or a few questions to literary works (for example, does it have fourteen lines? does it have a happy ending?), and proceeded rigorously, we would make strange collocations, would group texts that we felt, intuitively, did not belong together. And the attempt to classify on the basis of *all* textual aspects would be hopeless. We could not discriminate them in one text, or compare them with all the aspects of another text. If we decided to classify by means of a set of "significant" aspects, we would have to justify our criteria of significance.

Wittgenstein's famous remarks on "family resemblance" are relevant to these dilemmas but do not resolve them.[19] When we

19. Wittgenstein's metaphor is adopted by Alastair Fowler in *Kinds of Literature: An Introduction to the Theory of Genres and Modes* (Cambridge, Mass.: Harvard University Press, 1982), p. 41, to explain the way in which different works in a genre are interrelated. Fowler's use of this metaphor is criticized by Earl Miner, "Some Issues of Literary 'Species, or Distinct Kind,'" in Lewalski, ed., *Renaissance Genres*, pp. 23–25.

align a number of instances under the same concept, the reason is not, Wittgenstein says, because they share an "essence," but because of "a complicated network of similarities overlapping and criss-crossing: sometimes overall similarities, sometimes similarities of detail."[20] Texts are grouped together when they exhibit a number of features that belong to the set, even if they also have anomalous features. But as Wittgenstein clearly says, before we look for "family resemblance," we assume there is a "family": "Don't look for similarities in order to justify a concept, but also for connections. The father transmits his name to his son even if the latter is quite unlike him."[21] In other words, the taxonomy is prior to our observation and comparison of individuals, and is based on "external facts" of filiation.

Yet occasionally a naive literary historian will attempt to classify texts merely by observing similarities, and the attempts illustrate the difficulties. We may cite a passage from Allardyce Nicoll's *British Drama,* where he classifies some obscure plays written between 1550 and 1575.[22] He begins with dramas in "tragicomic" form, of which there are, he says, three subvarieties. "Moral interludes," the first subtype, include "abstractly named characters," much "farcical-comic business," and a Vice as a central figure. The "second group of plays shows the mixture of the serious and the comic in another way." Though "the plots are for the most part taken from classical sources," the "influence of the morality tradition is apparent." The style is "romantic." And so forth. The third group exploits conventions of chivalric romance. In connection with each subvariety Nicoll lists examples and discusses one play as a paradigm.

Classification is necessary for Nicoll's project, since he lacks space to discuss each play individually and, moreover, wishes to generalize. No one has classified this particular col-

20. Ludwig Wittgenstein, *Philosophical Investigations,* trans. G. E. M. Anscombe (Oxford: Basil Blackwell, 1968), p. 32.

21. Ludwig Wittgenstein, *Remarks on the Philosophy of Psychology,* ed. G. E. M. Anscombe and G. H. von Wright, trans. G. E. M. Anscombe (Oxford: Basil Blackwell, 1980), I, p. 923.

22. Allardyce Nicoll, *British Drama,* 5th ed. (New York: Barnes and Noble, 1963), pp. 61–66.

lection of plays before, though Nicoll is, of course, furnished with a fund of concepts, such as "morality play" and "chivalric romance," that he can apply. Armed with these, he observes the plays and tries to determine which ones most resemble which other ones. The taxonomy he makes does not reflect points of view that were current in the period he is discussing, that is, the playwrights he groups together did not have a special sense of belonging together, neither did these groups exist for their contemporaries. Yet Nicoll does not suppose, I imagine, that his categories are merely conveniences of exposition, as Croce would have maintained, but feels that they are objectively grounded in characteristics of the plays themselves, in differences and resemblances anybody may observe.

Yet it seems clear that other scholars using the same methods would have created different—probably very different—taxonomies. To show this, it is only necessary to point out that Nicoll's are unconvincing. The three groups are not clearly distinguished from each other. The first are "moral interludes," and plays in the second group show "the influence of the morality tradition." Obviously many plays might go into either group. The second group is "romantic" in style; the third exploits the conventions of chivalric romance. The criteria Nicoll uses to taxonomize are of different kinds. Some refer to subject matter ("chivalric romance," "classical sources"), some to types of character (the Vice), some to stage techniques ("farcical-comic business"). Obviously Nicoll is simply picking out whatever characteristics happen to strike him, and a different reader would be struck by different characteristics. Nicoll's classification is subjective and arbitrary.

Classification of texts into genres relies on a combination of observation and positivistic scholarship producing relevant external facts, and it also relies heavily on inference. We may follow Alastair Fowler, for example, as he argues that during the Renaissance the genre of georgic poetry flourished in England.[23] He cites Rosalie Colie, who maintains that a Renaissance genre evokes a system of values, a "set of interpreta-

23. Alastair Fowler, "The Beginnings of English Georgic," in Lewalski, ed., *Renaissance Genres*, pp. 105–125.

tions" or "fixes" on the world.[24] Referring to Renaissance books on gardening and to the work ethic of the Protestant reformers, Fowler argues that the climate of opinion was favorable to the georgic ethos. He says there was enthusiasm for model poems—Hesiod and Virgil's *Georgics*. He consults the conceptions of the genre in Renaissance critical writings. From all this he extrapolates "the idea of georgic" around 1600;[25] in other words, he decides how a reader would have recognized a georgic and what expectations that recognition would have activated. He instances many poems that by this idea are georgic or partly georgic, though he does not cite any reader who actually recognized one of them as such. Thus in dealing with genres, as with any taxonomy, the literary historian must establish a canon (what texts belong to the genre) and a concept. Both the canon and the concept are always more or less indefinite (Fowler says that the Renaissance conception of georgic was "unfocused").[26] Because it depends so heavily on inferences of the literary historian, the description of a genre may be no less creative or constructive than the writing of literary history is generally.

In his *Restoration Tragedy* Eric Rothstein is inclined to settle his canon by a bold stroke highly characteristic of this scholar. A play is a tragedy, he declares, if it says so on the title page. But he at once adds, or if it is "quite similar in form and tone to those that are labeled 'tragedy,'" thus reintroducing the interpretive, constructive process that he wants to avoid.[27] For how does Rothstein know which features of the plays labeled tragedy were actually criteria of tragedy and which were irrelevant to this question? To make this judgment he must first know the Restoration concept of tragedy. But Rothstein's excellent chapter on "Tragic Theory in the Restoration" shows that many and opposing ideas of tragedy were entertained. He has to compare the ideas, not always self-

---

24. Colie, *The Resources of Kind*, p. 8.

25. Fowler, "The Beginnings," p. 111.

26. Fowler, "The Beginnings," p. 109.

27. Eric Rothstein, *Restoration Tragedy: Form and the Process of Change* (Madison: University of Wisconsin Press, 1967), p. ix.

consistent, of Rymer, Dryden, Dennis, Filmer, Rowe, Rapin, and others, in order to produce a relatively unified concept (which is, of course, required) that actually belonged to no one in the period. Pondering at length a closely similar problem in the *Origin of German Tragic Drama,* Walter Benjamin decides that positivistic methods of taxonomy lead inevitably to a vortex of skepticism. Classification must proceed from the "perception of a higher order than is offered by the point of view of a scholarly verism."[28] He argues that "tragic drama" (*Trauerspiel*) is an idea, an original essence, and, as such, exists independently of the texts that manifest it. Benjamin recognizes, however, that his resort to idealist metaphysics is a desperate move. He can see no other solution.

Of course, a literary classification is usually derived not by one procedure but by several at once. Tradition, present interests, self-classifications of authors, views of contempories, and observed features of texts may all play a role. In *The Norton Anthology of English Literature* Robert Adams says, "One may well think of the metaphysical poets who followed Donne (Herbert, Crashaw, Vaughan, Cowley, Cleveland) as trying to draw out the traditional lyric of love and devotion by stretching it . . . to encompass new unities . . . In the opposite direction, Jonson and his 'sons' the Cavalier poets (Carew, Herrick, Suckling, Waller, Davenant) generally tried to compress and limit their poems, giving them a high finish."[29] In this typical example poets are divided into two schools; the poets of each school are listed; and rudimentary conceptualizations of each category are suggested. The taxonomy is traditional, but it is also grounded in affinities the poets asserted. And Adams maintains that each group had its own repertoire of thematic and/or stylistic characteristics.

Finally, taxonomies are also determined by the logical and aesthetic requirements of the literary history. In the simplest

28. Walter Benjamin, *Ursprung des deutschen Trauerspiels,* ed. Rolf Tiedemann (Frankfurt am Main: Suhrkamp Verlag, 1963), p. 25.

29. Robert W. Adams, "The Seventeenth Century (1603–1660)," *The Norton Anthology of English Literature,* 4th ed., ed. M. H. Abrams et al. (New York: Norton, 1979), p. 1053.

instances the literary historian attempts to organize classifications into an elegant system or structure. The groups of authors or texts are configured according to logical patterns of
simple antithesis, dialectic, part/whole, and so on. This is the
impulse behind the formerly common periodizations in *Geistesgeschichte* that, for example, defined the eighteenth century as The Age of Reason, and interrelated all eighteenth-
century texts as particular moments of this general quality.
The Romantic period might then be the age of imagination and
feeling, to be succeeded by the era of Realism. R. S. Crane,
who comments at some length on this feature of literary histories, cites as an example "Louis Cazamian's account of English literature from 1660 to the present, in which the literary
evolution is plotted in terms of a necessary alteration of phases
dominated by intelligence with phases dominated by imagination and feeling."[30] The logical interrelation of the concepts
presents the succession of periods as not only historical but
also intelligible. In other words, on the basis of the conceptual
relationships the historian elaborates a scheme of historical
change as simple reaction, dialectical process, cyclic alternation, or whatever.

Aesthetic considerations are a much more extensive, various, and complicated factor in literary classification than has
yet been realized. I have space to consider only one example.
In *Fin-de-Siècle Vienna* Carl Schorske groups together two
young Viennese writers, Leopold von Andrian and Hugo von
Hofmannsthal. His ostensible reasons for linking them are that
they were friends, belonged to the same artistic circle, came
from the same social class, and shared the same artistic "mission."[31]

While he classifies them together, Schorske also argues—
and this is an all-important move—that Andrian and Hofmannsthal are representative. Schorske compares them (im-

---

30. Crane, *Critical and Historical Principles,* p. 32. The work to which
Crane refers is Cazamian's portion of Emile Legouis and Louis Cazamian,
A History of English Literature (New York: Macmillan, 1926–27).

31. Carl Schorske, *Fin-de-Siècle Vienna* (New York: Alfred A. Knopf,
1980), pp. 303–304.

plicitly) with their contemporaries, and asserts that their family background and shared ideology were characteristic of their time, place, and generation. They belonged to what Edward Wechssler calls an *Altersgenossenschaft*,[32] and shared, Schorske says, "the values and spiritual problems of the young generation of the 1890s."

According to Schorske these authors were Aesthetes. This is, in fact, a traditional classification of their work in the 1890s. Once he has the concept (Aestheticism) and the texts (writings of Andrian and Hofmannsthal) in mind, Schorske can reason in a hermeneutic circle. As a literary movement Aestheticism was, Schorske says, not created in Austria but in France, England, and Belgium. Moreover, he assumes that his readers are more familiar with Aestheticism in its French or its Pre-Raphaelite forms. Hence he derives the content of the concept from accepted exemplars of Aestheticism in England, France, and Belgium, and applies it to the writings of Andrian and Hofmannsthal. As he goes back and forth between the foreign concept and the Austrian writings, he points out discrepancies, and thus he defines an Austrian Aestheticism. (He can generalize from Andrian and Hofmannsthal to Austrian literary culture because he has said that they are typical of Austrian writers of their generation.) The description of Austrian Aestheticism has been Schorske's goal all along.

Andrian and Hofmannsthal are models of Austrian Aestheticism, it turns out, because this concept is modeled on them. If Schorske had such other Austrian Aesthetes of the 1890s as Richard Beer-Hofmann or Felix Dörmann in mind, his description of Austrian Aestheticism would be different. Similarly his description of English Aestheticism is framed in terms of William Morris and the Pre-Raphaelites, and if Schorske had Swinburne and Wilde in mind, he could not maintain, as he does, that English Aesthetes were "engaged" in their society. His reasoning is controlled throughout by the examples he has chosen.

32. Edward Wechssler, *Die Generation als Jugendreihe und ihr Kampf um die Denkform* (Leipzig: Quelle und Meyer, 1930).

It becomes important, therefore, to know why he chose Andrian and Hofmannsthal as his examples, and the reason is a formal one. The theme of Schorske's chapter is the image of the garden in Austrian literature, and in writings of Andrian and Hofmannsthal this image is more powerful and elaborated than in other Austrian writers of the time. The coherence Schorske seeks to give his chapter dictates his use of Andrian and Hofmannsthal as examples, and the examples, as I said, shape his concept of Austrian Aestheticism. Thus Schorske's taxonomy is determined by the aesthetic requirements of his own work.

Literary classifications have generally been constructed by an intuitive synthesis of multiple considerations. Few literary historians have reflected upon the processes by which they obtained their classifications. They have worked naively and *ad hoc,* often without a distinct consciousness of the basis of their classification, whether it was received opinion, readings of the texts, narrative or aesthetic necessity, their own interests, or a combination of these and others. Almost never have literary historians asked themselves what considerations ought to be the basis of classifications. With rare exceptions, such as Benjamin, they have stopped at vague remarks to the effect that all classifications are unsatisfactory, a truth that does nothing to clarify which might be more acceptable, which less, and by what criteria. Such innocence is no longer possible. Literary historians may continue to classify by the same procedures and reasons as in the past. But they will have to reflect on their moves, and they will have to justify them specifically in their histories.

JOHN PAUL RUSSO

Antihistoricism in Benedetto Croce and I. A. Richards

My mind inclines to the concrete.
   De Sanctis

The idealist attack on science, the revolt against historicism, the neo-Kantian concern for values and human purpose in history: this forms the intellectual background of Benedetto Croce's *Aesthetics* (*Estetica*; 1902). A book with multiple valences, it is essentially a defense of poetry in the form of a dispute with literary history as it was practiced at the turn of the century. For several generations, with an exclusionary zeal, it defined how a particular line of defense might proceed. Although I. A. Richards did not acknowledge the common purpose, his *Principles of Literary Criticism* (1924) and *Practical Criticism* (1929) advance from positions that Croce had already secured. Moreover, Croce's ideal of a new literary history concerns what he called the "aesthetic" as opposed to the "practical" personality; it is text-oriented and essayistic or monographic in form; it denies the separation of literary history and criticism; it takes into account the literary historian's own immersion in history in the selection and prosecution of the task. Only Croce's explicatory tools were weak in comparison to Richards's. Thus in such works as *Coleridge on Imagination* (1934) and *Beyond* (1974), Richards comes closer than Croce himself to realizing this program.

   In *Estetica* Croce made it his mission to rescue aesthetics and the work of art from positivism, psychologism, sociology,

268

rhetoric, philology, and literary history itself.[1] Taine had valued scientific method to the extent that he could say "personal taste has no value whatever" (*A*, 393); yet Croce found his method contaminated by rhetorical theory and moralism, and by "definitions and doctrines" of the "wildest" thinkers (*A*, 392). Brunetière mistakenly framed his treatment of the literary genres in terms of an "evolution of kinds" (*A*, 449).[2] Spencer, "the greatest positivist of his day," made a "hotchpotch" of materialist, idealist, utilitarian, and aesthetic criteria (*A*, 388). For Croce, "aesthetic knowledge" and the "individuality" of the work of art (*A*, 17, 28) had been sacrificed to the search for origins (in psychology, society, race, other literary works) and to positivist methods by which "every mean little copier of a text, or collector of variants, or examiner of the

1. Abbreviations of works by Benedetto Croce cited in the text and notes are as follows: *A, Aesthetic as Science of Expression and General Linguistic* [*Estetica*], Douglas Ainslie, trans. (1902; New York: Noonday Press, 1964); *Au, An Autobiography*, R. G. Collingwood, trans. (Oxford: Clarendon Press, 1927); *DP, The Defence of Poetry: Variations on the Theme of Shelley*, E. F. Carritt, trans. (Oxford: Clarendon Press, 1933); *EL, European Literature in the Nineteenth Century*, Douglas Ainslie, trans. (1922; New York: Chapman and Hall, 1924); *GA, Guide to Aesthetics* (*Breviario di estetica*), Patrick Romanell, trans. (1912; New York: Library of Liberal Arts, 1965); *H, History: Its Theory and Practice*, Douglas Ainslie, trans. (1917; New York: Harcourt, Brace, 1921); *L, Logic as the Science of the Pure Concept*, Douglas Ainslie, trans. (1909; London: Macmillan, 1917); *PD, The Poetry of Dante*, Douglas Ainslie, trans. (New York: Holt, Rinehart and Winston, 1922); *PE, Problemi di estetica* (Bari: Laterza, 1910); *PL, Poetry and Literature: An Introduction to Its Criticism and History*, Giovanni Gullace, trans. (1936; Carbondale and Edwardsville: Southern Illinois University Press, 1981); *PPH, Philosophy, Poetry, History: An Anthology of Essays*, Cecil Sprigge, trans. (1951; London: Oxford University Press, 1966); *PS, Primi Saggi* (Bari: Laterza, 1919). Hereafter abbreviations and page references are enclosed in parentheses and follow citations.

2. Taine wanted to demonstrate that the "great laws governing the genera or species in nature are the same as those governing the literary genres." Brunetière, quoted in Giovanni Gullace, *Taine and Brunetière on Criticism* (Lawrence, Kan.: Coronado Press, 1982), p. 21. "The closer the work is to the point of perfection of the genre, the higher it is placed in the scale of literary values. Thus the *moment* will decide the value of a work of art. This will eliminate the individual as a judge of the work and will establish 'history' (that of the genre) as an objective literary judge" (p. 94).

relations of texts . . . raised himself to the level of a scientific man" (*H*, 293). Also lost were taste, value judgment, and the humanistic component. "Pseudo-scientific haughtiness diffused itself from Germany over the other European countries, and has now reached America, though in other countries than Germany it met more frequently with irreverent spirits, who laughed at it" (*H*, 293–294).

At issue in the "crisis of scientific reason" in prewar Europe were the nature of matter and time, the "conflictual plurality" of the subject, the "knowledge of the body," and the relation between the natural and human sciences.[3] In the latter category the problem was most serious in history. History stood "halfway between the humanities and the newly rising social sciences," writes Hayden White, and historians wavered "between the conviction that history was an art, an aspect of *belles lettres,* and the conviction that it was an empirical or possibly even a positivistic science."[4] By this time, too, the dominant school of literary method, German philology, had suffered a loss of purpose. "The view of antiquity as providing ideal standards for emulation could no longer be sustained," writes Hugh Lloyd-Jones on classical philology; "as the old classicists' picture of the ancient world became remoter, the afflatus that had set in motion the whole vast development became feebler. A dry and rigid positivism crept over the work of scholars." Outside Germany, the country "most affected" by German philology was Italy.[5]

3. Franco Rella, ed., *La critica freudiana* (Milan: Feltrinelli, 1977), p. 13. See also Andrew Arato, "The Neo-Idealist Defense of Subjectivity," *Telos* 21 (1974); *Crisi della ragione,* ed. Aldo Gargani (Turin: Einaudi, 1979), pp. 12–19; and Mary Hesse, *Revolutions and Reconstructions in the Philosophy of Science* (Brighton, Eng.: Harvester Press, 1980), pp. 167–186. In Croce's phrase, the "hard ice of positivism was beginning to melt" (*PS*, viii).

4. Hayden V. White, introduction to Carlo Antoni, *From History to Sociology: The Transition in German Historical Thinking* (Detroit: Wayne State University Press, 1959), p. xv.

5. Hugh Lloyd-Jones, introduction to Ulrich von Wilamowitz-Moellendorff, *History of Classical Scholarship,* trans. Alan Harris (1921; Baltimore: The Johns Hopkins University Press, 1982), p. xix.

In assailing the "superstitious cult" and "hypocrisy" (*A*, 391–392) of the sciences, Croce kept a sense of proportion. A place on the map had to be found for the scientific study of literature. In fact, he later came to regard the sciences dialectically as a "corrective reaction to the idealist metaphysics" of the previous generation.[6] Observing the same dialectic at work, one understands Croce's "Philosophy of the Spirit" (1902–1917) as a reaction to scientific positivism on the grounds of an *anti*metaphysical idealism. Yet Croce did not launch his critique of historicism primarily on behalf of idealist philosophy. "His thought is not a system," writes Raffaello Piccoli, "but a method"; his idealism, like Vico's, results from the "centering of [his] intellectual interests on the history of the human spirit."[7] Keeping science in its place, advancing his philosophical project, both served a larger goal. Croce adopted and to some extent renovated neo-Hegelianism to bring about a cultural renewal in which the traditional humanistic subjects, history and poetry, might once again play the central educative role.[8] A new type of literary history would replace historicism.

At the outset of his career in 1919, I. A. Richards cleared the boards by attacking historicism, idealism, aestheticism, and other contemporary critical theories including Croce's

6. M. E. Moss, *Benedetto Croce Reconsidered: Truth and Error in Theories of Art, Literature, and History* (Hanover, N.H.: University Press of New England, 1987), p. 11. For Croce's toning down of his attack on the sciences, see *H* 49 and *A History of Italy, 1871–1915*, trans. Cecilia M. Ady (Oxford: Clarendon, 1929), pp. 141, 240 (quoted by Patrick Romanell in *GA*, xi).

7. Raffaello Piccoli, *Benedetto Croce: An Introduction to His Philosophy* (New York: Harcourt Brace, 1922), pp. vi, 40. Piccoli, a Fellow of Magdalene College, Cambridge, died at forty-seven in 1933. Also a Fellow, Richards wrote his obituary, with a Coledrigean note of compliment: "With him the idealism of Croce had become not a position but a power—something to be applied rather than expounded" (*Magdalene College Magazine* 10/3 [1933]: 65–67). For this information I am grateful to the late Uberto Limentani, Fellow of Magdalene College.

8. Martin Jay refers to Croce's "neo-Hegelian humanism" (*Marxism and Totality: Adventures of a Concept from Lukacs to Habermas* [Berkeley: University of California Press, 1984, p. 1952]).

expressionism.[9] Writing in the spirit of Cambridge realism, he rejected Croce's idealist premises and deplored his "great influence" (*C*, 14; *L* 209, 214) in England where disciples were joining idealist aesthetics to a commonsense logic. Since Richards's first tutor in philosophy at Cambridge was the neo-Hegelian J. M. E. McTaggart, he had a close knowledge of his adversary: "Croce is far too careful a philosopher for his readers to be able to pick and choose between the parts of his doctrine" (*C*, 14). "Doctrine" is Richards's negative word for an outmoded system either lacking empirical foundation or interfering with aesthetic response. Elsewhere Richards speaks of Croce's "dogmatic" and "voluminous" works (*FA*, 15). But Richards was hasty in his judgment. He was so offended by Croce's antipositivist theme that he overlooked his struggle against historicism and other forms of what would come to be called "extrinsic" criticism. Richards scarcely realized to what extent they shared a common goal.

The two thinkers also shared much common ground. In their instinctive habits of mind they were antimetaphysical, immanentist, secular, and liberal. If as idealist and positivist Croce and Richards stood at opposite ends of the spectrum, they frequently take the language of their respective philosophies to reject historical, moralistic, and sociological approaches to criticism, to support the principle of continuity between life

9. "Four Fermented Aesthetics," *Art and Letters* 2/4 ns (1919): 186–193, in *L* below. Abbreviations of works by I. A. Richards cited in the text and notes are as follows: *B*, *Beyond* (New York: Harcourt Brace Jovanovitch, 1974); *C*, *Complementarities: Uncollected Essays*, John Paul Russo, ed. (Cambridge, Mass. and London: Harvard University Press and Carcanet, 1976, 1977); *CI*, *Coleridge on Imagination* (London: Kegan Paul, 1934); *FA*, *The Foundations of Aesthetics* (1922: New York: International Publishers, 1929); *FP*, "The Future of Poetry" (1960), in *So Much Nearer: Essays towards a World English* (New York: Harcourt Brace, 1968); *IT*, *Interpretation in Teaching* (New York: Harcourt Brace, 1938); *L*, *Selected Letters*, ed. John Constable (Oxford: Clarendon, 1990); *MM*, *The Meaning of Meaning* (with C. K. Ogden) (London: Kegan Paul, 1923); *PC*, *Practical Criticism: A Study of Literary Judgment* (London: Kegan Paul, 1929); *PLC*, *Principles of Literary Criticism* (London: Kegan Paul, 1924); *PR*, *The Philosophy of Rhetoric* (New York: Oxford University Press, 1936); *SP*, *Science and Poetry* (London: Kegan Paul, 1926).

and art, and to affirm the unity of form and content and poetic autonomy (*GA*, 25; *CI*, 25).[10] Moreover, an idealist theme in Richards extends from his early absorption in the values of English Romanticism to his studies in Coleridge and Platonism. Both Croce and Richards maintain the division of science and poetry (or the prosaic from the poetic), *what a poem does* from *how it does it* (*A*, 26–27, *GA*, 59; *PLC*, 320, *C*, 231). Their linguistics is pervaded by organicism. Each thinker repudiates the traditional rhetorical principle by which the single word or phrase is the unit of discourse. Instead they value the contribution of the word to the contextual whole, which alone has meaning (*A*, 160; *CI*, 101, *PR*, 48). Croce's concept of language as "perpetual creation" (*A*, 150) and the "impossibility of normative grammar" (*A*, 147) adumbrate Richards on the "proper meaning of superstition" (*PR*, 11) and "doctrine" of correct usage (*IT*, 247–263). Richards did not acknowledge their agreement, twice citing Croce's definition of the sublime ("The sublime (or comic, tragic, humorous, etc.) is *everything* that is or shall be so *called* by those who have employed or shall employ these words" [*A*, 90]) as an example of an "irritant" where words evoke "emotions irrelevant to the determination of the referent" (*MM*, 240; *IT*, 247).[11] Both Croce and Richards reject totalizing principles that limit human freedom. One of Croce's major disagreements with Hegel concerns the teleology of the Absolute Spirit.[12] Richards accepts William James's open universe over the theory of preformation. Finally, Richards and Croce separate poetry from moralism, but share the humanistic concern for value judgment and moral choice (*PPL* 296–308; *CI*, 139–40). For Croce, art has a "liberating and purifying

10. Evan Watkins, *The Critical Act: Criticism and Community* (New Haven: Yale University Press, 1978), pp. 20, 45ff.

11. However, Croce was merely defining the term *sublime* as a "pseudo-concept" (what Richards calls a "fiction" or Word Magic [*MM*, ch. 2]), pretending to universal validity but possessing only an empirical and limited definition.

12. In his later career Croce looked upon his philosophy not so much as a "system," but as a "series of systematizations" (quoted in Piccoli, *Croce*, p. 274). Cf. Ruggiero Romano, *La storiografia italiana oggi* (Rome: L'espresso strumenti, 1978), pp. 50–51.

function" (*A* 21, 393); it frees the individual from private bias and local history into a recognition of common humanity. In the "most valuable aesthetic experiences," writes Richards, we do not respond "through one narrow channel of interest," but "simultaneously and coherently through many" (*PLC*, 251).

For seven years, after leaving the University of Rome in 1886, Croce did research in the drama, theater history, and memorials of old Naples. "I had left behind me the bitterness and passion of the Roman political circles and entered a society of librarians, keepers of archives, scholars, antiquarians, and such-like good, worthy, gentle souls . . . not much given to thinking" (*Au*, 45). Was history mere archival work? Did he not write so that the theater and monuments of his colorful city might come to life? Further study on the influence of Spain on Italy, the beginning of a history of Italy since the Renaissance, provoked a deeper dissatisfaction. As he felt—it is a common enough experience for any scholar—his mind was being stocked "with lifeless and disconnected facts at the expense of much toil and with no constructive result" (*Au*, 52).

Then in 1893, in a single day, Croce wrote his first theoretical essay, "History Subsumed under the General Concept of Art." He wanted to "to combat the *absorption* of history" by the natural sciences and to counter psychological hedonism (the so called "English aesthetic" of Spencer, Grant Allen, and Vernon Lee [*FA*, 50]) by asserting the concept of art as knowledge (*L*, 327). While the sciences establish the knowledge of general laws and concepts, he argues, they miss the vital individuality of the historical and literary fact. "In the presence of an object, the human mind can perform only two operations of knowledge. It can ask itself: what is it?, and it can represent to itself that object in its concreteness . . . Whenever we assume the particular under the general, we make science; whenever we represent the particular as such, we make art" (*PS*, 23). History is not art, but it may be placed "beneath the general concept of Art" (*L*, 327) because, like art, it concerns particulars. Aristotle said that history deals with the particular, but that art is "more serious and philosophical" because it contains the universal (*Poetics*, 9.4). For the young Croce, history and art deal with the particular, and the difference is that "art produces a *possible* reality" and "history produces a *factual* reality."[13] Croce never abandoned this distinction. As he elaborated his system, however, he came to think that history must avail itself of general concepts in some way, and that aesthetic knowledge possesses a universal element that becomes real in and through the particular.

According to Croce's "Philosophy of the Spirit," reality or life unfolds within or *as* human consciousness (free, spontaneous "spirit") in four *a priori* modes of activity: two theoretical and two practical. The theoretical modes are the intuitive (or aesthetic) and the logical (or conceptual): "Knowledge has two forms. It is either *intuitive* knowledge or *logical* knowledge; knowledge we acquire by the *imagination* or knowledge obtained through the *intellect;* knowledge of the *individual* or knowledge of the *universal;* of *individual things* or of the *relations* between them: it is, in fact, productive either of *images* or of *concepts*" (*A*, 1). The two practical modes of spiritual activity are the economic and the ethical. These four are "distinct," irreducible, and exhaustive. We either know particulars or universals or we act in our particular interest or in the universal interest. In Croce's four modes, one recognizes the beautiful, the true, and the good, to which he added the economic (or useful). The four modes compete against, combine with, are mediated by one another in present consciousness, as consciousness intuits imaginatively, or makes intellectual concepts, or acts self-interestedly or morally. Reality or Spirit is the plenum of individual "histories," though Croce does not believe in some metaphysical entity such as collective consciousness. Rather, the "whole spirit" is present "in every particular man and at every particular instant of life"—and changing "at every moment" (*L*, 377; 315). The sum total of these histories is the Spirit or History.

The fundamental unit of Croce's system is the intuition (*intuizione*). Croce's "intuition" differs markedly from the ordinary English meaning, the knowledge of self-evident truths or the understanding that comes by way of nonrational processes.

13. Gullace, in *PL*, xxi.

His term is closest to *Anschauung* ("a looking at"), the forming of the image or "representation" in consciousness, the
"immediate object, or product, of Imagination."[14] Richards begins construction of his empirical model with "sense" or "impulse." Croce treats sensations and impulses as if they were
brute matter by comparison to mind, outside the circle of consciousness, as yet un*form*ed and given meaning by "spirit." A
sensation is an *im*pression, not an *ex*pression, which is always
an active process of the mind: "By elaborating his impressions,
man *frees* himself from them" (*A*, 21).[15] Croce's examples of
intuition (which is both the process and its product) include "a
moonlight scene by a painter," "the outline of a country drawn
by a cartographer," a "musical motive," the "words of a sigh-
ing lyric" or those same words "in ordinary life" (*A*, 2); what
"individuals experience, suffer and desire" (*L*, 293–294).[16] Beginning with particulars, history and poetry stand in closest
proximity to "individuality" (*A*, 30), to "concreteness" (*H*,
39), to the "pure palpitation of life" (*PPH*, 216). "[Croce] used
the term [art] as Vico used it, that is to imply the first form of
knowledge, that closest to reality."[17]

The act of forming the image cannot be separated from the
something that is formed, the intuition from its expression. In
Croce the intuition *is* the expression: "That which does not
objectify itself in expression is not intuition or representation,
but sensation and mere natural fact. The spirit only intuits
in making, forming, expressing" (*A*, 8). We experience a

14. Gian N. G. Orsini, *Benedetto Croce: Philosopher of Art and Literary
Critic* (Carbondale: Southern Illinois University Press, 1961), p. 33.

15. Orsini, *Benedetto Croce*, p. 128. "Activity is the deliverer, because
it drives away passivity" (*A*, 21). For Richards on idealism, materialism,
and sensation, see *CI*, 54.

16. A broad category that includes both ordinary perception and aesthetic perception, intuition is "the undifferentiated unity of the perception
of the real and of the simple image of the possible" (*A*, 4); the distinction
between the empirically real and the imaginatively nonreal is "extraneous."
Perception is the "knowledge of actual reality, the apprehension of something as *real*" (*A*, 3). Homer's gods are "real" as intuitions, not as perceptions.

17. Edmund E. Jacobitti, *Revolutionary Humanism and Historicism in
Modern Italy* (New Haven: Yale University Press, 1981), p. 62.

confused state of mental impressions, prior to their being transformed into expression by a meaningful intention. The aesthetic intuition (or more accurately, intuition-expression) may be verbal or nonverbal ("line," "color," and "sound"), but it is always in the mind and not the object. The spirit or human consciousness is "more real" than its external products. "What is called *external* is no longer a work of art" (*A*, 51). Croce gives the example of Leonardo standing for days at a time before the unfinished *Last Supper,* and answering his impatient patron: "the minds of men of lofty genius are most active in invention when they are doing the least external work" (*A*, 10). Croce's prejudice against the "external medium" of art has serious consequences for his practical criticism.[18] Richards was extremely critical of Croce's "confusion" between value and communicative efficacy (*PLC*, 255) and compared it to Pater's.

Raw sensation is the lower limit of intuition; the upper limit is logical knowledge, the second mode of spiritual activity. This mode depends upon intuitions which, on the basis of the laws of thought, it conceptualizes and universalizes. Without images of experience, the logical mill would have no grain to grind, but the grain can exist without the mill.[19] The logical mode is occupied with the elaboration of pure concepts. *This* river, *this* lake, *this* bay—these are intuitions; the concept is water, a universal. To depict the difference between an intuition and a universal, Croce speaks of the use of maxims in a play. By themselves maxims are "concepts" aiming at universal application. In the mouth of a protagonist like Polonius, however, maxims function mainly to individualize, to characterize, to express a particular intuition (*A*, 2). In contrast to the pure concepts and the laws of thought, Croce posits "pseudo-concepts," which are useful "fictions" or "limited generalizations . . . made out of a few instances erected into

18. Wellek, *Benedetto Croce*, p. 10.
19. Similarly, the two practical modes depend upon the two theoretical modes. "Knowing is independent of doing save in so far as it is the condition of doing, but doing is dependent on knowing as its condition" (H. Wildon Carr, *The Philosophy of Benedetto Croce: The Problem of Art and History* [London: Macmillan, 1917], pp. 136–137).

general classes."[20] Philosophy is the domain of the pure concepts and their relations; the sciences work mainly with the pseudo-concepts and are classified under the third or economic mode of spiritual activity. This pragmatic view of science has a parallel in Richards's adoption of Percy Bridgman's operationalism and Niels Bohr's complementarity.

Armed with his concept of the presentness and particularity of intuition, Croce distinguishes his idea of history from various forms of historicism. "True history"—and literary history is a branch of history—is the synthesis of the intuitive and the logical modes of spiritual activity, and the exclusion of the economic and ethical modes. "History expresses itself with judgments, inseparable syntheses of individual and universal," where the individual is the subject of the judgment, and the universal is the predicate (*H*, 60). Ideally, the historian gathers the intuitions of individual facts, applies logical concepts to them, and narrates: hence, history is the "narration of individual reality" (*L*, 305). But Croce accuses contemporary historians of pretending to employ pure concepts when they are only using pseudo-concepts, of appearing to write "true history" when they are writing "pseudo-histories," that is, rhetorical history, moralistic history, patriotic and nationalist history, even "universal" history. (The vaster the canvas is, the more pronounced the bias inevitably becomes.[21]) In rhetorical pseudo-histories, the ethical mode converges upon the intuitive and logical modes in the historian's consciousness. Similarly, in poetical history, a hedonistic or pedagogic "extrinsic end" is assigned to poetry (*H*, 42). One or two generations normally suffice to prove the limitations of pseudo-histories: they show evidentiary incompleteness, misinterpretation of

20. Carr, *Benedetto Croce*, p. 88; Orsini, *Benedetto Croce*, p. 112.

21. "It is true that conformably to certain industrial ways of thought which have crept into intellectual life, there is an expectation (but it is as vain as Noah's expectation of the return of the raven) of a new history of national art and letters, or of a new history of international artistic time-periods, or indeed of a new universal art history, to be generated out of the multiplicity of such essays and monographs. But in truth the romantic ideal of a general, national, or universal history now survives solely as an abstract ideal" (*PPH*, 349).

evidence, conscious or unconscious bias; they are constantly being "out-dated"; there is always a new spirit of the age. "Sociological or general histories of art and letters" may have a certain usefulness as reference guides, "aid to memory," or "education of the unlearned." Yet they lack "true intellectual inspiration or originality" and ought to be called "handbooks or manuals" (*PPH*, 349). In pseudo-history a fact can be "*correct*" or "*certain*" by convention or even an empirical test, but not "*true*" (*H*, 27–29). What, then, is true history?

True history brings to life sources, documents, and narratives, which otherwise remain as chronicle. "History is living chronicle, chronicle is dead history"; "history is an act of thought, chronicle is an act of will" (*H*, 19). Centuries may be neglected by historians, with documents and works of art slumbering as chronicle, before some present concern stirs an interest and they are given new meaning and purpose. Renaissance and Enlightenment historians skipped over the Dark Ages before Romantic historians revived them. "*First comes history, then chronicle,* then history again in a contemporary reader" (*H*, 20). Without the middle stage, there can be no revival and hence the importance of documentation, textual accuracy, and so forth. Nonetheless the vehicle of "reanimation" is the historical intuition. Metaphors of life and death— as everywhere in Croce—underscore the opposition. History is always "*of life*"; "proper commemoration of the dead is the knowledge of what they did in life, of what they produced that is working in us" (*H*, 92). By contrast Croce deplores the "cold indifference" of philological history (*H*, 30, 34, 36). Croce cites a monk writing at the turn of the first millennium in Monte Cassino: "1001. *Beatus Dominic migravit ad Christum*. 1002. *Hoc anno venerunt Saraceni super Capuam*. 1004. *Terremotus ingens hunc montem exagitavit*." The monk who wrote it must have grieved the loss of Brother Dominic who "migrated towards Christ," must have feared the wanton destruction of the Saracens above nearby Capua and the convulsions of an earthquake (*H*, 19). This is true history. Other monks may have felt nothing but their cold fingers when they copied the document as chronicle. The young conspirator Boscoli, condemned to death for plotting against the Medici, complained

to Della Robbia, "Get Brutus out of my head!" because the
example of Plutarch's Brutus inflamed his passion for liberty
and brought him to the stake. This is Brutus as a moment of
rhetorical or "practicistical" history, not history "as thought,"
a true historical intuition (*H*, 43).

History and chronicle are the product of "two different spiritual *attitudes*" (*H*, 19). So crucial is the historian's attitude
with regard to subject matter that what is chronicle to others
may be history to us, when read "in our heart" for its fullest
human meaning. The narration of history "springs directly out
of life," is conditioned by the desire to research the past and
make that research "a present and not a past concern" (*PPH*,
498). As David Roberts remarks, "Croce was among the first
to insist that the historian is necessarily active and creative, on
the basis of a preexisting concern that in some sense 'pre-
figures the field.'"[22] At the moment, Croce admits, the Pelo-
ponnesian war, Mexican art, and Arabic philosophy hold no
interest for him. Hence "at this present moment" the histories
of these subjects are not histories at all, "but at the most simply titles of historical works. They have been or will be histories in those that have thought or will think them, and in me
too when I have thought or shall think them, re-elaborating
them according to my spiritual needs" (*H*, 13). These needs
arise in the same way that needs arise in other areas of life.
Now, Croce writes, Hellenic life is "present in me": "it solicits, it attracts and torments me, in the same way as the appearance of the adversary, of the loved one, or the beloved son
for whom one trembles" (*H*, 14).

The presentness and particularity of the historian's intuition
enshrines itself in Croce's celebrated paradox: "Every true
history is contemporary history" (*H*, 11). What is past is made
present and vital in the act of historical judgment and narration. In this way the past influences the present and the

22. David D. Roberts, *Benedetto Croce and the Uses of Historicism*
(Berkeley: University of California Press, 1987), p. 151. "For Croce, the
deepest purpose of humanistic education was to indicate this human responsibility and to establish the bases for affirmation and confidence"
(p. 351).

"spirit" grows upon itself, is a "continuous *surpassing of it-self*" (*L,* 319). True history stands forth as an ideal, since it is virtually impossible to eliminate the interference of the practical modes, personal bias, and error. As the attempt is made, one approaches true history, and Croce introduces "humanity" as a conceptual universal. "Catholics and Protestants, Revolutionaries and conservatives are . . . more in agreement than they were formerly; because something has passed and penetrated from each to each, or rather the *humanity,* which is in both, has become elevated" (*L,* 292). Likewise, we all agree that Aphrodite did not sleep with Anchises, that Romulus and Remus were not suckled by a wolf. The Catholic writers who insist on disputing the Immaculate Conception are as rare as those anticlericals who write "in little democratic journals of the inferior sort or of degraded taste" (*L,* 293).

The emphasis on the historian in whom history "lives" means inevitably that history must suffer the perils of life, too, and the greatest peril is the forgetfulness of chronicle. We are finite human beings, conditioned by our time and circumstance: "To forget one aspect of history and to remember another one is nothing but the rhythm of the life of the spirit, which operates by determining and individualizing itself, and by always rendering indeterminate and disindividualizing previous determinations and individualizations, in order to create others more copious. The spirit, so to speak, lives again its own history without those external things called narratives and documents; but those external things are instruments that it makes for itself, acts preparatory to that internal vital evocation in whose process they are resolved" (*H,* 25). The vertigo that accompanies futile attempts at "universal histories" and "definitive systems" (*H,* 62) should force us back to the finite, "the concrete, which is grasped by thought and which lends itself as a base for our existence and as point of departure for our action" (*H,* 53). One of the tensions in Croce's work is that he wants the historian to be deeply involved in his own historical situation and at the same time as free as possible from the practical modes. Historians should concentrate on a particular problem in the essay or monograph, not for the sake of increased specialization but because in that way alone can they capture "living, active history, *contemporary history*" (*H*, 53–54). In this respect, he is his own best example, as the premier historian of European liberty during the Fascist period.

Numerous implications for literary history follow from Croce's insistence on the presentness, particularity, and living quality of the intuition. The *pars destruens* of Croce's critical project extends from detecting interference from the three other modes to the abuse of pseudo-concepts such as periods, schools, meters, genres, and rhetorical ends. "To a great extent" writes Renato Barilli, "Croce's method is a subtracting procedure; one of the first operations he performs is precisely the clearing up of the field from the cumbersome layers of eloquence besetting any literary work."[23] In Croce's view, literary historians have failed to detect the "commingling" of the "pure intuition" with the other modes. In parts of the *Divine Comedy* Dante "was not, properly speaking, composing poetry" but an "ethico-polito-theological romance" (*PD*, 84). Even in the fifth canto of the *Inferno*, a passage of most intense lyricism, one discovers lines serving as "a small wooden bridge to cross from one green band to the other" (*PL*, 109). No one objects to this "conventional or structural aid" (*PPH*, 325). Still, it is not poetry.

Similarly unpoetic are the "informative and glossarial parts" of poems, plays, and novels, as well as descriptions of antecedent facts, reports of unseen events, epic genealogies, and the use of characters who function "to permit the progress of the action" and who do not "reach poetic intensity" (*PL*, 109). Although Tolstoy's philosophical commentaries in *War and Peace* "do not lack importance," they impair the "beautiful poetic movement" of the novel (*PL*, 151). The logical mode has intervened. Likewise Schiller, whom Croce reveres as a critic (*DP*, 4–5), is "always intellectualistic" in his poetry; as he grew older, he "did not lose the gift of imaginative spontaneity, which he had never possessed, nor the moral enthusiasm and the polemical energy, which he had possessed and retained" (*EL*, 35). Tasso's Catholic allegory in the *Gerusa-*

---

23. Renato Barilli, *Rhetoric*, trans. Giuliana Menozzi (Minneapolis: University of Minnesota Press, 1989), p. 101.

lemme liberata is "not something artistic" (*G*, 80) (in general, allegory is inorganic: "a sort of cryptography" [*PL*, 40]). Nor are Petrarch's scholastic "conceits" essentially poetic by comparison to his "lofty, graceful, melancholic verses" (*G*, 80). The Austrian censors inadvertently did Manzoni's poetry a favor when they cut "patriotic" stanzas from an ode in *Adelchi;* the passages belonged to the pragmatic modes (*PL*, 151). Leopardi's poetry suffers from a "prosaic tone" (*EL*, 124) and a "large amount of didacticism." In "Bruto" and the "Canto notturno," the poet interrogates his characters as a prosecutor would an accused: this is oration, not poetry. Metastasio and the Arcadians, baroque and eighteenth-century verse, is rhetoric and eloquence. At the same time Croce appreciates why Manzoni, who likewise deplored seventeenth-century rhetorical conceits as lacking real feeling, could say a "touch of rhetoric, 'discreet, subtle, tasteful,' is indispensable" (*PPH*, 299).[24]

The critic's primary task is to separate the poetry from the nonpoetry, that is, the residue of the three other modes, lesser poetry, "imperfections," or "the ugly" (*PL*, 103; *G*, 67). *Poesia e non poesia* (1923) is the title of one of Croce's books of essays. Its English title, *European Literature in the Nineteenth Century,* gives an entirely different impression.[25]

If the poet is not at fault in mixing the modes, the literary historians might be, as when they write on the occasion of poetry with their personal agenda foremost in mind. The poem ceases to be of poetic interest and becomes a vehicle of some other intention. Emphasis on the logical mode makes a poem

24. As Barilli remarks, "The danger is that poetry may become some kind of polarity at the limits, almost unattainable, almost unrealizable, never experienced as actually existing, if it is not accompanied by an inevitable dose of eloquence" (*Rhetoric*, p. 101).

25. The distinction between poetry and nonpoetry sometimes leads to serious lapses. "The *Odyssey* is a work of art, but not intrinsically of poetry"; the *Iliad* is "at the head of all great modern poetry, the *Odyssey* is an exquisite example . . . of the literature of travel and adventures" (*Poesia antica e moderna,* quoted in *PL*, lxx–lxxi). This, according to Giovanni Gullace, is because of "the rationality of its construction, the moral tone, the technical skill with which the work was carried out" (*PL*, lxxi).

into a document in the history of ideas. The practical mode appeals to utilitarian or political concerns. Moral ideals become uppermost in the minds of critics who permit the ethical mode to interfere with the intuitive mode. In every case, Croce thinks, the literary experience becomes infected with other ends. "Such work will redound to the benefit of the history of philosophical methods and ideas, of moral conflicts and social institutions. It will constitute a chapter in the history of philosophy, civilization, politics, but it will no longer be history of poetry and art as such" (*PPL*, 343). Croce notes how often, in contrast to excellent works of art, "mediocre," "wretched," or "bogus" works of art better serve the needs of historical documentation on account of "their greater nearness to practical life and to intellectual abstractions" (*PPL*, 343). "Intellectualistic" criticism measures the "advancements of art against the advancements of philosophy" (*G*, 75). Ariosto is weak because of a "weak" philosophy; Tasso is "strong" because of his stronger one. Eliot made this criticism of Shakespeare as opposed to Dante. But the question remains, does Croce subtract too much?

In opposition to current practice, Croce asserts that "any attempt at an aesthetic classification of the arts is absurd" (*A*, 114). He rejects the employment of the genres, schools, rhetorical tropes, meters, notions such as sophisticated versus folk poetry, categories of the sublime, the pathetic, and so on. They are "pseudo-concepts," useful perhaps for a given purpose, but more often than not standing between the reader and the text. Moreover, none of these concepts can ever decide a case between poetry and nonpoetry. "All the books dealing with classification and systems of the arts could be burned without any loss whatever" (*A*, 114). Vicenzo Monti's school "has little or no value, but that is only because all poetical schools have little or no value"; his verse lacks "feeling for real things" and inhabits "a corner of the world which is called 'literature'" (*EL*, 21, 27). In a late essay "Poetry, the Work of Truth: Literature, the Work of Civilization" (1948), Croce pays tribute to the mission of "literature" but leaves no doubt as to the higher calling. As for life-and-times biographies, the "advantages that the knowledge of the author's practical life offers to poetry do not amount to much" (*PL*, 163). (Richards would not have said it differently.) Worse still are the "frigid products of philology" (*H*, 30) conceived "as merely a learned *exercise*," "without connexion with life" (*H*, 33). Period histories are "mythological," understood in the "naturalistic" sense, except when the terms are "employed empirically—that is to say, when chronology is used in chroniclism and erudition in a legitimate manner" (*H*, 115). Reviewing Joel Spingarn's *Journal of Comparative Literature* in 1903, Croce writes that "these are merely erudite investigations, which in themselves do not make us understand a literary work and do not make us penetrate into the living core or artistic creation."[26] At the same time, he had no wish to discount gains made in historical method, which provides the "complementary knowledge" (*H*, 15) before the higher act of imaginative "re-creation."

These qualifications must be underscored. Lest Croce be accused of subjective relativism, he has a habit of giving back with one hand what he has taken with the other. He admits that classifications (periods, genres, poetic diction, meters) can be useful preparation. Readers may fail to understand a text "for want of subsidiary knowledge" or from "incompatibility of temperament," or "inattention" (*PPH*, 500). (Richards's *Practical Criticism* is primarily concerned with the analysis and removal of such obstacles.) If Croce disputes the value of the genres, he concedes that the distinction between heroic and love poetry may serve as an "empirical," "classificatory" device suitable in "fixing roughly the different features of the love poet Petrarch and of the ethico-religious poet Dante" (*PPH*, 331). Croce can be extremely harsh with the "dilettanti" of poetry who fail to apply themselves to the "nec-

26. René Wellek, *Four Critics: Croce, Valéry, Lukács, and Ingarden* (Seattle: University of Washington Press, 1981), p. 12. Comparing Carducci's tender "Era un giorno di festa" and Heine's ironical "impressions" on a similar event, Croce cautions: "Heine goes on to make merry over a lady confessing a long string of sins to a young friar. The narrator sees only, greedily, the fair one's hand. Bringing this page into relation with Carducci's poem, even in a note, goes against the grain—it seems a profanation, or worse. The page should be read at another time when in a mood for broad jokes" (*PL*, 960).

essary and often slow and painful philological preparation"
(*PL*, 121). "To listen to poetry's voice," he says, "it is necessary to get close to it, and philology prepares the way" (*PL*,
87). He agrees with Longinus, the "strongest critic," who said
that criticism is "extremely hard labor" (*PL*, 121).

The importance of historical erudition brings us to the *pars
costruens* of Croce's project. The critic first makes an "intuitive re-creation" of the motifs and feelings of the "artistic personality" in the poem (*PL*, 142). This readerly act tells that
"pure poetry" is a "rare flower" (*EL*, 364), that only a "few
dozen" poets of "universal humanity, its measure and its equi-
librium," remain out of "thousands" in the nineteenth century
(*EL*, 361).[27] It were better to say that literature only becomes
"poetic" when the poetic language has received sufficient "intensity" to permit re-creation of the pure intuition or "vision."[28] Significantly, Croce speaks of "lyrical intuition" after
1908, because a short lyric—or rather, the lyric impulse—is the
norm, though theoretically intuition can embrace an epic.

Following upon the intuition, the critic gradually builds up
an idea of the "individuality" of the work of art and the "aesthetic personality" behind it. Every author has a *characteristic*
(*caratteristica*): a specific "content," a "feeling" (*PL*, 142), a
"central motif, a character, an action, a situation or—to put it
more exactly—an emotion: the musician's motif, the painter's
macchia [patch], the architectural line."[29] The characteristic of
Ariosto is the clarified moment of "cosmic harmony," the
"movement of things in their emerging, conflicting, and coming again to a peaceful agreement" (*PL*, 142). The characteristic of D'Annunzio is a "dilettante of vital sensation"; the poetry fails in reaching for "spiritual interests." His "fierce
lustfulness" is pretentious—there is no lust, only narcissism—
and despite his large poetic endowment, his late work is repet-

27. Croce defends Carducci whose verse had not appealed to modern
taste (which lacks "ethical and aesthetic discipline"). Carducci is a "heroic
poet" who possesses "complete humanity"; "Battle, glory, song, love, joy,
melancholy, death, all the fundamental chords of humanity resound" in his
poetry (*EL*, 367).

28. Carr, *Benedetto Croce*, p. 181.

29. Quoted in Orsini, *Benedetto Croce*, p. 109.

itive and conveys "a sense of poverty, the poverty of a Midas" (*PPL*, 971). A characteristic is not a formula, warns Croce. In practice, however, formulae appear more or less "rigid and hard," and hence "after the momentary satisfaction, our discontent even with the most elaborated critical formulae, including our own, which have been produced through so much mental tension, brain work, and scrupulous delicacy" (*PL*, 143).

To write literary history it is not sufficient merely to experience the "intuitive re-evocation" (*PL*, 144). "Sensibility is an essential moment of criticism; but it is not criticism" (*PL*, 121). Crocian scholars point out that neoclassic critics deeply admired Shakespeare: their taste was excellent. Yet they accused Shakespeare of not observing the dramatic unities or mixing his metaphors or failing to mete out poetic justice. Their judgment was faulty and the literary history of Shakespeare suffers accordingly.[30] In other words, criticism differs from taste. With taste, one recreates the *subject,* the aesthetic personality and its movement of thought and feeling: the first mode of spiritual activity. With judgment, one adds the *predicate,* applying the categories of the logical mode to the process of elucidation. Just as there is a difference between the intuition of history and the analytical narration of history, so there is an aesthetic intuition and a literary history: "pure intuition is poetry and not history, and to return to it is equivalent to abolishing history" (*L*, 289). At the same time, the critic does not settle for a "rational equivalent" (*PL*, 140) of the intuition, such as a logical prose paraphrase (Richards advises such paraphrase as an act preparatory to criticism). That is keeping the two modes too far apart.

To link the logical mode to the intuitive re-creation the critic makes a "characterization" (*caratterizzazione*), defining the fundamental motifs "with a formula announcing the successful inclusion of the feeling of the single work of poetry in the most suitable class which he knows or has thought out for the occasion" (*PL*, 143). "Characteristic" contains the irreducibility of the pure intuition. "Characterization" requires the organi-

30. Moss, *Benedetto Croce,* p. 105; Orsini, *Benedetto Croce,* p. 103.

zation (not merely the assemblage) of characteristics within a "psychological class or type." Given the uniqueness of the intuition, this can only be "by approximation" (*PL*, 143). As true history is the "narration" of "individual reality" (*L*, 305), so literary history is "the study of the characteristic in a single artist," "the study of his personality and his work, which are really one and the same" (*PPH*, 348): "What was Leopardi's life? By this I mean the spiritual process through which man expresses and shapes his own feelings, defines and particularizes his own thought, asserts his aspirations in action, and in a general way develops the germ which he bears within him, realizing more or less completely, yet substantially, his own ideal. To employ a crude but expressive metaphor, his was a strangled life" (*EL*, 116).

Both localizing the characteristic and making the characterization direct critical discussion to the true source of the poetic intuition, the character, the "whole man . . . who thinks and wills, and loves, and hates; who is strong and weak, sublime and pathetic" (*DP*, 25). Croce was so suspicious of any type of categorization, so defensive against extrinsic criticism, that only reluctantly did he come to admit the logical mode into criticism at all. G. N. G. Orsini points out that, remarkably enough, in the 1902 edition of *Estetica* "criticism was merely taste," that is, the intuition.[31] This would have made the critic into a kind of artist. In adding the logical mode, Croce was moving well beyond aestheticism.

The critic has proceeded from the characterization of the individual works to the individual character behind them, and thence to the entire work. "The aim of this constructive work—which is the highest that the critic is called upon to accomplish and in which good critics of single poems sometimes show themselves to be inadequate or even uninterested—is the forging of an instrument analogous to that used for the interpretation of a single poem, an interpretation which serves to give an orientation concerning the character of the whole work of the poet" (*PL*, 164). The critic separates out unsuccessful poems from the complete works; uncovers what may be an

31. Orsini, *Benedetto Croce*, p. 130. See also p. 143.

exception to the fundamental character; distinguishes the ideal personality of the poet from the practical personality; and disposes of misleading and deprecatory labels (naming the *Georgics* a "didactic poem" when it is "poetry" [*PL*, 143]). Some artists have single, others complex characteristics, "two or more fundamental states of mind" (Dante's passage from the *stil nuovo* to the *Comedy* [*PL*, 164]):

It will be shown how a given artist began by imitating existing art, whether near to him or far from him in time, sympathetic or unsympathetic or even antipathetic to his temperament. In these imitations (it will be shown) he will proceed all the more clumsily and incoherently by reason of the energy of his own temperament, until, becoming aware of his difference from those others, he finds himself and rises to the height of an original production. It will be shown how another artist in his youthful years joyfully poured forth the inspiration bestowed upon him already perfect, as by the bounty of nature. But then he soon exhausted his vein, and it was of no avail that he sought every device for perpetuating his first successes, imitating and caricaturing himself, or imitating and striving to outdo others, until he relapsed into silence or found some other line of work as a critic, scholar, or politician.   (*PPL* 348–349)

The Crocian characterization bears a deep affinity with the criticism of De Sanctis, Saint-Beuve, and the nineteenth-century character study with its origins in Romantic criticism. The premise is the authenticity of individual character as the unit of history.[32] Croce differs from his predecessors in his more limited use of historical materials and his greater focus on the text.

As characterization is the "summit" (*PL*, 144) of criticism, it is also the summit of true literary history. Poetry is a "historical fact" (*PPH*, 314); "the criticism of poetry is the history of poetry" (*PL*, 191). The intuitive and logical modes are mediated by present consciousness which is the (individual) historical action. To move beyond the two theoretical modes is to fall into pseudo-history, for example, the history of the genres, comparative literature, period histories, nationalist histories,

32. A concept examined by Theodor W. Adorno in *Minima Moralia* and *The Jargon of Authenticity*. See also Watkins, *Critical Act*, pp. 38, 54–55.

"propaganda" (*EL,* 360) (Croce disapproved of the labels "Italian" poetry, "French" poetry, and so on). To a certain extent, Croce's characterization resembles Pater's localizing of the specific "virtue" of a writer (in the Preface to *The Renaissance*). But Croce does what Pater *says* a critic ought to do, not what Pater himself *does*. More academic and impersonal, Croce does not vie with his subject matter. He deplores impressionistic and aesthetic criticism: the critic is not an artist and does not write another "poem." The forms that Croce proposes for "literary-artistic history"—"still in the formative stage" (*PPH,* 346)—are the critical essay and the monograph. In what other forms could a theory devoted to individualization be more adequately exemplified? Given historical specialization, Croce was making a virtue of necessity. The essay and monograph "have become increasingly common media of critical and historical exposition," far outdistancing general or universal histories (*PPH,* 349). His *European Literature in the Nineteenth Century* consists of twenty-five characterizations—"few dozen . . . free intelligences, each one with his own physiognomy" (*EL,* 361)—with little or no attempt to connect them by general lines of development or recurrent themes.

Croce is aware of the objection that the "essential concept of history, which is progress," may be lost in the process of individualization, treating the "history of poetry as the very judgment of single poems" (*PL,* 148). Is it sufficient that the only true history and genuine progress are the individual history and progress that went into the labor of poetic creation? Croce believes that this is the case not only for poetry but for all human enterprise, where general progress is always linked to "definite" and "concrete" beauties, truths, and moral acts (*PL,* 148). A reader steeped in history perceives the "perpetual enrichment," "from Homer to Dante, from Dante to Shakespeare":

It may seem that the identification of the judgment of poetry with its history breaks up history into a multiplicity of single histories, placed one beside the other, thus destroying the order of succession which is indispensable to historical thought. But the judgment of poetry not only does not deny this order; it does not even remotely prescind from it. On the contrary it presupposes and reaffirms this order continually. Who could ever seriously understand and think of the *Divine Comedy* if it were placed earlier than, or at the same time as, the *Iliad* . . . Every work is properly interpreted and re-evoked only in its historical position, in which all preceding works converge in it together with all preceding history of which they are a part. (*PL,* 147)

That moment of convergence is the present consciousness of the critic about to commence the characterization. In sum, "there is nothing to be added in order to conclude with certainty that the esthetic judgment of a poem contains its history . . . that the judgment is the history of the poem" (*PL,* 146).

Besides the history of poetry there is the history of criticism where Croce must of necessity permit the logical linkages. He strongly believed in the literary history of interpretation, which has become of serious importance today in reader-response criticism and the revival of the history of taste: "Where the tradition is broken, interpretation is arrested" (*A,* 126; *PPH,* 330). It is worth noting that part two of *Estetica* contains a history of aesthetics; a long section of his *Logica* is a history of logic; the final part of *Teoria e storia di storiografia* is a history of historiography. In each volume he places his own contribution in the line of thought. He follows this same practice in studies on Dante and Shakespeare. Critical monographs should contain "by general indications or in full detail, the history of previous characterizations" (*PL,* 144). The critic forms part of an unbroken chain of human effort and study, and for all of his sharp rebuke to philologists and historians, he has deep respect for the scholarly enterprise:

The complete reproduction of the past is, as every human work, an ideal, which is realized *ad infinitum,* and, for this very reason is always realized according to what is permitted by the structure of reality at each moment of time. Is there not in a poem a nuance whose full significance escapes us? No one will want to claim that that nuance, of which we now have a dim vision that does not satisfy us, will not manage to become more precise in the future, as a result of studies, reflection, and the rise of favorable conditions. (*G,* 72–73).

Croce sees the history of criticism as a common humanistic effort of many generations. He must have been thinking of the critics who always feel the need to belittle previous criticism to establish their own reading when he pondered: "Thought passes, but generates other thoughts, which, in their turn, will excite other thoughts. In the world of thought also, we survive in our own children; in our children who contradict us, substitute themselves for us and bury us, not always with due piety" (*L*, 319).

Croce came to philosophy from history. In 1911 Richards began his undergraduate career at Cambridge in history and switched within a year to philosophy because "I couldn't bear history"; too much of it "ought not to have happened" (*C*, xxiii, 256). This prejudice against historicism was not on account of its scientism—it was less against historicism than a more fundamental antagonism to history itself. This antagonism had its origins in his utopian impulse, nurtured by a Romantic and Victorian radical tradition (with a touch of British Whiggism). Late in life he said he "hated the past" for its evil and suffering. Nothing could be done about what had happened. One could only do something about the future; so he looked forward, "even now" (1972).

As a result, the few references to the concept of traditional literary history scattered through Richards's writings are uniformly negative. In an interview in 1968 he was forced to concede that some poetry presented obstacles that historical criticism might remove. Milton was the interviewers' example. The "turning point" was Milton, replied Richards, after him "things become more intelligible": "professional instruction, as it were, in English literature might very well stop after Milton" (*C*, 265). But, as if to say this was an unwilling concession, he added, "what most people need . . . more than anything else is to hear [Milton] really well read aloud." The interviewer argued that Pope's poetry—after Richards's "turning point"—could not be fully appreciated without some study in the social, political, scientific, and philosophical materials to which he constantly alludes. Admitting room for "footnotes and commentary of some sort," Richards declared that Pope "at his greatest, the opening of, say, the second book of the *Essay on Man*, doesn't need any introduction" (*C*, 265). If the same question were put to Croce, he might have said that the footnotes and commentary mean that the "[*Essay on Man*] was not a good example of genuine poetry" (*PL*, 34) but of literature; it lacks originality and powerful feeling, is "art for art's sake . . . an amalgam made possible by accurate and subtle work" (*PL*, 63, 66). Both Richards and Croce feel that great art should be able to communicate without excessive commentary.

The allusiveness and obscurity of modernist poetry should have tested Richards's "turning point" after which professional instruction is unneeded. But, according to Richards, the allusions to Shakespeare, Marston, Donne, Browning, and Ruskin in Eliot's "Burbank with a Baedeker" are mainly justified on grounds of "emotional aura," not for the sake of teasing the reader's ingenuity. The latter would form a proper response, say, in a poetry of wit (*PLC*, 2nd ed., 290). With regard to the tangled network of allusions in Eliot generally, if the reader "is used to great poetry" and "has read the lines slowly and carefully enough to give them time to take shape to him *as sounds*," the reader may receive an "impression very rarely made by anything but great poetry" (*C*, 175). (Out of context, the statement can mislead; Richards always insists on the relation of sound and meaning [*PLC*, 128–129, 267–268; *PC*, 229–233]). Richards emphasizes the feelings over reference (or *through* reference) in Eliot's poems. These feelings, which are "deep," "passionate," "intricate," "coherent," and "sincere" (*C*, 175), govern the references, though the "imaginative realization" of the feelings as opposed to the references may take many readings, "even a lapse of years." As far as the references themselves, readers might better make their own "happy guesswork" of the "links in the poet's thought." If the poet supplied these links, by which Richards means the associative logic of the poem, he might have "impaired the concentration of the poetry and deadened the astonishing emotional resonance of his phrasing." Nonetheless, Richards concedes the use of "a gloss to be read apart from the poem at the reader's discretion" (*C*, 175). His attitude recalls Croce's: the necessity of taste (being "used to great poetry"), the "aesthetic intuition" or "re-creation," the emphasis on feeling, the danger of mixing the logical and practical modes in the (re-)creative act, the concession to erudition. Richards complained that Robert Lowell's sonnets contained too much local detail that would within a generation require heavy documentation (interestingly Lowell's revised title for the collection is *History*).

The need for a concept of literary history might have arisen in Richards's theory of communication. Put briefly, the theory stipulates that "under certain conditions, separate minds have closely similar experiences" (*PLC,* 176). To understand a writer one has to have common reference points. Communication happens when "one mind so acts upon its environment that another mind is influenced" (*PLC,* 177). If we move beyond mere pointing at objects and into language as the vehicle of communication, *A* ought to have high powers of description and *B* an "extraordinarily sensitive and discriminating receptive ability" for excellent communication. Here is an opportunity for Richards to reach beyond the immediate linguistic context of the author into the social and historical realities. Instead, he discusses the powers of poetic language to prevent miscommunication in the form of unwanted ambiguities. Attention is thrown onto the text and the reader's response. A "sincere" response follows the intentions and patterns laid down by the artist as closely as possible, without the interference of stock responses, irrelevant associations, or private hobby-horses. "Sincerity" is obedience to the "*tendency towards increased order*" (*PC,* 285) of which the artist is generally a master. In his first book he cited "contact with the personality of the artist" (*FA,* 9, 74) as fifteenth in a series of definitions of beauty, setting it in his preferred grouping under the name of "Synaesthesis." Thus, the ground Croce covers with "intuitive re-creation" is crossed by Richards with the theory of communication and "sincerity." Like Croce, too, Richards demands that the act of sincerity follow a schedule of "unremitting research and reflection" (*PC,* 287).

If Richards devotes more attention to the reader's responses than Croce, his treatment of the artist's psychology remains abstract. To borrow a phrase from Coleridge, Richards does not describe the artist, but the "poet in *ideal* perfection," the poet who appeals to the "*all in each* of human nature," largely removed from the historical setting. He values the "availability of experience" in the memory, organization, "normality," and universality. But apart from a poet's creative moments, Richards has little interest in the life. Coleridge and Shelley were the only writers on whom he ever speculated at length in a biographical vein, and the narrative development in these studies is sketchy. He said he preferred the "disappearance of all poets" and a "return to the anonymity" of the Homeric rhapsodes, ballad composers, and Old Testament prophets (*FP,* 150–151). In his poem "The Ruins" he wrote, "And words it is not poets make up poems." A favorite quotation from Kipling was, "Seek not to question aught beside / The books I leave behind."

Since Richards did not construct a concept of new literary history, as did Croce, the question remains what kind of literary history can be inferred from his theory and practical criticism. Though he deplores the biographical part of criticism, in his early criticism he places strong emphasis on the artist's "intention" within the poem, the "speaker's . . . aim, *conscious or unconscious,* the effect he is endeavoring to promote" (*PC,* 182). In "Nineteen Hundred and Now," written in 1927, he gives the aesthetic intentions of Huxley, Wells, Shaw, Lawrence, Eliot, and Joyce that resemble Croce's "aesthetic personalities" in *Poesia e nonpoesia* (1923). Richards measures the distance between the life of a writer and his imaginative use of it in essays on Hopkins (1926), Dostoevsky (1927), and Forster (1927), brief paragraphs in *Practical Criticism,* and a short essay on Lawrence's poetry (1933). Croce had defined the difference between the aesthetic and the practical personality. Increasingly, however, Richards's published criticism came to resemble his lectures in substance as well as style. The focus is on language; we do not find authors even as aesthetic personalities, but speakers of individual poems. Sometimes the speakers disappear into the linguistic thicket. Lectures in 1957–58 on Platonism and mysticism in Shakespeare's "Phoenix and the Turtle," Donne, Marvell, and Keats are textbook close readings.

In these and other essays Richards demonstrates a power of explication which Croce lacks, and which might have enabled him to rescue many a passage relegated to "nonpoetry." Typ-

ically, Croce depicts the feeling in a brief passage of "pure poetry" or names the general feeling in a poem. Rarely does he
analyze imagery and feeling in a complete poem (a notable exception is his essay on Carducci's lyric "Era un giorno di
festa" [*PPL*, 956–960]). Even his sensitive paraphrase of the
imagery in Leopardi's elegiac "Silvia" has no reference to
sound, stanzaic pattern, line-break, or rhythm beyond a few
observations on the poems with which it is categorized: "soft
and flexible" rhythm, "full of harmonies" (*EL*, 126–131). In
the final stanza of "Silvia" Leopardi addresses Hope as "dear
companion of my new age," and Croce objects to the figure on
the grounds of "abstract" allegorism, an example of Leopardi's "lapses into aridity," "of one tone into another," "of poetry into what is different from poetry." This is a serious
charge—what Richards would call a failure to unify—against a
poem Croce said was "perhaps [Leopardi's] masterpiece."
But, with his micrological method, would Richards have leveled the charge? More likely he would have found something
in the poem to justify the transition from Silvia to Hope: the
"pleasing/uncertain future" in the mind of the young girl in the
second stanza; the "expectation" and "promise" of the girl
and the poet that coalesce in the fourth stanza and remain in
the poet's heart after her death in the fifth; even the play of the
name "Silvia" and "salivi?" ("are you climbing towards?"),
respectively the opening and (to emphasize the poem's direction) closing words of the very first stanza; and many other
subtle touches. The classical personification of Hope is no
ghost in the sixth and final stanza when she appears as the dear
companion.

Two of Richards's books exemplify Croce's demand to rewrite literary history in essayistic or monographic form and to
focus upon the "internal dialectic" of the writer's art (*PL*,
348). *Coleridge on Imagination* begins with a long review of
the history of interpretation, another Crocian tactic, and then
proceeds to "translate" Coleridge's metaphysical concepts
into modern psychological terms. The dialectic lies in
Coleridge's attempt to assimilate Hartleyan associationism,
Kantianism, and Christian apologetics, and also arises between Coleridge's metaphysics and Richards's psychological

model. Richards intends to "re-design" Coleridge's "speculative apparatus" (inner sense, fancy and imagination, understanding, reason . . . *mind*) and prove its usefulness in contemporary criticism, making clear where post-Coleridgean
"terms," "distinctions," and "technical devices" become op-
erative (*CI,* 2). Croce would have approved the critic's simultaneous elucidation of historical materials and their application
to a present concern. In fact, Richards's larger goal is to show
how the imagination functions in myth-making, to expose the
myths of the Nazi propaganda machine (*CI,* 170), and to expand upon Coleridge's "new theoretic order" and vision of the
"rectified mind and the freed heart" (*CI,* xxiv). In Croce's conceptualization, two historical times intersect, Coleridge's
"documentary" time, and Richards's presentness in the 1930s.

More than any other of Richards's works, *Beyond* fulfills
Croce's ideal of new literary history. The book is a series of
essays on the dialogues between central human figures and
their gods. Homer, the author of Job, Plato, Dante, and
Shelley, each interrogates the deity on justice, human suffering, immortality, and the nature of the soul. Job seeks to penetrate the mystery of injustice in a universe ruled by God, and
God in response speaks past him to the mystery of power and
creation. Socrates apprehends the Idea of the Good, but will
only describe "its offspring" in the mind. Within each dialogue, as well as between dialogues, "different and opposing
positions are not only present but *active,* thereby sustaining
tensions without which their hold and sway in our tradition
would be far slighter" (*B,* 60). From the closest readings, Richards leaps to review the matter from the remotest distance, as
the prose modulates from analytic detachment to tortuously
worded dialogues of the mind with its inmost self, to sermons
addressed to a world public on the wrongdoing of Homer's
Olympians, the rational highmindedness of Plato's Good, and
Shelley's incandescent revolutionary idealism. The "internal
dialectic" is central to the structure of each essay.

If *Beyond* meets the requirements of Croce's new literary
history, *The Foundations of Aesthetics* (written with C. K.
Ogden and James Wood; 1922) does not succeed as a Crocian
history of a discipline. Forgetting a plea for toleration (*FA,*

6–7), Richards virtually declares war on the history of aesthetics. The theory of imitation, which dominated Western aesthetics for two thousand years, receives half a page; Richards's favored synaesthesis, a quarter of the book. Richards and his co-authors seize upon the weak points in moral theories, social theories, formal theories. Little attempt is made to set the theories in their historical context, though the groupings correspond roughly to the classical, Romantic-Victorian, and modern periods. Croce would not have objected to the polemical tone. He would certainly have questioned the absence of "piety" and the reduction of many theories to caricatures, including the prejudicial, mismanaged description of his own expressionism. By comparison, Croce's part two of *Estetica* is more conventional in form, more judicious in scope, though it too has polemics and caricatures. Hogarth and Burke are poorly dealt with, and Coleridge shares a sentence with Carlyle (*A*, 258–260, 352). While numerous minor critics are examined, Johnson is never mentioned. Nietzsche and Ruskin are hurried off in a paragraph each; while deserving respect, Ruskin is "hasty in analysis" and Nietzsche's *Birth of Tragedy* is "vague" and "does not bear criticism" (*A*, 382, 412). Nonetheless, Croce's learning is greater than Richards's, and part two of *Estetica* bespeaks what Croce asked of critics, a "reverence for tradition and history" (*EL*, 361).

The program of critical reform that Croce envisioned combines (1) "historical erudition" (*A*, 129), for "it is impossible to absorb and relive the experience of a work of art without a certain historical culture" (*PL*, 348); (2) "personal taste" (*GA*, 69), whereby Croce reclaims the subjective element which had been submerged by positivist methods; (3) judgment as to the specific nature and value of the work of art, because taste does not provide reasons, and the intuitive and logical modes are autonomous (*PE*, 52–53); and (4) the critic's own "expression" of "historical representation" (*A*, 130–131), the need to give feeling, life, and "beauty of form" to writing (*L*, 300); Croce did not approve of high-flown rhetorical writing. His style is direct, unpoetic, and often moving, but never sublime or "pathetic." He believed that "historical or critical thought, though expressed in a poor or outworn style, will maintain its virtue as thought" (*PPH*, 544).

For all his desire to convey the particular intuition, however, Croce wanted Richards's microscopic eye and his micrological method.[33] Croce was caught between a modern theory and an antiquated methodology, though he infused the portrayal of the "aesthetic personality" with great force and originality. On the other hand, what Richards gained in rescuing the most fugacious linguistic details led, in his work and in that of New Critics, to the gradual loss of the personality into textuality. This need not have happened. In biographies of Keats and Johnson, for example, W. Jackson Bate has demonstrated how a proper balance between life and work can be secured. Nevertheless, Croce and Richards realized that the study of the past was not being served by contemporary literary historians, and they redirected attention to the work of art. It is a testimony to their humanistic achievement that, after them, the shape of "true" literary history could never be the same.

33. It is possible that Raffaello Piccoli introduced Richards's works to Croce. Although Croce's personal library contains many books of English criticism from the Decadence up to World War I (Pater, Wilde, Symons, and others), chronologically *Richards's Principles of Literary Criticism* (1924) and *Practical Criticism* (1929) are the last major works of criticism from the English-speaking world in the collection (housed in the Istituto Italiano per gli Studi Storici which he founded in Naples).

Contributors

ERNST BEHLER, Professor of Comparative Literature and Germanics at the University of Washington, has written extensively on European Romanticism, medieval and modern history of thought, and contemporary critical theory. He is the editor of the critical editions of Friedrich Schlegel, A. W. Schlegel, and the new edition of Nietzsche's works in English.

RONALD BUSH is Professor of Literature at the California Institute of Technology. He is the author of *The Genesis of Ezra Pound's Cantos* and *T. S. Eliot: A Study in Character and Style,* and the editor of *T. S. Eliot: The Modernist in History.*

PAUL A. CANTOR is Professor of English at the University of Virginia. He is the author of *Shakespeare's Rome, Creature and Creator,* and, most recently, the *Hamlet* volume in the Cambridge Landmarks of World Literature Series.

RALPH COHEN, Kenan Professor of English, University of Virginia, is also Director of the Commonwealth Center for Literary and Cultural Change and editor of *New Literary History.* His collection *The Future of Literary Theory* was published last year.

ALASTAIR FOWLER is Regius Professor Emeritus of the University of Edinburg, and is currently Visiting Professor at the University of Virginia. His most recent book is *A History of English Literature,* and he is currently working on *The New Oxford Book of Seventeenth Century Verse.*

JOHN FROW is Professor of English at the University of Queensland, Australia, and the author of *Marxism and Literary History* as well as numerous articles on semiotics, discourse analysis, and literary theory.

ÜLKER GÖKBERK teaches in the Humanities and the Department of German at Reed College in Portland, Oregon. She is currently working on the literature of minorities in the Federal Republic of Germany.

JON KLANCHER is Associate Professor of English at Boston University, and the author of *The Making of English Reading Audiences, 1790–1832.* He is currently writing a study of the institutional contexts of English Romanticism.

JEROME MCGANN is Commonwealth Professor of English, University of Virginia. His most recent book is *Towards a Literature of Knowledge.* The final two volumes of his edition *Byron: The Complete Poetical Works* are scheduled to appear in late 1990 (vol. 6 and 7).

MARK PARKER is an Assistant Professor of English at Randolph-Macon College. His articles on Lamb and Austen are forthcoming. He is currently working on a study of the essayists of the *London Magazine.*

DAVID PERKINS is Marquand Professor of English at Harvard University. His most recent book is *A History of Modern Poetry* (2 vols., 1976, 1987) and he is completing a book entitled *Is Literary History Possible?*

MICHAEL VALDEZ MOSES is Mellon Assistant Professor of English at Duke University. He has published articles on nineteenth- and twentieth-century British fiction and on contemporary Third World literature. He is currently completing a book on *Tragedy and Modernity: Political History and the Novel.*

JOHN PAUL RUSSO is Professor of English, University of Miami, Florida, and has recently published a biography of I. A. Richards.